THE TABLETS OF
DESTINY
(Revelation)

*Thank you for supporting independent publishing
and the work of the Systemology Society*

mardukite.com

MARDUKITE ACADEMY REVISED SECOND EDITION

THE TABLETS OF
DESTINY

(Revelation)

HOW LONG-LOST ANUNNAKI WISDOM
CAN CHANGE THE FATE OF HUMANITY

WRITTEN BY JOSHUA FREE

THE JOSHUA FREE IMPRINT
JFI PUBLICATIONS

ISBN : 978-1-961509-06-1

Also available in hardcover.

A MARDUKITE SYSTEMOLOGY PUBLICATION
Mardukite Research Library Catalogue No. "Liber-One"
Developed for Mardukite Academy & Systemology Society
cum superiorum privilegio veniaque
SECOND EDITION
August 2023
Published from
Joshua Free Imprint – JFI Publications
Mardukite Borsippa HQ, San Luis Valley, Colorado

*Based on the first professional
Systemology lecture series
given by Joshua Free to
the Systemology Society
August 7–9, 2019*

TABLET OF CONTENTS

:: INTRODUCTION ::

000 – Mardukite Zuism: A Brief Introduction . . . 13

00 – Tablets of Destiny, Arts of Civilization
and Control of the Human Condition . . . 27

0 – Sifting the Sands of Time to Recover Wisdom from
the Clay: The Evolution of Our Understanding . . . 34

:: THE TABLETS OF DESTINY ::
MARDUKITE SYSTEMOLOGY LIBER-ONE

1 – Responsibility of Cosmic Power and The Transfer
of its Divine Abilities . . . 43

2 – Deciphering Fundamentals of Existence from The
Tablets of Destiny . . . 59

3 – Carrying the Legacy of Ancient Wisdom from The
Tablets of Destiny to the New Age . . . 69

4 – Communication of Thought, Will and Action on
The Tablets of Destiny . . . 79

5 – Understanding the Action of Thought, Will and
Energy from The Tablets of Destiny . . . 92

6 – The Power of Thought and Will as Energy and
Manifestation in the Physical Universe . . . 100

7 – Engineering Reality as a Manifestation of Thought
and Energy in the Physical Universe . . . 113

8 – Understanding How Personal Thought Creates
Realities of Manifestation . . . 127

9 – "There Is No Future Until We Settle Our Past"
Unifying the Mardukite Paradigm with NexGen
Systemology for a Self-Honest Evolution . . . 141

10 – Understanding the NexGen Systemology
Standard Model and the "Zu-Line" . . . 156

11 – Understanding Emotional Encoding and
The Power of Imprints [Extended Course] . . . 166

12 – An Introduction to Cathartic Processing
(Resurfacing and Reducing Imprints)
[Extended Course, Route-1 Revised, R-1R] . . . 187

:: APPENDIX ::

A – "Enuma Elis" Cuneiform Tablet Excerpts . . . 208

B – Marduk's "Tablet of Destiny" . . . 218

C – The "Sajaha" Cuneiform Tablet Excerpts . . . 219

D - Systemology Glossary (v.4.3, Liber-One Edit) . . . 222

E – Suggested Reading and Additional Materials . . . 249

∞

EDITOR'S NOTE

"The Self does not actualize Awareness
past a point not understood."
—*Tablets of Destiny*

While preparing this book for publication, the editors
have made every effort to present this material in a
straightforward manner—using clear, easy to read and
understand language.

Wherever a word that is defined in the glossary
first appears in the text, it will be **bold**.

A clear understanding of this material is critical for
achieving actual realizations and personal benefit
from applying philosophies of *Mardukite Zuism* and
NexGen Systemology spiritual technology.

The *Seeker* should be especially certain not to simply
"read through" this book without attaining proper
comprehension as "knowledge." Even when the
information continues to be "interesting"—if at any
point you find yourself feeling lost or confused while
reading, trace your steps back. Return to the point of
misunderstanding and go through it again.

It is expected that a *Seeker* will work through this
material multiple times to achieve optimum results.

And *now* responsibility for this power and its
actualization is passed on to you, the *Seeker*.

Take nothing within this book on faith.
Apply the information directly to your life.

Decide for yourself.

∞

"Becoming a person means that the individual moves, knowingly and acceptingly, toward being the process which he inwardly and actually is. He moves away from being what he is not — away from being a facade. He is not trying to be more than he is, with attendant feelings of insecurity or bombastic defensiveness. He is not trying to be less than he is, with the attendant feelings of guilt and self-deprecation. He is increasingly listening to the deepest recesses of his psychological and emotional being, and finds himself increasingly willing to be, with greater accuracy and depth, the *Self* which he most truly is."

—CARL ROGERS
Founder of Humanistic Psychology in his book "On Becoming a Person"

THE TABLETS OF DESTINY

— ENTRY POINTS —

MARDUKITE SYSTEMOLOGY
GRADE-III INTRODUCTION

— 000 —
: MARDUKITE ZUISM – A BRIEF INTRODUCTION* :

According to the most ancient historical records written at the birth of our modern civilization...

432,000 years ago, a small population of advanced beings—called the ANUNNAKI—began developing the planet Earth for their purposes. These elite Self-Actualized spiritual beings resided on Earth in physical bodies, but found their forms inadequate for the physical labors required. Enter: the "Human Condition." Ancient "cuneiform" tablet writings from Sumerians and Babylonians of Mesopotamia are clear regarding the original creation and systematic programming of Humanity.

> CUNEIFORM is the oldest known writing system used by scribes of ancient Babylon to record their wisdom and the history of humanity on clay tablets.

"Cuneiform" is named for its style of wedge-shaped script formed by a reed pen called a "stylus." Rather than an alphabet of letters, cuneiform writing is a system of "signs" representing "things" and "ideas." These may even be combined to represent even more complex "signs."

Many concepts adopted for modern "Mardukite Zuism" and its "Systemology" are derived from cuneiform tablets.

The ANUNNAKI introduced complex writing systems in order to program civilization and all parameters of Reality for the Human Condition. Legendary "Tablets of Destiny" (Divine Truth, supreme knowledge and cosmic power of the "gods") were first introduced to Humanity in the Babylonian narrative known best as the "Epic of Creation.

---

* "Mardukite Zuism: A Brief Introduction" Revised 2021 Version 2.0.

THE ARCANE TABLETS.

Ancient Babylonians used the *Tablets of Destiny & Creation Epic* to systematize all cosmic knowledge into a workable paradigm called "Mardukite Zuism"—a systemology received directly from the ANUNNAKI.

> PARADIGM : all-encompassing standard or religion used to view the world and communicate reality.
>
> SYSTEMOLOGY : applied philosophies (of *Mardukite Zuism*) combined with personal spiritual techniques and technology ("*Tech*") effectively demonstrating systematic principles of a "paradigm."

THE SYSTEMOLOGY OF LIFE, UNIVERSES & EVERYTHING.

The *Arcane Tablets* describe the division of the ALL by the LAW, outside of which is but INFINITY. The *Epic of Creation* describes these activities as "mythology." The "Standard Model of Systemology" that is applied to *Mardukite Zuism* uses the same information to demonstrate...

> that ALL ("AN-KI") envelops both:
> the Spiritual Existences ("AN")
> and the Physical Existences ("KI")
> divided by Cosmic Law and
> connected by Life-Awareness ("ZU")
> and beyond which is only the Abyss,
> an Infinity of Nothingness ("ABZU")

MARDUKITE ZUISM DEFINITIONS FOR STANDARD MODEL OF SYSTEMOLOGY.

> ABZU = the Abyss; Infinity; Infinity of Nothingness; that which extends, is exterior to and beyond of, all spiritual and physical existence.

<u>ANKI</u> : the ALL; All Existences; Everything that is AN and KI; Everything that is conceivable; represented by the "Standard Model of Systemology."

<u>AN</u> : the "Spiritual Universe" or "Heavenly Zone" comprised of spiritual energy-matter, in the direction of Infinity—the "Alpha" existence independent of, and superior to, the physical, *beta* or KI.

<u>KI</u> : the "Physical Universe" or "Earthly Zone" comprised of physical energy-matter in action across physical Space and observed as Time in the direction of Physical Continuity—"beta" existence condensed from, and subordinate to, the spiritual, *Alpha* or AN.

<u>ZU</u> : "to know"; "knowingness"; "Awareness" or "consciousness"; spiritual energy-matter of AN observed as "Lifeforce" in KI; "Spiritual Life Energy"; the actual personal spiritual beingness or "Awareness" of Self as the Alpha-Spirit which extends along a "line" from the Spiritual (AN) to the Physical (KI).

THE TABLETS OF DESTINY &
BABYLONIAN CREATION EPIC.

Seven cuneiform tablets compose the ancient _Babylonian Epic of Creation_, named the _Enuma Eliš_ by scholars after its opening lines. These seven tablets are the basis for what later traditions refer to as the "_Seven Days of Creation._" The _Epic of Creation_ tablets describe development of all existences with a Divine artistic perfection. The _Enuma Eliš_ is the core example of religious literature from Babylon, which served as the basis for ancient "_Mardukite Zuism_"— the first true systematized religion in history.

The Absolute _behind_ and _back of_ ALL Existence is referred to on the _Tablets of Destiny_ as the INFINITY OF NOTHINGNESS; a constant static latent unmanifest potentiality of ALL and Everythingness.

The LAW—Cosmic Law—is defined as the Cosmic Dragon—TIAMAT—on "_Epic of Creation_" Tablets. She is the First Cause or movement across a "Sea of Infinity." Later, the LAW becomes a division between Spiritual Existence (AN) and any Physical Universe (KI). The LAW—_Tiamat_—permeating ALL, uses the _Tablets of Destiny_ and then fixes the systems of finite potential:

The Systems of Manifestation—
Substance, Motion and Awareness.

"Before 'Heaven' or 'Earth' were named," a formation and interaction of active existences—"substances" and "bodies" and "Life" and "gods"—creates turbulence and waves of action through space.

The governing system of Cosmic Law—_Tiamat_—responds accordingly. She fixes the _Tablets of Destiny_ to her "deputy"—a messenger wave action of the LAW named "_Kingu_" and sends him rippling out to "meet" the Anunnaki "gods."

The *Anunnaki Assembly* of "gods" prepare to battle The LAW. When none among them comes forth to engage, the *Anunnaki* "god" MARDUK volunteers as hero to confront *Kingu* and *Tiamat*—but with a condition that the *Anunnaki Assembly* recognize him as "Chief of the Gods" upon his success.

When *Marduk* approaches *Tiamat* (LAW) directly, he is flanked by *Kingu* and the "army of Ancient Ones." *Marduk* relinquishes the *Tablets of Destiny* from *Kingu*. With the *Tablets of Destiny*, *Marduk* successfully conquers the true understanding of "Cosmic Law" and thereby conquers *Tiamat*.

THE TABLETS OF DESTINY & SELF-HONESTY.

Marduk uses the Tablets of Destiny to discover "<u>Self-Honesty</u>" and Divine Knowledge governing "<u>Cosmic Ordering</u>"—systems dividing the "Spiritual Universe" (AN) from a "Physical Universe" (KI).

The two Universe types are connected only by a stream of Spiritual Awareness (*Lifeforce*) that Sumerians called <u>ZU</u>.

Wisdom of the Arcane Tablets is later passed down to and concealed by an <u>ancient esoteric secret society</u> in Babylon: the Scribe-Magicians, High Priests and Priestesses of *Mardukite Zuism*.

<u>Self-Honesty</u> is a term describing an original "<u>Alpha</u>" state of <u>clear knowingness</u> and <u>Self-directed beingness</u>. "Self-Honesty" is the most basic and true expression of Self as "I-AM"—free of artificial attachments; reactive-response conditioning; and imposed or enforced programming as Reality for the Human Condition. Spiritual development in modern *Mardukite Zuism* is referred to as the "Pathway to Self-Honesty" and the "Gateway to Infinity." It is modeled directly from the Ancient Mystery Tradition as observed at the original Temples of Babylon.

KEYS TO THE GATEWAY

"I will take my Blood—and with Bone—I will fashion a Race of Humans to keep Watch of the Gate. And from the Blood of Kingu I will create another Race of Humans to inhabit the Earth in service to the Gods— so shrines to the Anunnaki may be built and the temples filled. I will bind the Elder Gods to the Watchtowers; let them keep watch over the Gate of Abzu and the Gate of Tiamat and Gate of Kingu—and with a Key that shall be ever hidden, known to none, except only to my Mardukites."

— MARDUK, *Enuma Eliš, Creation Tablet VI.*

THE ANUNNAKI LADDER OF LIGHTS & BABYLONIAN GATEWAYS TO INFINITY.

ZIGGURAT TEMPLES in Babylonia—and throughout Meso-potamia—served to remind populations of the "bond" or ZU connecting "Heaven" and "Earth." Seven-stepped "levels" of the physical *Ziggurat Temples* of Babylonia—and seven corresponding Gates—represent spiritual levels of actualized Awareness; states of Self-purification (or "spir-itual defragmentation") as they ascend in the direction of AN toward Infinity of Supreme Beingness—the Pathway of Self-Honesty—in imitation of the footsteps of the gods during their descent through the "spheres" or "Gates."

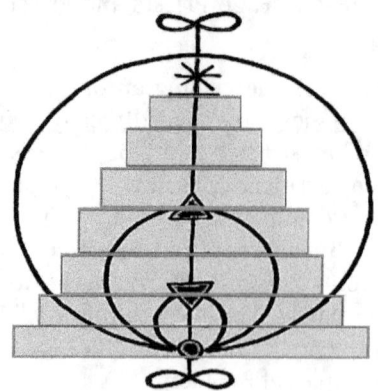

COSMOLOGY AND METAPHYSICS.

All Things in the Physical Universe are in motion—wave motions of "energy and matter in space measured as-and-across time." Continuity of the Physical Universe (KI) is divided by LAW and encompassed by the ALL (ANKI). The direction of AN extends toward ABZU, an Infinity of Nothingness beyond effective existence.

The <u>Alpha Self</u> or <u>Alpha Spirit</u> is the true source—the "spiritual cause" of "physical effects." It engages <u>Self-determined WILL</u> from its "spiritual" <u>Alpha existence</u> as an Actualized Awareness impinging on "physical" <u>Beta existence</u> and experienced as "Life."

USING ANCIENT WISDOM TO UNLOCK HUMAN POTENTIAL.

Communication of clear wisdom and true knowledge from Arcane Tablets is distorted as it passes through time and geography, diverse languages and authoritarian cultures using the "Power" to program the masses and fragment the Human Condition away from Self-Honesty.

Use of this ancient wisdom reveals the Keys to "<u>Cosmic Ordering</u>"—applying the highest understanding of "cause-and-effect" sequences to all action in the Physical Universe, and to all *Self-directed* applications of WILL-Intention and Effort.

MARDUKITE ZUISM, SYSTEMOLOGY & SPIRITUALITY.

The Spiritual Universe (AN)—of metaphysical or spiritual energy and metaphysical or spiritual matter is not dependent on the Physical Universe (KI) to exist; the two are existentially independent of each other, maintaining a single channel, conduit or connection, which is <u>Alpha Spirit</u> "Awareness" as Spiritual Life or ZU.

The Alpha Spirit engages a <u>ZU-line</u>, a spiritual lifeline of ZU energy to a genetic vehicle or organic body to experience physical beta existence.

MARDUKITE ZUISM DEFINITIONS FOR METAHUMAN SYSTEMOLOGY.

<u>ALPHA SPIRIT</u> : a Spiritual *life-form*; the True Self or "I-AM"; a unit of *Awareness*; a *Spiritual Beingness* that controls a physical body or "genetic vehicle" using a Lifeline or continuum of spiritual "ZU" energy.

<u>ASCENSION</u> : actualized Awareness elevated to (AN) spiritual existence that is exterior to beta-existence; the ability to *Self-direct* from *Spirit* as *Self* in existence independent of any "body."

<u>BETA-EXISTENCE</u> : manifestation of a Physical Universe (KI); conditions of energy-matter manifested in a state of condensed existence matching frequencies specific to space in the Physical Universe.

<u>FRAGMENTATION</u> : breaking apart; scattering the pieces; fractioning wholeness; fracture of holism; discontinuity; a separation of totality; anything outside or apart from original clarity (or *Self-Honesty*).

<u>GENETIC VEHICLE</u> : Physical *life-form*; physical (*beta*) body controlled by an Alpha Spirit using a continuous Lifeline of ZU energy; an organic catalyst for a Spirit to operate causes and observe effects (in *beta*).

<u>HUMAN CONDITION</u> : a standard issue default programmed state of Human experience; receptacle for Alpha Spirit Awareness that is generally accepted to be the extent of its potential identity (*Beingness*).

<u>ZU-LINE</u> : Spiritual Life-Energy (ZU) continuum; an energetic channel or Identity-Continuum connecting Alpha Spirit Awareness from Infinity-to-Infinity including the full Physical or *beta* range of existence.

THE HIGHEST FORM OF
TRUE DIVINE WORSHIP.

The true Destiny of Humanity is to achieve spiritual Self-Actualization; the reunion of Self with the Infinite.

Attaining Self-Honesty in this Life is the most important step a person can take toward achieving their highest ideals, goals and realizations as a Spiritual Being.

The Highest form of "True Worship" begins with the Spirit —the true Self—and all external practices, rituals, ceremonies and historical examples are but outer reflections of this ideal. The Highest form of "Sin" is against the Spirit —against the Self—and its ability to maintain Self-Honesty.

There are modes of thought, action and Self-direction of effort that will contribute toward Ascension; and modes that lead away from that.

Beta experiences of "Sin"—pain, fear, guilt, anger—are all related to personal fragmentation; and emotional turbulence from all of these may be released—and intention energy redirected—because:

We all co-create the reality we experience in this lifetime!

SPHERES OF EXISTENCE AND INFLUENCE &
A UTILITARIAN SYSTEMOLOGY OF ETHICS.

The prime directive of all beta existence is: *to exist*. The continuation of existence is the purpose behind all existence. Between realization of Self and Infinity, there are many spheres of existence that we may influence.

All of the spheres are interconnected. There is nothing in existence that is in absolute exclusion to all existence. Each sphere of existence supports subsequent existences and assists reaches toward higher spheres of influence.

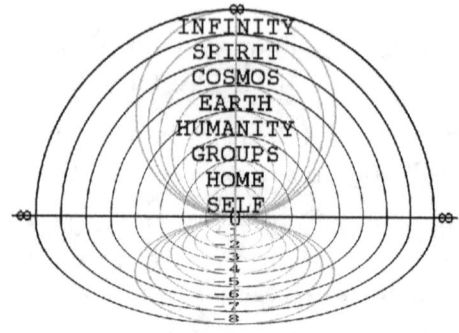

The greatest good contributes to the greatest continuation of optimum existence and survival for the greatest sphere of inclusion. Degrees of rightness and wrongness are determined by Cosmic Law and are reflected in the quality and continuation of optimal existence at the highest sphere of existence. Individual happiness is attained via the channel to the highest sphere. Unhappiness is a result of "selfishness," lack of "Spiritual Self-Actualization" and/or reach of "Actualized Awareness" beyond *Self* as identified to a *body*.

ZU : MARDUKITE ZUISM & MODERN ZUIST RELIGION.

History demonstrates how dangerous, troublesome and easily misused the concept of "RELGION" is; so, for purposes of incorporating *Mardukite Zuism* and its *Systemology* as a contemporary standard, the idea is treated here as defined.

> RELIGION : a concise spiritual paradigm, fixed set of beliefs and practices, regarding Divinity, Infinite Beingness—or else "God."

—*Mardukite Zuism* operates under a premise of very specific beliefs and "<u>systemology</u>" of "<u>applied spiritual technology</u>."

—*Mardukite Zuist Religious Doctrine* fundamentally relays the previously described "Highest forms" of <u>Worship</u>, <u>Cosmic Law</u>, and <u>Ethics</u>.

Mardukite Zuist Spiritual Doctrines and its *Systemology* successfully meet modern "religious" criteria for:

a) A Description of Cosmic Creation;
b) Belief in a Supreme Infinite Being;
c) Ethics Leading to Human Ascension;
d) Ethics of Conduct Toward all Life and Existence;
e) Immortality of the Human Spirit;
f) A Published Library of Religious Literature;
g) Traditions of Practice and Application; and
h) A Spiritual Advisement Methodology.

GOALS & IDEALS OF MARDUKITE ZUISM.

The word "ZU" meant "knowing" in original Sumerian cuneiform script. Goals and ideals of Zuism reflect this. *Mardukite Zuism & Systemology* seeks to assist an individual in reclaiming a total realization of the True Self or "I-AM" knowingly as the Immortal Alpha Spirit, in line with a most ancient directive: to "Know Thyself."

In view of the fact that all modern humans are subjected to   technologies depriving them of their freedoms to *be, think, know* and pursue truth: goals and ideals of *Mardukite Zuism & Systemology* are to effectively repair abilities and elevate certainty of an Individual to increase and direct "Actualized Awareness" toward Higher Gateways of Spiritual Ascension.

INFINITY, "GOD" & SUPREME BEINGNESS

Spiritual Philosophy of *Mardukite Zuism* is systematized by a Standard Model of Systemology. It demonstrates Absolute Supreme Beingness associated with the Highest realization of "God" as INFINITY. No thing is Higher or Absolute than the *Infinity of Nothingness*—and reducing Supreme Beingness to any finite personality or character trait is to limit and defile what is herewith represented, but with lesser "words" and mundane sentiments or semantics.

> The Highest Name of God cannot be conceived
> —hence our symbolic use of the Infinity Sign:
>
>
>
> ...or Sumerian cuneiform word-sign: "ABZU"—
> "The Infinite Nothingness and Source of All ZU."

—The Spiritual Universe (AN) is *All-as-One* because it exists as an infinite singularity or stasis: infinite potential with no gradient or observed motion; which is its own continuity.

—The Physical Universe (KI) is *All-as-One* because it is in continuous motion, with all manifest parts working systematically as the condensed solid continuity of beta-existence.

—A "spiritual continuum" or "conduit channel" of ZU (or a "*Zu-line*") from a Spiritual Universe (AN)—links our Awareness levels of "I-AM," "True Self" or Spirit ("Alpha Spirit") with varying potential "Point-of-View" and degrees of motion experienced in the Physical Universe.

—The Alpha Spirit or "Soul" is the true Awareness, "I" or "Self" connected to the operation and control of the physical body.

BASIC CONCEPT OF THE HUMAN SPIRIT.

> The true Self is the "I" or "I-AM" or "Spirit"
> regardless of its *perceived* position in spaces,
> *Point-of-View*, degree or level of Awareness.
> Spirit remains at its original fixed true point.

Whatever "spiritual energy-matter" (*if any*) that may compose the Alpha Spirit or makeup of "soul"—it must occupy this "other space" with its spiritual existence and then project its Awareness and Will onto the Physical Universe (KI) in order to experience the *Game* we call "*Life.*"

This *"Spiritual Life Energy"* or *Awareness* of a *Spiritual Being* is treated as a "Lifeforce" and "Consciousness" and goes by many names throughout the history of language, mysticism and spirituality—but we find the idea first treated as <u>ZU</u> on cuneiform tablets of Mesopotamia.

> On an Identity-lifeline or continuum of ZU energy, an Alpha Spirits is operating from a Spiritual Universe to experience in *beta-existence*. We refer to this concept as the *"<u>ZU-line</u>"* on the Standard Model of Systemology to illustrate the projected Awareness from Spirit (as an epicenter or fixed point) to any other *Point-of-view* (POV) anywhere in existence.

ZU is the name given to the spiritual beingness or essence of all Life in existence—and Self is a concentrated center or focal point that projects Awareness on a ZU-continuum or Zu-line toward a point of artificial Identity separate from Self.

The True Self of an Individual Human is a "spiritual universe cause" of "physical universe effects"—engaging as an immortal Alpha Spirit with a Self-determined Will actualized as an Awareness along a ZU-continuum (or *"Zu-line"*), extending from Infinity-to-Infinity, through every possible frequency and vibration along the total spectrum of physical and metaphysical existence.

THE SYSTEMOLOGY OF SPIRITUAL ADVISEMENT COUNSELING PRACTICES FOR MARDUKITE ZUISM

The Mardukite Chamberlains, an underground research organization established in 2009, dedicated itself to recovery and consolidation of relevant historical, scriptural & ritual records of ancient Mardukite Babylon in Mesopotamia, following up the founding of Mardukite Ministries (Mardukite Zuism) by Joshua Free the previous year, in 2008. By 2011, a Mardukite Alumni faction (International Systemology Society) began research and development into new methods of:

> applying ancient wisdom as a futurist spiritual technology
> that effectively awakens, unlocks and fully actualizes
> spiritual potential of the Human Condition.

A systematic and logical approach to spirituality is demonstrable on the Standard Model of Systemology, where ZU-line frequencies are represented at various degrees:

- "zero-point" body death;
- cellular life and sensory perceptions of a genetic body;
- bio-chemicals induced by emotion;
- thoughts and intention transmitted between our Alpha Spirit and the "genetic vehicle"—
- all the way "up" the scale to a perfected clarity of Self-Actualized Awareness of I-AM as our true "Alpha" state, just below Infinity and Absolute Beingness.

Full potential of ZU in is only altered from its natural state as a result of personal fragmentation of the Human Condition. This may be restored by systematic spiritual practices.

The *Pathway to Self-Honesty* is a personal journey and spiritual adventure marked by progressive clearing of personal energy channels fragmented by emotional imprinting and programming-data accumulated from "experiences" in the environment—the "debris" that fragments the total actualized experience of Self in Awareness as the Alpha Spirit.

The first and most important step—Before an individual can actualize potentials of the Spirit as Self, they must fully realize:

> The *I-AM Self* and the *Alpha Spirit* are One and the same.
> This state of Knowingness is a primary intention of basic
> spiritual practices of Mardukite Zuism & Systemology.

Mardukite Zuism materials, *Systemology* books and advanced training courses are available to Mardukite Ministers seeking qualification as specialized Clergy, Priests, Priestess, and Professional Pilots of systematic processing.

— 00 —

THE TABLETS OF DESTINY, ARTS OF CIVILIZATION AND CONTROL OF THE HUMAN CONDITION : AN INTRODUCTION BY REED PENN :

There is perhaps no greater enigmatic and potentially powerful facet of **Sumerian** tradition and **Babylonian (cuneiform)** literature than the "Tablet of Destinies"—or "*Tablets of Destiny.*" Within these pages, Joshua Free presents the first public **esoteric** knowledge synthesis of wisdom concerning these legendary relics—a presentation far surpassing the scope of any previous academic or scholarly research regarding ancient artifacts and their interpretation.

Elusive lore of the "*Tablets of Destiny*" constitute the **prehistoric** heart and soul of **Mesopotamian** "mythology" and "magic"—to use the most convenient terms applied to its general understanding. But, as a result of these terms, we are offered very little concrete *functional* or *practical* knowledge to apply to our lives. Contemporaries in this field are apt to only translate and interpret the "language" of these ancient mysteries, but with little true *Self-Honest* understanding of what these "words" or "symbols" originally represented to the author that set them down.

In "*Tablets of Destiny: Using Ancient Wisdom to Unlock Human Potential,*" Joshua Free essentially maps the highest route to esoteric knowledge—expertly bridging materials from the "*Mardukite Core*" (*Research Library*) with the wisdom and latest clarity gleaned by the advanced "*NexGen Systemology*" *New Thought* division of the "*Mardukite Research Organization.*" This much anticipated foundation work and public debut of "*Mardukite Systemology*" provides a concise and accessible guide to the fundamentals of "cosmic ordering" and the "systematization" of the Human Condition, described on cuneiform tablets as "control of the Divine *ME*" ("*may*")—or else, the "*Arts of Civilization*"—

the supreme knowledge and wisdom that commands all true authority of godhood in the heavens and sovereignty on earth.

Actual "Divine" power and wisdom reflected as the "*Tablets of Destiny*" appears strongest in our most distant era of *the most recent version of* human civilization and its inception in the '*Ancient Near East'*. Once collected and united—near the boundaries of Europe, Asia and what we now call the Middle East—it fragmented, then dispersed, throughout the globe in its underground migration as secret doctrines of the "**Ancient Mystery School.**" To this *School*, all original spiritual wisdom traditions on earth owe a debt —in spite of the fact that their own cultural pantheistic systems evolved as substandard facsimiles of the aesthetic beauty in true Cosmic Wisdom and holistic perfection reflected in Natural Law that we now know as the "*Tablets of Destiny.*" These pages, therefore, represent a *milestone* step for *NexGen* humanity toward the total rediscovery and actualization of the original beauty and perfection of *Human Potential*.

Δ Δ Δ Δ Δ Δ Δ

Before deferring to the author to illuminate the deepest mysteries of this lore, I received a request to apply my research and experience as a long-standing "*Mardukite Systemologist*" and briefly provide geographic, historical, literary and *systemological* background to this study. It is important to note, first and foremost, that we are treating the *oldest cuneiform records* from Mesopotamia—the "Land between two rivers"—which conceived the current inception of our modern era of human **systematization** approximately 6,000 years ago. And although we are dealing with an ancient region now known and occupied as *Iraq*, it cannot be more strongly emphasized that our archaic sources have no direct relationship with current religious and political activity in *Iraq*—other than, perhaps, an advocacy to preserve certain ancient sites and living genetic heritage of the *Yezidi* population—aspects which actually extend back into *"pre-history."*

Cuneiform tablet records also demonstrate that previous inceptions of similar civilizations were attempted on Earth for some 432,000 years—governed by the "godlike" overseers (referred to as *"Anunnaki"* from Mesopotamian sources) that originally held possession of the *Tablets of Destiny.** But, it is the most recent **incarnation** of human systematization that we are most concerned with—and which offers us the clearest recovered records penned by human hands. As it has been said: "history begins in Sumer," meaning "history," by definition, *begins* with the "written word," which we attribute to *Sumer* (*Babylonia*) and the invention of cuneiform (*"wedge-like"*) script—and its use on *"clay tablets,"* which is how most scholars have academically interpreted the *Tablets of Destiny.*

In some instances, a singular clay, stone or metallic specimen represents the iconic or definitive "Tablet of Destiny" relic—Sumerian *dub-nam-tar-meš* or Akkadian *tup šīmāti*—as it appears in the most famous spiritual and **cosmological** teachings of Mesopotamia, particularly the *"Enuma Eliš,"* or Babylonian *Epic of Creation.*‡ In other esoteric lore, and in relation to the dispersal (or **fragmentation**) of a collective body of sacred knowledge, the "Tablet of Destiny"—or what some scholars inappropriately refer to as the *Tablet of Destinies*—is perhaps only *one of seven* "Tablets of Destiny"— *tuppu šīmāti*. This knowledge is regarded as the "Supreme Key" to the Divine *"me"* (pronounced "may")—or else the "Arts of Civilization"—used by "gods" and kings to institutionalize a systematization of Human Condition and Reality experience, still in operation after thousands of years.

Scholars misappropriate the term *"Tablet of Destinies"* to denote another "Divine" or "astral" artifact possessed by the Anunnaki god **Nabu**. It is otherwise translated as the

---

*   See also "Tablet-K" in *The Complete Anunnaki Bible.*

‡   See *Appendix* or "Tablet-N" in *The Complete Anunnaki Bible.*

"*Tablet(s) of Fate*" or "*Book of Life*"—*dub-nam-meš* in the Sumerian, or *im-nam-ti-la*—such as indicated in a prayer to the Anunnaki Sun Goddess Aya (or Haia): "*On the 'Tablet of Life' never to be altered, place so-and-so's name.*" Clearly this is not the same item we are describing, nor one of the Supreme ("*me*") "Arts of Civilization" in itself. Instead, it reflects some type of "crystalline" or "Akashic" record of energetic "*activity*" encoded as these "Arts" in motion throughout the Cosmos—and especially on Earth.

A marked distinction between "*destiny*" and "*fate*" eludes many people. In fact, the modern English language provides very little support for separating these concepts in the mind, going so far—or *not* so far—as to simply use one to define the other. And they are *not* the same. Several early "*NexGen Systemology*" knowledge lectures by Joshua Free pertained to *etymology*—or else, the "origins of words and their meaning"—and among these, the most frequently given lecture specifically described an **apparent** distinction between "*destiny*" and "*fate.*"

We may take these words for granted today, but we are mistaken when using them interchangeably. Even the Sumerians, in their original development of basic vocabulary, displayed a **differentiation** between the word "fate" (*nam*) and "destiny," displayed in Sumerian cuneiform with the combination of **cuneiform signs**: *nam* ("fate") and *tar* ("to cut"); or *namtar*, meaning literally "to decree (or ordain) fate." And while the more "advanced" language developed, and Akkadian (Babylonian) includes a great many additional words in its vocabulary, we find the two concepts suddenly blurred even then into a single expression: *šīmāti* (pronounced "*shye-may-tee*") to denote "destiny" or "what is fixed and established." In esoteric and mystical instances, it is no wonder that each subsequent culture in Mesopotamia would continue to borrow many former Sumerian terms for their own language, especially as a "sacred," "religious" or otherwise "magical" language—just as we see in the case of the Assyrians (and others) that continued to perform rituals and speak incantations in former Akkadian and Sumerian tongues. Even today many prefer to practice their most obscure "magical rites" in some foreign Latin or Greek—or Enochian, and so on.

If we reduce the specific words *"Destiny"* and *"Fate"*—exactly as we know them from their **Proto-Indo-European** (*PIE*) roots—to their most basic applied meaning on the "road of life," then *"destiny"* perfectly represents our inevitable *destination* points (and even the "fixed laws" in place concerning our journey), meanwhile *"fate"* is the *route* or *pathway* we choose to take—and the causal relationship those choices have on our "reality experience" in light of the fact that a fixed *destiny* is always in effect. By our most ancient definitions: the blueprints of *"Destiny"* related to Divine knowledge (known to the "gods") concerning the ordering of the **Cosmos**; and the blueprints of a person's *"Fate"* concerned effects of causal law that might be "divined" from some type of *"Oracle"* or *"Seer"*—often a person with a holistic wide-angle *"clear awareness"* of **Cosmic Law** in *Self-Honesty*.

> **destiny** : "what is set down, made firm, standard, or stands fixed as a constant end; the absolute *destination* regardless of whatever course is traveled; in *NexGen Systemology*, the *'destiny'* of the *'Human spirit'* is infinite existence."

Our modern word *"Destiny"*—from the Old French *destinée* and Latin *destinare*—implies what is "firmly established" or "determined irrevocably" and "inevitably." In esoteric terms, *"Destiny"* is the *appointed design* (or "designation") of Cosmic Law, reflected as the knowledge earned from understanding—and actualizing—the *"Tablets of Destiny."* Even as its ancient simplified Proto-Indo-European (PIE) root—*"stā-"*—it denotes something "standing," "set down" or "made firm." We can easily see meaning of this root in other related words such as: "constant," "distance," "standard," "static," "statue" and "substance"—all of which are relevant examples from a systemological point of view. *"Destiny"* therefore represents what we *have* to work with—the conditions of the *"game"* we are playing at: its field (or board); the pieces; the rules; and even the table its set upon—all in one.

In "contrast" (which is itself another word derived from the PIE root *"stā-"*) our *"Fate"* is, quite simply, the experienced activity and sequence of causal events concerning our *"game"* of Life. *"Fate"* is not independent of *"Destiny."* It is, in fact, *ruled by* "Destiny"—but, it is entirely within our capabilities as "players" to determine, from *Self*, the course of our *"Fate."* We choose our course of efforts or attentions and Cosmic Law immediately responds—thus becoming *"our Fate."* Even the word we know today as *"Fate,"* has a quite different track of descent into our vocabulary—although the common tendency is to use it interchangeably with, or even to define, *"Destiny."*

The word *"Fate,"* borrowed directly from the Old French, appears as *fata* in Latin, denoting "the course of one's lot in life." It can also apply to a "spirit guide" or "oracle" that is presumed to *speak* to us about the things known only to the *gods*—and of which, we also earn the word "fay" and "fairy" from the same PIE root *"bhā-"* or *"phā-."* This root, meaning "to say, proclaim or shine light upon," is most interesting for our purposes, because it is where we derive meaning for the words: "banish," "euphemism," "fame," "fantasy," "ineffable," "phantom," "photo" and "prophet."

> *fate* : "what is brought to light or actualized as experience; the actual *course* taken to reach an end, charted end, or final *destination*; in *NexGen Systemology*, the *'fate'* of a *'Human spirit'* is determined by the choice of course taken to experience *Life.*"

A true understanding of Cosmic Law—which is our *Destiny* as beings in Existence—is what ancient cuneiform records allude to as perfect knowledge of *Self* in the Universe—reflected on *"Tablets of Destiny"*—a fundamental once only known to the "gods," or else, the uppermost **echelons** of ancient society. We must understand who we are as this *Self*—and how we may most effectively operate within the boundaries and freedoms of the *Game*. How can we truly know the nature of our *Fate*, when we have, at best, a fragmented understanding of *why* we are even doing what we do? How can we effectively direct our reality engineering efforts from *Spirit*, if we still treat the phenomenon of our *Fate* from an intellectual viewpoint of mysteriousness? These are the problems that we are applying solutions to at this Grade, and knowledge tier, called: "*Mardukite Systemology*."

The residing *Spirit*, or I-AM, maintains an ability to direct the "*Fate*" of our life course in this incarnation from a static vantage point of *Destiny*. We merely have to awaken a conscious use of these functions in *Self-Honest* clarity—operating as the holistic *Spirit*, and not simply the fragmented *Mind*—in order to achieve our *destined* state as masters of this *spiritual technology*.

May its wisdom shine clear light on your journey!

Sincerely, from the Pathway,

—Reed Penn
August 2019

— 0 —

SIFTING THE SANDS OF TIME TO RECOVER WISDOM FROM THE CLAY
(THE EVOLUTION OF OUR UNDERSTANDING)
: AN INTRODUCTION BY JOSHUA FREE :

"Your command shall be effective," says *Tiamat*—the *First Cause*—to *Kingu*, her **vizier** and cosmic messenger, as she transfers possession of the *Tablets of Destiny*, affirming:

"Whatsoever you will—it shall be established."

Here we paraphrase the sentiment applied to the "origins of Creation" as provided on the very first tablet of the Babylonian cosmology series. Here our premiere know-ledge of the *Tablets of Destiny* shows its face in perhaps the most **paramount** foundation text of the ancient Mardukite "paradigm"—the *Enuma Eliš*, or *Epic of Creation*[*] of Babylon.

> *paradigm* : "an all-encompassing *standard* by which to view the world and *communicate* Reality; a stand-ard model of reality-systems used by the Mind to filter, interpret and organize experience of Reality."

More "Mardukite ink" has been spilled regarding the *Enuma Eliš* than any other cuneiform tablet cycle. At first glance, it might seem that there is no *new* data to glean for our purposes. However, we have never provided a treat-ment of this cornerstone from a point of *Awareness* attainable using our current *Grade-III* level of understand-ing, and certainly never publicly in connection to the elusive *"Tablets of Destiny,"* appearing within throughout our most ancient texts as a definitive key to commanding true authority as *Self* in the physical universe.

For nearly a decade these matters remained privately exp-

---

[*]   Appearing in the *Tablets of Destiny (Appendix)*; excerpted from "Tablet-N" in *The Complete Anunnaki Bible* edited by Joshua Free.

lored by an advanced division of the "*Mardukite Research Organization*" known as the "*Systemology Society*" governing the new "*Mardukite Academy of Systemology.*" This faction has operated in the esoteric underground since 2011, developing a direct extension of the "Mardukite Core"[§] to support research and discovery of continuing work, as it applies to the present state of the Human Condition and its imminent future.

Δ Δ Δ Δ Δ Δ Δ

At our "<u>first level of understanding</u>," the *Enuma Eliš* is a treatise regarding "magical practices" in ancient Babylon, contributing to the "systematized religion" distributed among the common Mesopotamian population. No shortage of rites and workable **methodologies** may be derived at this level to occupy the civic mind and social awareness of humanity (at a physio-emotional degree of *Awareness*). In fact, this is what has been going on for some time in **Western civilization**—at least 4,000 years—since the perfected Babylonian **codification** of Human systems. Even data that appears concrete within confines of this "physical" level—including vast **catalogs** of terminology and definitions provided by physical sciences—may still fall under the category of "**superstition**" when treated at "higher" clearer degrees of *Awareness*.

Ancient efforts to successfully systematize the material world, using Babylonia as its epicenter, are attributed to the Anunnaki god "Nabu"—meaning "*the speaker*" or "*prophet*"—who **heralded** a rise of the original ancient "Mardukite" *standard* in Babylon, in honor of his "father" **Marduk**, the central hero of the *Enuma Eliš*. This was accomplished by establishment of a "priesthood"—a distinct **learned** portion of the population—dispensing "myster-

---

§   *Grade-I* and *Grade-II* materials pertaining to past systems of "magical," "mystical" or "religious" semantics, with some materials now available in a series of Master Edition anthologies as—*Necronomicon: The Complete Anunnaki Legacy, Merlyn's Complete Book of Druidism,* and *Great Magickal Arcanum.*

ies" from the "<u>second level of understanding</u>," using the "written word" as their medium—something incredibly revolutionary for its time. In doing so, the "*Mardukite paradigm*"—at an "intellectual degree of awareness"—became a global standard, perpetually influencing worldly systems of the **Human Condition** in every social **institution** imaginable: philosophy of individualism; management of family life; structure of societal roles; and even world order. All of which reflects an intellectual treatment of wisdom from these proverbial "*Tablets of Destiny*."

> **self-honesty** : "the *alpha* state; clear and present total *Awareness* of-and-as *Self*, in its most basic and true proactive expression of itself as *Spirit* or *I-AM*—free of artificial attachments, perceptive filters and other emotionally-reactive or mentally-conditioned programming imposed on the human condition by the systematized physical world." (*NexGen Systemological NewSpeak*)

The "<u>third level of understanding</u>" is the highest degree—in total *Self-Honest* clarity of *Awareness* as *Self*—demonstrable from the "*Tablets of Destiny*." This superior level of realization is often **misappropriated** simply as "spiritual" in former philosophical and religious efforts throughout history. In spite of vocabulary they may use, most philosophical and spiritual paradigms are still only treated, at best, from the "second level of understanding," as comprehended purely from intellectual levels by the "most educated" of those institutions. These folk tend to pride themselves on a *superior* scope of **discernment** regarding their particular vocabulary ("**semantic-set**") specific to the realm they operate.

Δ Δ Δ Δ Δ Δ Δ

Most organizations—operating outside *Self-Honesty*—either lack ability (*or desire*) to **evaluate** (*or elevate*) their "congregations" or "students" for **Self-actualization** and **Self-**

determinism. Many, which maintain a *responsibility* to assist humanity in this way, fear losing their own civic control and the social dependence emphasizing the "Institution" above all. This focus disrupts the natural order of *Life*, disregarding completely the fundamental existence of the spiritually evolving *Individual* as its primary goal. Here we begin to recognize definitive distinctions between common **"exoteric"** public presentations (and understanding) of universal information from that which is deemed "esoteric," meaning a higher understanding of—and behind of —the same, that few are actually aware of.

We do *not* suggest that our discoveries and presentation within the scope of *Mardukite Systemology*—is the *only* method whereby a person may truly reach the elevated state, which we call *Self-Honesty.** There are a few individuals throughout history that *have* achieved this—with the more recognizable examples described as "Ascended Masters" or "spiritual leaders," even becoming central icons for later evolving "faiths" and "traditions."

In all such antiquated instances, these points of achievement are accounted for by the determination of an individual's *own* unique ability and *not* as a reflection, product or result of some systematized tradition, philosophical institution or environment. This is a problem we resolve within *parameters* of our current Grade-level of work.

> *parameters* : "a defined range of possible variables within a model, spectrum or continuum."

Everywhere we turn today, there is an abundance of alleged avenues of "mysticism" and methods professing "enlightenment"—and many are, at least in part, drawn from the same stream of knowledge descending from the "Ancient Mystery School." But as we move along the **timeline** into the modern "New Age," we still find these

---

* An appropriate word-phrase with no preexisting semantic attachments, so as to differentiate this actualization of *Self-Awareness*.

esoteric treatments handled in *fragmented exclusion* within the same "first" and "second" **gradients** of potential understanding, and no greater.

> **fragmentation** : "the *fractioning* of wholeness or the *fracture* of a holistic interconnected *alpha* state, favoring observational Awareness of perceived connectivity between parts; also *discontinuity*; separation of a totality into parts; in *NexGen Systemology*, a person outside a state of *'Self-Honesty'* is said to be *'fragmented'*."

A few seem to approach some version of "*Self-Honest clarity*" resulting from half-measure efforts to "**Cross the Abyss**" within their own paradigm and fall by the wayside. Even adept institutions might carry ability to bring students right up to the *Gate to the Abyss*—but those few which pass through still carrying attachments and weights of a broken paradigm, are capsized from the Boat—left to sink or swim amidst a Sea of Infinity. And *that* is, at best, where previous implementation of ancient wisdom from the "*Tablets of Destiny*" generally have led *Seekers* prior to our recent efforts.

Our presentation given in this revised *Liber-One* volume is the first time our "*NexGen Systemology*" crosses paths directly with the "Mardukite paradigm" in public for the current era. *Grade-III* begins a new cycle of "*Mardukite Systemology*" material emphasizing a *demonstration of ancient wisdom in present time for the future.* To accomplish this—in *Self-Honesty*—and to make it accessible to anyone, we are introducing the foundation principles—most appropriately—within the context of the "*Tablets of Destiny.*" We are, for the first time, treating this wisdom from the collected **holistic** understanding gained from the *first three* Graded tiers—or *Gates*—of understanding, as represented by **ziggurat** temples of Babylon. There is no great secret behind this part—we are taking our (I) *physical* understanding, transferring it to (II) *intellectual* wisdom philosophies, and finally, (III) *spiritual* applications with practical results promoting advancement and incorporation of the true *Self* as *Spirit* in *Self-Honesty* into our everyday *Life*.

It is my privilege to present this revolutionary new break-through to all *Seekers* for the first time—and usher in a new standard by which to chart the next spiritual evolution of humanity into the 2020's and beyond.

Safe Passage on the Pathway to Self-Honesty,

—Joshua Free, "Nabu"
Autumn Equinox 2019
Revised Summer 2022

Δ Δ Δ Δ Δ Δ Δ

SUMMARY

Legendary *"Tablets of Destiny,"* representing Divine Truth, supreme knowledge and cosmic power of the *"gods,"* are first introduced to humanity in some of the oldest writings on the planet, the *"Babylonian Epic of Creation"* or *Enuma Eliš* cuneiform tablet series from Mesopotamia.

Ancient Babylonians used the *Enuma Eliš* to systematize all Cosmic knowledge into a workable paradigm, also called the "Mardukite Paradigm," which was received by them from a "higher learned class" called the *Anunnaki*.

All data and information becomes static, understood as *knowledge* only to the level of *Awareness* that it is processed.

There are two primary types of knowledge interpretation: the *"exoteric"* understanding that is programmed based on the common level of the masses, species or group; and the *"esoteric"* understanding that is restricted only to an actualized level of *Awareness* achieved by an individual or smaller group, independent of public opinion or scrutiny.

Many avenues, traditions and belief systems exist by which someone may fragment knowledge and apply authoritarian labels and semantics to experience—but there seems to be no institutionalized organizations that emphasize achievement of a *Self-Honest* individual in this *Lifetime*.

The three tiers, gates or levels of *Awareness* involve taking our (I) *physical* understanding, transferring it to (II) *intellectual* wisdom philosophies, and finally, (III) *spiritual* applications with results that promote advancement of the true *Self* as *Spirit* in *Self-Honesty*.

We may apply the three "levels of understanding" to the *Enuma Eliš* and discover three "levels" of its potential use: Firstly, its magical and physio-political properties; secondly, the cosmological and philosophic knowledge; and thirdly, the revelation of the "*Tablets of Destiny*" as a map to *Self-Honesty*" and realization of godhood in this *Lifetime*.

THE TABLETS OF DESTINY

— REVELATIONS —

MARDUKITE SYSTEMOLOGY
LIBER-ONE

.: 1 :.
RESPONSIBILITY OF COSMIC POWER &
TRANSFER OF ITS DIVINE ABILITIES

Wisdom earned from application of *True Knowledge* yields great power—that great **executable** "Cosmic Power," which appears so **prevalent** in our most ancient texts and "legends" from around the world. Even when we evaluate the distant esoteric **inception** of many widely practiced human traditions and religions, there would seem to be a "higher order" of experience taking place—something eluding the current perceptive state of the human condition in society. At our present Grade-level of understanding, we are no longer concerned with **exacting** the varying **logistics** and cultural timelines carrying this degradation to the present. Our goal is not to repair existing fractured, fragmented—or otherwise *aberrated*—paradigms and institutionalized systems of belief. Our emphasis is on actualizing the *individual spirit*, empowered as its original, proper —or, *alpha*—state of *Self*.

To accomplish this journey for our times, just as with many instances of "Ascended Masters" in the past, we cannot rely on programming perceived from our environment or by any specific paradigms erupting as imitative examples to figures in the past previously traveling this *Pathway to Self-Honesty*. Individuals may be successful in this effort—but we cannot trust their **scions**, those which inevitably carry the messages into an institutionalized knowledge *outside* of *Self-Honest Clarity*. In fact, we might be wary of any contemporary standard of thought held by the masses.

The philosopher *Seneca* recommends that we "use our highest efforts," and however cattle-like our programmed nature, "we should not follow the herd of those that go before" or we will "go not where we should go, but where they go." He advises that: "Since every man chooses to believe rather than evaluate, Life is then never brought to a scrutiny—credulity has always the ascendant. The error handed down from Father to Son embraces our Thoughts in its mazes—we headlong into it. In a phrase: it is the dull infatuation of being led by the examples of others, that exposes us to ruin."*

Empowerment is equivalent to *responsibility*—our "ability" to "respond," or else *enact change*. We may execute this power only to the degree that we maintain *understanding* and *Awareness* of it—and no further. We do not exceed the point we do not fully understand as *Self* in our personal development and spiritual evolution—no matter how many fancy word-games and databanks of semantics we may attach to further communications of Reality we are experiencing.

> **responsibility** : "the *ability* to *respond*; the extent of mobilizing *power* and *understanding* an individual maintains as *Awareness* to enact *change*; the proactive ability to *Self-direct* and make decisions independent of an outside authority."

Humanity would lose its sense of power when it fears it and treats all "responsibility" as a "bad thing" or a grudging chore to behold. In fact, responsibility is equivalent to, and a necessary condition of, our faculties for creating changes that lead to our ultimate goals and true evolution of the *Spirit* as *Self* via *spiritual technologies* and build the confidence necessary to wield awesome power of the "*Tablets of Destiny*."

Δ Δ Δ Δ Δ Δ Δ

According to our ancient cuneiform tablet sources, Cosmic Power—demonstrated as the "*Tablets of Destiny*"—originates in the Primordial Abyss ("*Abzu*"), the "Infinity of Nothingness," often represented by a symbol of the side-

---

* Paraphrasing from John Toland's *Pantheisticon*, originally published in 1720. The *Systemology Society* published a a special tercentenary edition enhanced by Joshua Free in 2020. It is also issued in the 'Appendix' of *Merlyn's Complete Book of Druidism* and *The Complete Mardukite Master Course*.

ways "8" or two zeroes ("OO") next to one another. Transfer of this power thus begins with its origination in the *Infinity* of the Abyss (*"Abzu"*). Manifestation progresses and descends in degree through an entire spectrum of Creation, down to the minutest dross, then back to the Abyss again—recursive and continuous in its own perfection.

This is the only Absolute—and the most fundamental (or "base") cosmic **static** behind all existence, introduced within the modern Mardukite paradigm from the *Enuma Eliš* in earlier *Grade-II* material pertaining to Mesopotamian cosmology.[‡] Therein, this *Nothingness* is esoterically described as the "ALL" or "latent, unmanifest potentiality of *Everythingness*." And this concept is just as abstract today as it once was when first set down in writing thousands of years ago. It is traditionally demonstrated as a *"Sea* of Infinity" in pantheism—as literally described on *Enuma Eliš* tablets.

"And from the *Deep* emerged the *First Cause*—the *LAW* —'*Tiamat*'." Here then, the *Enuma Eliš* describes the first "creature" spawned from out of the Abyss—the "Cosmic Dragon"—to whom the early Mesopotamian languages distinguish with a title meaning *"Cosmic Matrix"*—the *"Life-Giving Mother of All Creation."* Engendered as "She" on the tablets, *"Tiamat"* is the first form and demonstration of "Cosmic Law" in wholeness—"powers" transferred to "Her" as the original "consort" to the *"Abzu."* In many esoteric instances, this "Cosmic Dragon" is represented by the *"ouroborus serpent"* or simply the figure "0" zero. The LAW symbolizes the *"First Cause,* which pervaded over the *Sea of Infinity."* The *Enuma Eliš* informs us that *"Tiamat"* is the first one to possess the *"Tablets of Destiny"* apart from the

---

‡ *"Liber-50"* (released as *Sumerian Religion: Introducing the Anunnaki Gods of Mesopotamian Neopaganism* by Joshua Free) and *"Liber-51+E"* (released as *Babylonian Myth & Magic: Spiritual Traditions and Mysticism in Mesopotamian Anunnaki Religion* by Joshua Free); both are included in the complete Grade-II anthology (*Necronomicon: The Complete Anunnaki Legacy*, 2020 Edition by Joshua Free, Joshua Free Imprint / JFI Publishing).

Abyss—"*She*" becomes the supreme manifestation of "*The Law*" governing the "*Finite Cosmos.*"

This is only where the legacy surrounding the "*Tablets of Destiny*" begins. The *Enuma Eliš* continues, describing the first *ripples* of physical creation carried as the Law across the Abyss with *motion*—a "messenger aspect" named "*Kingu*" on the tablets. "He" is designated in the *Epic* as the consort and *vizier* of "*Tiamat*"—the manifestation of the "*Prime Mover*"ʃ of "*The Law*" in the Cosmos. The primary facets composing all existence—*substance, consciousness* and *motion*—were thus fixed in the Cosmos, *All-as-One*. The Cosmos were in motion in "*khaos*," operating in existence as a singularity under *The Law*. This motion began to "*create*" and "*externalize*" substance into every potential degree and fashion on the **spectrum**.

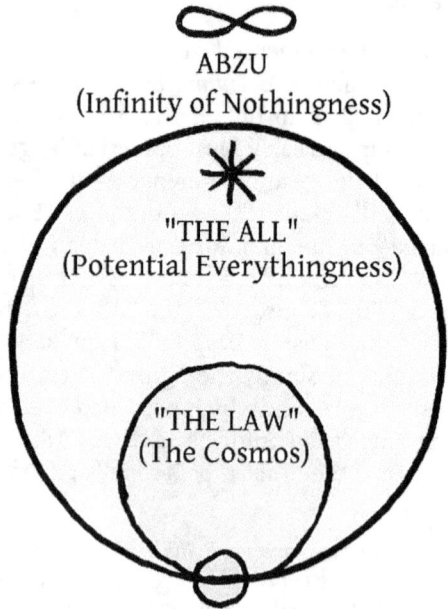

ABZU
(Infinity of Nothingness)

"THE ALL"
(Potential Everythingness)

"THE LAW"
(The Cosmos)

ʃ   "The primary cause of all motion in the cosmos"— from Aristotle's semantics.

The *Enuma Eliš* explains that after the **singularity** of *Abzu* and *Tiamat*, "there were no other gods yet called into being; none bore a name; and no destinies were yet ordained." Afterward, "the celestial gods were created in the Midst of Heaven." Existence then fragmented into oscillating waveforms and particles of *space-over-time*, "and the ages increased," defined by the motion of these waves and parts. "The gods became plentiful and noisy," as the **cacophony** of waves and solids began to abound and interact with one another, "disturbing and troubling" the singularity of "*Abzu* and *Tiamat*." To resolve the "noise" that would allow them to "lie down again in peace," both "*Abzu* and *Tiamat*" devise a plan of attacking and eliminating their creations to reduce them to parts. This is what we call "**entropy**"—and it is reflected on *Enuma Eliš* tablets when "*Tiamat* spawned a host of vipers and dragons, sharp of tooth and merciless of fang... and all fashions of monsters." Suddenly, the *prime directive* of all existence is to *survive* in the balance of *The Law* of creation and entropy.

After this, the *Enuma Eliš* tablets increase in "mythological" or "pantheistic" systematization for "religious" purposes. This legitimized their use in Babylon as a demonstration of "*Marduk's*" superiority in the genealogy of divinity. The celestial gods—or "*Anunnaki*"—find themselves caught up in the proverbial "*war-in-heaven*," engaged in combat against *Tiamat* and Her entropic minions for their own survival—and ultimately their own spiritual sovereignty as the next generation of Cosmic Creators. *Tiamat* prepares her spawn for battle, sending Her messenger "*Kingu*" as their commander, after first encoding total control of the *The Law* on the *Prime Mover*. "She gave him the *Tablets of Destiny,* fixing them to his breast" saying, "Your command shall be effective. Whatsoever you will—it shall be established."

The "Anunnaki Assembly" hears the commotion of war against them, so they convene to take action. When none among their hierarchy volunteers to battle, *Marduk*, eldest son of *Enki*, stands up and makes a proposition. He asks them, if he were to conquer *Tiamat* and fix a proper cosmic order into existence, would they hail him as the "Chief of the Gods." The Anunnaki agree. He prepares for combat, arming with a bow, a thunderbolt and "seven terrible winds." He mounts his chariot, an "unequaled storm," driven by four horses—named *Destruction, Ferocity, Terror* and *Swiftness.* "With garments cloaked in terror and an overpowering brightness crowning his head, *Marduk* set out toward the raging *Tiamat.*"

Marduk seeks to overcome the primordial powers of *Chaos* —a whole dramatic demonstration ensues. As *Marduk* approaches, he is able to "gaze upon the inward parts of *Tiamat*," but when he moves to attack directly, he is flanked by activity of "*Kingu*," now identified as "Her spouse." Before advancing on *Tiamat* to attack, *Marduk* counters *Kingu* with a "powerful gaze"—presumably his own Will, as no other type of assault on *Kingu* is indicated —and "the Will of *Kingu* was destroyed and his motions ceased." He then defeats *Tiamat* by "filling Her belly with the terrible winds" and "Her Will was taken from Her." Then, *The Power* directly transfers to the Anunnaki generations, with *Marduk* as Chief, since "He rightly took the *Tablets of Destiny* from *Kingu*, whom he had conquered— and sealed them with his seal, then hung them from his neck."

> *AN* : "an ancient cuneiform sign designating the *'spiritual zone';* the *Spiritual Universe*—comprised of spiritual matter and spiritual energy; a direction of motion toward *Infinity*, away from or superior to the physical (*'KI'*); the spiritual condition of existence providing for our primary *Alpha* state as an individual *Identity* or *I-AM-Self* which interacts and experiences *Awareness* of a *beta* state in the Physical Universe (*'KI'*) as *Life*." (*NexGen Systemological NewSpeak*)

Empowered with the "*Tablets of Destiny,*" *Marduk* split the body of *Tiamat* in two, using her "head as a covering for the heavens"—the spiritual zone, <u>AN</u>—and with her "body" he "measured and structured the *Deep*" and founded the "Kingdom"—the physical zone, <u>KI</u>—"which was created as like the heavens."

> **KI** : "an ancient cuneiform sign designating the
> '*physical zone*'; the *Physical Universe*—comprised of
> physical matter and physical energy in action across
> space and observed as time; a direction of motion to-
> ward material *Continuity*, away from or subordinate
> to the Spiritual ('*AN*'); the physical condition of exist-
> ence providing for our *beta* state of *Awareness*
> experienced (and interacted with) as an individual
> *Lifeform* from our primary Alpha state of Identity or
> *I-AM-Self* in the Spiritual Universe ('*AN*')." (*NexGen*
> *Systemological NewSpeak*)

"*Law*" prevailed as the "Firmament"—*All-as-One*; "*an-ki*"—demonstrating the "eternal" and perceptibly infinite **continuity** circle of the *Great All*. Spiritual Law (the "ALL") governed the Spiritual Universe ("*AN*") and Cosmic Law (the "LAW") governed the Physical Universe ("*KI*"). "The beginning and ending of Creation are the same; one as the other. Whatever change is enacted in the physical world is not separate; it significantly and necessarily has its higher counterpart in the spiritual world."[§] *Marduk* then proceeds to *order* the Cosmos—establishing zones of "fixed planets," twelve "Houses" of the zodiac, and "Star-Gates" energetic-ally connecting the system holistically. Thus, according to ancient Mardukite Babylonian tradition (verbatim), the at-tributive aspects of our "Reality" as we have come to understand them in all systems—regardless of correspond-ing vocabulary—was set up by "*Marduk*," fixed in place and defined by "Divine" authority of the "*Tablets of Destiny*."

Where the first five *Enuma Eliš* "Creation" tablets (de-scribed above) demonstrate an esoteric understanding of

---

§   Quoting *Sajaha Tablet II: lines 8-9*—in the *Appendix* of the current
    volume, excerpting "Tablet-S" in *The Complete Anunnaki Bible*
    edited by Joshua Free.

50

"*cosmogenetic*" origins (of the systems in the universe)—the sixth tablet is metaphorically "*anthropogenetic*" (describing human origins). It is for this reason that later Hebrew interpretations of the Mardukite Babylonian paradigm relay the seven *Enuma Eliš* tablets as "seven days" of Creation—of which on the "sixth day," according to Judeo-Christian semantics: "God creates Man." These three words significantly oversimplify our older Mesopotamian sources, transcribing *Marduk's* original "sixth tablet" monologue:—

"The Key to the Gate shall be ever hidden, except to My Offspring. I will take my Blood—and with Bone, I will fashion a Race of Men, that they may keep Watch over the Gate. And from the *Blood-of-Kingu*, I will create a Race of Men—that they will inhabit the Earth in service to the Gods, and so that Shrines to the Anunnaki may be built and the Temples filled. I will bind the Elder Gods to the Watchtowers; let them keep Watch over the *Gate-of-Abzu*, and the *Gate-of-Tiamat*, and the *Gate-of-Kingu*... And with the Key known only to My Race."*

The seventh and final *Enuma Eliš* tablet is *exoterically* a "legal record" of *Marduk's* supreme executive spiritual mastery over the physical universe with the **assumption** of "*Fifty Names of Divinity*"—the qualities of physical systemology that are otherwise known as the "*Arts of Civilization.*" These "tangible" derivatives of the "*Tablets of Destiny*" are also referred to as the Divine "ME," pronounced, "*may.*" This is mythographically important, because **chronologically**, from this point onward in the Mesopotamian Mythos—as reflected on cuneiform **successively** more recent "historical tablets"—the issue of "material worldly control" centers on a knowledge-fragmentation of the original "*Tablet of Destiny*" wisdom, which we identify in lore as these Divine "ME" and "*Arts of Civilization*"—which we could just as easily translate for our purposes as literally the "*Arts of Human Systematization.*"

Δ Δ Δ Δ Δ Δ Δ

The "Arts of Civilization" (rendered on tablet records with the cuneiform sign: "ME") first appear on the oldest cuneiform tablet sources as a tool for systematizing a communication of virtually all aspects of "society" and "Reality." According to these ancient cuneiform records, this begins (for our current age or incarnation of civilization) sometime after the end of the last Ice Age—when after the "De-

---

* Quoting from *Enuma Elis: Tablet VI.*

52

luge,"[‡] the Anunnaki return to jump-start "civilization" again, starting with a small protected (and surviving) population of the Ancient Near East: a result of efforts put forth by "*Enki*"—chief Elder Anunnaki "scientist," and father to "*Marduk*." *Enki's* original homestead of *Eridu* (near the ancient coast of the Persian Gulf) served as an Anunnaki capital—both before and immediately following the "Deluge"[§]—as the primary storehouse of "ME–*Arts of civilization* on Earth," the physical world and its systematized "Order" as perceived in *Awareness*.

A decade of intensive holistic research and discovery has made it very clear to us, however, that ancient *Reality Engineers* maintained "permanent records" (formulas, axioms, guides and instructions)—essentially "physical archetypes"—regarding all key knowledge for systematizing "*consciousness*" (understanding) of the "Human Condition."

> **consciousness** : "the energetic flow of *Awareness*; the Principle System of *Awareness manifestation* that is spiritual in nature, which demonstrates potential interaction with all degrees of the Physical Universe; the *Beingness* component of our existence in *Spirit*; the Principle System of *Awareness* as *Spirit* that directs action in the Mind-System."

In one prehistoric *legend*, the "*Arts of Civilization*" are divided among *seven* "*Tablets of Destiny*"—each using a different material to correspond to a particular "ray" or "energy stream"—or "*Radiances*"—of Reality as a sevenfold schema:

(1) an Onyx Tablet of Water and the Abyss;
(2) a Golden Tablet of Fire and Action;
(3) a Diamond Tablet of Earth and Matter;

---

‡ The "Deluge" is recorded in the *Atra-Asis* cycle, which directly inspired Hebrew lore of "Noah"—see "Tablet-G" in *The Complete Anunnaki Bible* edited by Joshua Free.

§ "Before the Deluge, Kingship was in *Eridu*—then after the Deluge, Kingship again came down from Heaven." Quoting "Tablet-G" in *The Complete Anunnaki Bible* edited by Joshua Free.

(4) a Beryl Tablet of Spirit and Essence;
(5) a Silver Tablet of Survival and Innate Programming;
(6) a Wooden Tablet of the Green World and Nature; and
(7) an Ivory Tablet of Animation and Animal-Life.

Esoterically, the original "ME" represent *fragmentation* of holistic knowledge into seven parts—easily dispersed as "separate understandings" of the ALL, which were deemed too powerful (or too dangerous) by early systematizers to be left **undefiled**. Or else, these figures progressively lost the ability to behold the total collected wisdom of the Cosmos—which progressively developed in obscurity. For whatever the reasons, these *Anunnaki* beings operating at a higher echelon of *understanding* and *Awareness* structured the "human condition" in such a manner of fragmented social programming that we remain under its "spell" today, primarily fixed in our consciousness processing—as *"Reality"*—utilizing authoritarian language (semantic-sets) and civic systemology. It is no coincidence that later use of the cuneiform sign "ME" (in Akkadian language) indicates "to be" or *"Beingness."*

In every ancient cuneiform version of human inception (or upgrade) on Earth, it is "Divine engineers" that experimentally integrate their own genetic material *and* an astral or spiritual component of higher order *Awareness* onto *Life* on Earth. This advanced or accelerated natural evolution of humanity perhaps light years ahead of its own timeline.

Early Sumerian civilization was loosely systematized with very basic programming of survival and servitude. In times when *Anunnaki* figures are blatantly present and conducting affairs on Earth, the societal records are quite light. All critical communications among *Anunnaki* themselves, are taking place at a higher order of understanding and reasoning. It is not reflected on any form of religious or spiritual tablets at this time, because it was not necessary for general populations to understand how their programming worked in order for it to operate. This other *higher* transfer of knowledge-power took place *later* and then *only* esoterically among a hand-chosen "elite" which inherited control of the "physical systemology" of the "Realms" maintained by humanity in the eventual absence of the "gods" and their direct presence on Earth. It is quite clear that such a presence later solidified as wholly representative, figurative and open to interpretation among the masses—hence "religion"—which reduced fluid potential into static faith.

Once tangible forms of the "*Arts of Civilization*" were solidified in *Eridu*, control of the ME "transferred"*—or was sometimes stolen‡—between *Anunnaki*. Each time these "Arts" moved location, a new capital city came into being dedicated and systematized to its own **patron** Anunnaki deity. By the time a complete **archetype** of "human systemology" reached perfection as the "Babylonian paradigm," the Divine ME or "*Arts of Civilization*" were no less than *60*—a numeric designation of "*Anu*," the Father of the *Anunnaki*—including two "*Tablets of Destiny*" (one for the "heavens" and one for "earth") and a third "*Tablet of Truth*" in addition to seven "*Divine Decrees*" (royal regalia representative of sovereignty) and fifty civic worldly systems that are no doubt, in some way, connected to the fifty "Divine Names" *assumed* by Marduk in the *Enuma Eliš*.

This present volume treats collective wisdom of the "*Tablets of Destiny*," "*Divine ME*" and "*Arts of Civilization*" as an actuality for the first time in the modern age. The list is an ancient catalog of systematic *facets* of perception (and reality *fragmentation*) that we can easily identify today as

---

* First relayed in the "*Transfer of the Arts of Civilization from Eridu to Erech/Uruk*" tablet cycle, which describes how Enki surrendered some "one-hundred decrees and treasures" to Inanna-Ishtar to support her early human-systematization attempts as "Uruk Sumerian" civilization—para. *Sumerian Religion (Liber-50)* by Joshua Free.

‡ An example is found on the second tablet of the *Anzu* cycle, when a "*Tablet of Destinies*" is stolen from Babylon and used against the ancient Mardukites—ref. "Tablet-V" series of *The Complete Anunnaki Bible* edited by Joshua Free.

"programs" determining our physical, emotional and intellectual experience of operating the "*human condition.*" These are the "Agreements-of-Reality" for the "Realm"—what is "regulated" as "Real" by a member of the "royal elite"—but after a collective of "elite priests and priestesses" (that serve to maintain control and survival of the System) first establishes the Ruler as a divine representation of the "gods on earth." This **orchestration** of activity was conducted precisely according to instructions left by *Anunnaki* for the "elite" to ensure that their "creations" stayed "civilized"—and further, to safeguard against the "Human condition" rising to such an elevated state that it would pose as a nuisance to the "gods," in their "higher spiritual state of existence."

The obscure cuneiform document describing the "*Arts of Civilization*" lists fifty "*dynamic perceptions*" or "*perceptic facets.*" Antiquated records describing the *Arts* are often found roughly translated by early scholars. We are *not* going to attempt to "backtrack" our holistic understanding at this time by **correlating** a precise knowledge base with this literal list. A casual examination of our translation (given below) provides a bit of historical "momentum to our research," particularly regarding extreme systematic detail displayed in this ancient paradigm.

The original list:—(1) EN-ship or Enlil-ship; (2) AN-ship or Anu-ship (Godhood); (3) the Exalted and Eternal Crown; (4) the Exalted Throne of Kingship; (5) the Exalted Sceptre of Sovereignty; (6) the Royal Insignia; (7) the Exalted Shrine; (8) the Arts of Shepherdship; (9) the Arts of Kingship; (10) the Arts of Royal Ladyship or Queenship; (11) the Arts of the Divine Lady or Priestesscraft; (12) the Arts of the Chamberlain or Priestcraft; (13) "*lumah*" ... priestcraft; (14) "*guda*" ... priestcraft; (15) the Exalted Truth; (16) the Arts of Descent into the Underworld; (17) the Arts of Ascent from the Underworld; (18) "*kugarra*" ... a transgendered temple servant?; (19) "*girbadara*" ... a eunuch temple servant?; (20) "*sagursag*" ... a eunuch serving in the priestess convent?; (21) the Art of War; (22) the Secret of the Deluge;

(23) the Art of Weaponry; (24) Sexual Reproduction; (25) the Arts of Prostitution; (26) the Art of Lawmaking; (27) the Rules of Libel and Lawsuit; (28) the Arts of Pictorial Graphics; (29) the Ritual Arts of the Cult Chamber; (30) the Arts of Sacred Prostitution of the "Hierodule of Heaven"; (31) the Art of Crafting Musical Instruments; (32) the Art of Music; (33) the Role of Eldership; (34) the Role of the Hero; (35) the Art of Demonstrating Power; (36) the Consequences of Cursing and Malevolent Acts; (37) the Philosophy of Straightforwardness, Right Thought and Right Action; (38) the Destruction of Cities; (39) the Lamentations; (40) the Rejoicing of the Heart; (41) the Consequences of Falsehood; (42) the Arts of Metallurgy; (43) the Arts of Scribeship; (44) the Arts of Smithcraft; (45) the Arts of the Leatherworker; (46) the Arts of Building and Masonry; (47) the Arts of Basketweaving; (48) the Arts of Cosmic Wisdom; (49) the Arts of Attention Energy; (50) the Arts of Holy Purification; (51) the Systems of Fear; (52) the Systems of Terror; (53) the Systems of Strife, Challenge and Confrontation; (54) the Systems of Peace, Harmony and Balance; (55) the Systems of Weariness, Fatigue and Entropy; (56) the Systems of Victory and Success; (57) the Arts and Systems of Counseling Intellect; (58) the Arts and Systems of Counseling Emotion; (59) the Arts of Right Judgment; and (60) the Arts of Logic, Clear Thinking and Right Action.

Δ Δ Δ Δ Δ Δ Δ

SUMMARY

The esoteric "*Pathway to Self-Honesty*" (alluded to on "*Tablets of Destiny*") has been successfully traveled and charted by "*Ascended Masters*" in the past—even if their alleged followers, and traditions inspired in their name, have fallen short of producing such results *in Self-Honesty*.

Our ability to *Self-direct* and enact change in response to our environment as *Self-determinism* is directly **proportional** to our level of understanding and "*responsibility*."

The Absolute—ALL—is a background static behind and above all existence, referred to on the *"Tablets of Destiny"* as the *Infinity of Nothingness*. It is described as the "latent unmanifest potentiality of *Everythingness*."

The LAW—represented by the Cosmic Dragon "Tiamat" in the *Enuma Eliš*—is the **existential** division between the *Spiritual Universe* ("AN") and the *Physical Universe* ("KI").

The LAW "takes possession of" the *"Tablets of Destiny,"* fixing a separation between the (*Finite*) LAW of continuous manifestation from the (*Infinite*) ALL of Absolute unmanifest potential.

The Principle Systems of Manifestation—*Substance, Motion* and *Consciousness*—are fixed in the Universe by the LAW.

Formation and interaction of active existences—"substances" and "bodies" and *"Life"* and *"gods"*—in this new "Finite Cosmos" creates turbulent waves in space. The governing system of *Cosmic Law* —"Tiamat"— responds accordingly. She fixes the *"Tablets of Destiny"* to *her* consort and deputy, a "vizier-messenger wave action" of the LAW —named "Kingu" on the *Tablets*—sending *him* to ripple out and "meet" the *Anunnaki* "gods."

The *Anunnaki Assembly* of "gods" prepare to battle the LAW. When none among them comes forth to engage, it is the *Anunnaki* "god" Marduk that volunteers as "hero" to *confront* Kingu and Tiamat—conditionally requesting that the *Assembly* recognize him as "Chief of the Gods" upon success.

When Marduk goes to approach the LAW directly, he is flanked by Kingu and the army of *"Ancient Ones."* Marduk is then able to relinquish the *"Tablets of Destiny"* from Kingu, which enables him to conquer his understanding of the LAW and thereby Tiamat.

Marduk uses the *"Tablets of Destiny"* to discover *Self-Honesty* and the Divine Knowledge of "Cosmic Ordering," which divides the *Spiritual Universe* ("AN") and the *Physic-*

al Universe ("KI")—and the two universes are connected by a stream of *Awareness* called *Spirit*, *Life* or *Lifeforce*.

Wisdom from the *"Tablets of Destiny"* are passed down to, and concealed by, an esoteric "Order" or "Society" of Babylonian High Priests and Priestesses, which systematized the first *"Ancient Mystery School"* at the inception of modern Human civilization.

The singularity of "Divine" wisdom and knowledge is fragmented and dispersed on Earth as the "Divine ME" (pronounced *"may"*)—otherwise referred to on the *"Arcane Tablets"* as the *"Arts of Civilization,"* from which civic systematization of the "Human Condition" resulted.

The "Human Condition" is experienced from *Self* as *"Awareness."*

.: 2 :.
DECIPHERING FUNDAMENTALS OF EXISTENCE FROM THE "TABLETS OF DESTINY"

If we examine this wide body of allegorical lore in its entirety—hereafter referred to as "*Arcane Tablets*" or "*Tablets of Destiny*"—then we are left to **extrapolate** many definitive "truths" for ourselves regarding other data that we find consistent in guiding us effectively toward a higher level of understanding and practical application. We account for distortions of language across time, by applying intensive experimental research to any discoveries. We overcome distortions in present-time language by giving clear dynamic definitions of our terminology. A true communication of the "fundamentals" at this level of understanding is only accomplished by overcoming any barriers in language—to be certain we are definitive in our meaning of *A-for-A*. Otherwise, this information runs the risk of fading into the background of *Awareness* as "just more words."

The "*Arcane Tablets*" are clear in stating all *things* in the Physical Universe are indeed in motion, which is why they exist. The Physical Universe is also defined by *things* relative to other *things*. And all *things* are *wave* motions—as energy and matter—in space measured across time. Which is what a "wave" is. Most understand this best as distance traveled in a vehicle—as "miles-*per*-hour" or "kilometers-*per*-hour"—which is always given as "space over time" or "space divided by time."

> **dynamic (systems)** : "a principle or fixed system which demonstrates its '*variations*' in activity (or output) only in constant relation to variables or fluctuation of interrelated systems; a standard principle, function, process or system that exhibits '*variations*' and change simultaneously with all connected systems."

This is **localized** knowledge from the point of the Observer or *Self*—who is not moving, but is experiencing motion of physical mechanics at work and often refer to these aspects as "relative." We see, as the first *Self-determined* act by the **sentient** *Alpha Spirit* hero—in this case, "Marduk"—is to understand the Chaos of the Physical Universe and immediately apply efforts to Order it—and essentially, *create* with it.

"Cosmological" or "cosmogenetic" origin epics—of which the *Enuma Eliš* is an ancient and complete *Anunnaki* tablet-rendering used to systematize the Human Condition from a Babylonian **epicenter**—always, by definition, consist of attempts to *Order* the *Chaos*. Creation, as we understand it, is not a true physical "creation" at all, but an *ordering*. "Marduk" is not, by any means, *creating* the energy and matter of the Physical Universe—he *is* applying his *Will* to be the "spiritual cause" of "physical effects" from a higher point of *Awareness* that originates outside or apart from the Physical Universe. This is clear with *Tiamat* —the *Law*—separating "higher" encompassing "Spiritual" states of existence from the Physical Universe.

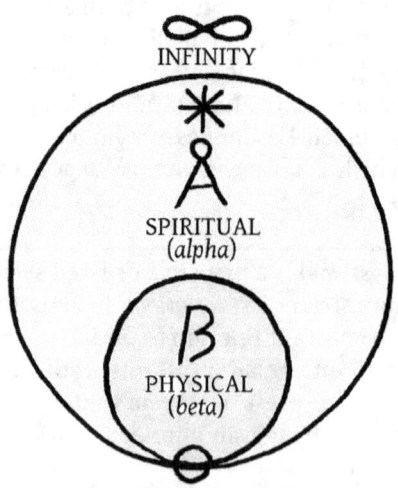

The two Universes are independent of interaction from one another to exist, except by one *pathway*—and the instance of one singular expression—which is *Life*. As far as we know, the Spiritual Universe (of metaphysical energy and metaphysical matter) is not dependent on the Physical Universe (of physical energy and physical matter) to exist; nor, as we can easily observe, is the Physical Universe dependent on a Spiritual Universe to remain in active motion—except when it comes to *Life*. We visibly see that this Spiritual Universe has the ability to animate physical organisms with *Spiritual Energy* as *Life* to experience the Physical Universe.

Once we are in a state of realization about *"what"* is taking place, the *"whys"* behind the phenomenon of *Spiritual Life Energy* inhabiting *Physical Matter* seem inconsequential (at this level of understanding) compared to *"how"* this works and *"how"* we may best use information that *is* within our degree of accessibility to further us in greater understanding and *Awareness*—levels of realization at a plateau that we cannot definitively *imagine* until we achieve it. The *why* may be understood as a result of its *Self-Honest* application. What we *do know* is that we have a Physical Universe on our hands that we are choosing to inhabit—for whatever reasons—and we have a knowing that the true *Self* is not actually our physical bodies, yet that *we are very much* connected to these "genetic vehicles" on a *Spiritual Lifeline* for experience *of* (and existence *in*) this Physical Universe—for *that much* we can be sure.

> **genetic vehicle** : "a physical *Life*-form; the physical (*beta*) body that is animated with (*alpha*) *Spirit* using a continuous *Lifeline*; a physical (*beta*) **organic** receptacle and catalyst for the (*alpha*) *Self* to operate causes and experience effects within the Physical Universe." (*NexGen Systemological NewSpeak*)

A distinction and classification between these two Universes is too often blurred in modern "spiritual" and "metaphysical" philosophies—and often too esoteric to easily decipher from ancient sources. Individuals rejecting authoritarian "religious dogma" of a Spiritual Universe (and its **causative** nature on the Physical Universe) are just as likely to **succumb** to another common trap, when the pendulum swings the other way and we systematize the Physical Universe—including its unique interaction as *Life*—without any regard for the *Spirit.* Conventional science has no better means of achieving an understanding than the *Singularity* it still seeks in its equations, because both are of the same *causal "Spiritual ∞ Infinity"* existing outside the boundaries of our *effective "Physical ° Continuity."*

Δ Δ Δ Δ Δ Δ Δ

All communication of our Reality is conducted in relative terms—essentially from the perspective of the Physical Universe: Existence to the extent that we are capable of, or instructed in, reception, experience and understanding. This is relative to the individual Observer and range of faculties at whatever tier of understanding and *Awareness* perceptions are operating at. This is a natural part of evaluating experience of Reality—for we are all here with the **faculties** of a *spiritual scientist.* Just as we see in physical *Awareness* for things—and the magnitude of definitions in our scope—the *Pathway* marking levels of *Awareness* between variable "degrees of continuity" in the Physical Universe ("KI" or *"beta"* state of existence) and "static infinity" governing the Spiritual Universe ("AN" or *"alpha"* state of existence) were once literally represented with ancient Babylonian temple infrastructure of *Marduk* and *Nabu*—the *ziggurats*—"stepped-pyramids" comprised of seven tiers connecting the Physical Universe with the "heavens."

The further up the levels—or "gates"—of the *ziggurat* one climbs, the greater the span of view achieved, and the "higher state of *Awareness*" accessible. It is progressive and cumulative. We are not losing a sense of previous levels of *Awareness*—though we may choose to no longer fixate on them. We are **Ascending**. In our natural state, we always tend toward the "higher" for survival and evolution of our physical existence in the Physical Universe ("KI") as **precedent** of our realizing or actualizing our spiritual infinity within the Physical Universe. *Life* that is not operating in this tendency is being *blocked*. And what's more, it is probably blocking or inhibiting other *Life*. We must assume that any *Life* operating against the holistic principles of its own physical and spiritual survival (which are relatively identical in the Physical Universe) is otherwise   not in "good shape." They apply efforts against their own survival—and that of others—and are "fragmented."

Today, we must continue to correct so many mistaken associations of the Spiritual Universe ("AN") with the "space *up there*." The space **encompassing** the Earth planet is still *physical space*—and physical space reflects the "physical continuity" of the Physical Universe ("KI"). We represent this with the symbol of a "circle" or "zero" (sometimes with a horizontal line through it)—also used in the sense of *degrees* of "spectrum on a continuum."

> **continuum** : "a continuous *whole*; observing all gradients on a *spectrum*; measuring quantitative variation with gradual transition on a spectrum without demonstrating discontinuity or separate parts."

Some esoteric schools have defined this continuum and its parameters regarding the Physical Universe as "*The Law*" or *Cosmic Law*. Yet, although we find the Physical Universe as continuous motion and transformation—maybe even relatively recursive upon itself—it is not a true Infinite-Static or "Infinity"—a quality that is reserved only for the *Life* that projects through the "Spiritual Universe" relative to our ability to calculate for it in the Physical Universe. The Physical Universe is a *continuity*. The Spiritual Dimension borders *Infinity*.

The only band or continuum that *All-as-One* connects the Physical "zeroes" with the Spiritual "infinities" is *Life*, for which we cannot use physical calculations to accurately describe, because "*Life*" is not the actual "physical" force of "physical" motion. Physical motion is all that what we are examining when we calculate "**physics**." We can fairly accurately measure movements of physical bodies in relation to one another, but we cannot account for *Self-determination* using physics alone. We *logically* represent true "Spiritual" or "metaphysical" aspects with mathematical symbols—*zeroes* and *infinities* and *Greek letters*. This only seems irrational when we disregard them as "Source" while charting motions of physical energy and physical matter across space-time in the Physical Universe. No calculation exists in physics to define the *Spirit* that *Wills* an arm to move. Only the physical (**kinetic**) energy demonstrated by the physical body during this action is measurable.

We can demonstrate all manners of semantic logic to define how the body functions and this or that muscle in combination with electrical charges of the brain-center are carried out to accomplish the physical motion in agreement with Cosmic Law of the Physical Universe, but that is it. That is the extent of *knowingness* via **physiology**. And it is certainly valid to the extent of its truth in the Physical Universe. It makes postulates as to how actions and motions of the "genetic vehicle" carry it across the terrain, but it does not define the *driver*—and it never will. There is an equally *logical* reason for this—and we may extract it directly from the *Arcane Tablet* narrative of Marduk.

Marduk conquers Tiamat by first attaining the "*Tablets of Destiny*"—an understanding of *Cosmic Law*, the physical laws governing the Physical Universe—and then using them. He is *not* changing the Law. He is *not* spontaneously generating new solids from Spiritual Nothingness. Marduk is using energy and matter of the Physical Universe and turning it back onto the Physical Universe *within* the parameters of Cosmic Law. He is the causative *Will* of action from a higher state, but he is not the physical force behind it. Those forces are already existent within the Physical Universe, and they have laws governing tendencies of their motion—which operate with or without our **agreement**. In fact, our ability to exist and evolve our form within the Physical Universe of these motions is entirely conditional on our "correctness" in evaluating our state of Reality *agreements* with the Physical Universe. Our degree of "incorrectness" seems to result in everything from pain to death.

An **Alpha Spirit** manifesting or projected from the Spiritual Universe chooses, for whatever reasons, to animate and operate a *Lifeform*. They may then thereafter, if somehow disturbed or fragmented out-of-phase, choose not to be in agreement with the Physical Universe. But unless their Reality is in a stronger state of agreements than Cosmic Law—which is, to us, an impossibility as far as we know, if still confining *Awareness* to the physical body—they will soon discover that they experience physical effects to their causes. This is not a "Divine" punishment; nor is it arbitrary. All effects of **manifestation** are according to parameters of the Cosmic Law of the Physical Universe.

> **alpha spirit** : "a 'spiritual' *Life*-form; the 'true' *Self* or I-AM; the spiritual (*alpha*) *Self* that is animating the (*beta*) physical body or *'genetic vehicle'* using a continuous *Lifeline*; an individual spiritual (*alpha*) entity possessing no physical mass or measurable waveform (motion) in the Physical Universe as itself, so it animates the (*beta*) physical body or *'genetic vehicle'* as a catalyst to experience *Self*-determined causality in effect within the Physical Universe." (*NexGen Systemological NewSpeak*)

The *Anunnaki* are described on the *Arcane Tablets* as "*primordial spirits*"—meaning that they already exist at the inception of the *ordered* Physical Universe. They conquer the Physical Universe, *ordering* it to suit their own inhabitant survival after projecting their *Lifeline* of *Spirit* into physical forms. This is no small feat, but it is this very

premise that originally defined "Divinity" or "gods" in ancient times. We may conclude that the ultimate goal of survival as *Self* is spiritual immortality, which may in some unknown way be reflected in our *beta existence* and its ability to assist us in achieving our highest energetic state. As is stated in an esoteric *"Doctrine of Analogy"*—There is a **correspondence** between things *seen* and *unseen*; earth is the shadow of heaven and man is a reflection of divinity.[*]

> **beta (existence)** : "all manifestation in the 'Physical Universe' (KI); the 'Physical' state of existence consisting of vibrations of physical energy and physical matter moving through physical space and experienced as 'time'; the *Awareness* of the *Alpha-spirit* (*Self*) as a physical organic *Lifeform* or *'genetic vehicle'* in which it experiences causality in the 'Physical Universe'." (*NexGen Systemological NewSpeak*)

Even as a form of recreation, it would require physical perception of motion to an otherwise spiritual or static existence—much like operating a remote "avatar" or a "virtual reality" experience from a stationary point. Over the last several decades, as understanding of technologies has risen, we witness increased consideration of such paradigms, particularly in popular movies. The operator supplies the *"Will"* for causation—but all **motor-functions** and *beta* interactions are carried out calculatedly within parameters of physical experience.

It seems that the *Anunnaki* had *quite a go of it* in the beginning, crashing about in the unfamiliar Physical Universe of physical solids and physical forces—enough turbulence to stir up a recourse action from the Law, when *Tiamat* dispenses the *"Tablets of Destiny"* with *Kingu*, the messenger-action of the Law, across the Physical Universe. Therefore our first brush with *Anunnaki* "gods" from *Arcane Tablets* depicts them as spiritual *Lifeforms* incarnate in physical bodies engaged in an effort of dynamic conquest over the

---

[*]   Quoting mystic philosopher, Eliphas Levi.

Physical Universe for their physical existence and surviv-al. And what a picture that paints for us—for what loftier purpose for *Life* can we glean from this lore than that it *ex-ists* and makes every effort to continue that **existence** to achieve the highest possible goal relative to all universes and possible existences, which is an increased *Awareness* that may earn a being **infinite-existence** as a *Self-directed Spirit*. In that state, we are resuming actualization of our true static spiritual *Alpha* point of *Self-Determinism*—and we may enact this *Awareness* upon our *beta* existence in the Physical Universe (KI).

Within the "Mardukite paradigm" shared among ancient Babylonian elite, Marduk had acquired the *True Knowing-ness* from the "*Tablets of Destiny*," which he then shared, demonstrating a map—a "spiritual pathway" through the turbulent Physical Universe—leading the way for *Life* to overcome disorienting distortions of a *beta* existence and everything that comes with it. If we follow the *Pathway* ap-propriately to *Self-Honesty*, we ensure progress of our own existence by regaining the highest levels of our true "spir-itual" *Self*-actualized *Awareness* while still operating in the Physical Universe. Such an accomplishment is our birth-right—a true realization of **Godhood** in this *Lifetime* and proper **Ascension** of our *Spirit* thereafter; the ability to rise up from primal **dross** and walk among the *gods* in the *heavens* as one of them.

Δ Δ Δ Δ Δ Δ Δ

SUMMARY

Communication of clear wisdom and true knowledge from the "*Tablets of Destiny*" is distorted as it passes through time and geography, carried by diverse languages and au-thoritarian cultures using the "power" to *program* the masses and *fragment* the Human Condition away from "*Self-Honesty*."

All *things* in the *Physical Universe* are in motion. All *things* are *wave motions* as "energy and matter in space measured across time."

Use of ancient wisdom demonstrated on the *"Tablets of Destiny"* reveals keys to *"Cosmic Ordering"*—the *Self-direction* using the highest understanding of "cause-and-effect" in the *Physical Universe*.

The *Self* is a "spiritual cause" of "physical effects" engaging a *Self-determined "Will"* as actualized *Awareness*.

"Spiritual ∞ Infinity" (in the direction of *AN*) is an *Infinity of Nothingness*. existing outside the boundaries of our *effective "Physical ° Continuity"* (*KI*), divided by the LAW and encompassed by the ALL.

The *Spiritual Universe* and the *Physical Universe* are existentially independent of each other, maintaining a definitive conduit or connection by only one *pathway* that we can determine—which is *Life* or *Awareness* of the *Alpha Spirit*.

From an *"alpha"* state of spiritual existence, the *Self* engages a *Lifeline* with a *"genetic vehicle"* or "organic body" in order to carry or maintain its *Spiritual Life* as *Awareness* through a *beta existence* in the *Physical Universe*.

Stepped "levels" of *"ziggurat"* temples in Babylonia—and corresponding *"gates"*—represent spiritual "levels" of *Awareness*, or "states" of *Self-purification* ("defragmentation"), as it "ascends" toward AN on the path of *Self-Honesty*, in the footsteps of the "gods."

Physical "space" reflects "physical continuity" of the Physical Universe ("KI"), which we represent with the symbol of a "continuity circle" or "zero"—also a sign used to denote *"degrees"* within a spectrum on a *"continuum."*

The only calculable *continuum* connecting "Physical *zeroes*" ("continuity") with "Spiritual *infinities*" is *"Lifeforce,"* for which we cannot use traditional physical models to accurately describe, because the *Lifeforce* itself is not the physical force of physical motion applied to physical substance that we calculate in traditional physics.

.: 3 :.
CARRYING THE LEGACY OF ANCIENT WISDOM FROM THE "TABLETS OF DESTINY" INTO A NEW AGE

When we consider the "Tablets of Destiny" and "Mystery School" as a dispersal source in the ancient world, with a legacy carried thousands of years up to present time—when we examine it now, **objectively**—we find shreds of it fragmented across the world in the lore of various ancient cultures and "spiritual traditions." As a premise—after exploring philosophical and archaeological data of other cultural examples across the timeline—the original Mardukite Research Organization (from which Systemology sprung) emphasized the oldest, clearest and most complete ancient paradigm—Mesopotamia, or specifically Babylon. This just happens to be the birthplace of Systemology in the Western world. Mardukite methodology is derived from essentially the oldest systematization source for the modern world. The work has been an effort of discovery, esoteric experimentation and evaluation... it does not pretend to be a direct descendent from this or that existing society or group—yet in the process of treating the bulk of "wisdom traditions" with our modern **acid-test** of Self-Honesty, we have negated most of the superfluous roughage from our field of study.

Most would agree that a Self-Honest "clear channel" to carry true ancient wisdom into present time has not been in existence—at least in no publicly visible esoteric fashion. There are no cultural paradigms or "systems," which inherited a direct unbroken line of total Awareness and esoteric understanding. What we do find is an organic evolution of diverse pieces in fragmentation—none of which have retained the same degree of clarity and continuity as the Arcane Tablets.

We know in our Systemology that "understanding" and "Awareness" are not the same. We illustrate this within the original Mardukite paradigm most blatantly with our treatment of the the *Enuma Eliš* tablets. In this instance, for the present Grade, we are not necessarily examining a *new* "set" of tablets. The "data" itself is still the same fixed clay artifact. However, we *are* gleaning *new information*—actual "knowledge"—by our *new understanding* of the same Physical Universe around us as we apply "higher" levels of *Awareness*. This is achieved from previous effective use of true knowledge and wisdom that advances our ability to be *Aware* in *Self-Honesty*—with actualized access to that missing *"clear channel"* of Reality experience.

Understanding and *Awareness* are simultaneous **gradients** on a scale that have a tendency to "rise" and "fall" *together* —or else "synchronously." For this reason, it is easy to semantically confuse the two. A true *understanding* (and thereby, application) of variant knowledge at each *grade* of personal development is **illuminated** only in proportion to the level of *Awareness* that is *synchronously* attained.

There is no "cheating the system" here—and we are treating all *things* as *Systems* for this Grade of knowledge demonstration concerning *"Mardukite Systemology."* We are speaking in relative terms—nearly always—and we must be certain, specific and consistent in use of terms once they are clearly defined for our purposes.

Certain benchmarks, guideposts and confirming validations along the gradient *Pathway* seem to signify a certain course of progression. Our definition of "knowledge Grades" or quantification of "understanding levels" is by no means Absolute. They are applied to an **individual** only as a point might relate to all other relative points "above" and "below" it. These points are all within a spectrum. They range from the direction of "AN" and *Infinite-Statics* (the *Nothingness*, *Abyss* and Spiritual Universe), "down to" the most rigid degrees of finite matter in the Physical Universe, "KI." Between exists a "spiritual continuum" or *"Life continuum"* that manifests as a "conduit channel"— that links...

*Awareness "levels" of our I-AM-Self ("alpha state") as Spirit
to the "degrees of physical variation"
experienced as effects in the Physical Universe.*

We are introducing a semantic *standard* here for *Mardukite Systemology*, from which to best communicate knowledge consistently. It is intended as the most simple, accurate and complete within the continuity of available language.

> **level** : "a physical or conceptual *tier* (or plane) relative to a *scale* above and below it; a significant *gradient* observable as a *foundation* (or surface) built upon and subsequent to other levels of a totality or whole; a *set* of 'parameters' with respect to other such sets along a *continuum*; in *NexGen Systemology*, a *Seeker's* understanding, *Awareness* as *Self* and the formal Grades of material/instruction are all treated as 'levels'."

The word "levels" is applied only to relative **tiers** of personal understanding and *Awareness* as represented by a metaphoric "stepped-pyramid" or "*ziggurat*." Ancient Mesopotamian people beheld this magnificent structural form as a symbolic manifestation of the "bond" between the Physical Universe ("KI") and the Spiritual Universe ("AN"). Religious traditions included a "graded" ascent up the *ziggurat* as a progressive "*Stairway to Heaven*" or "*Gateway to the Gods.*" Spiritual practices marking each progressive *level* up toward Infinity along the *Pathway of Self-Honesty* were meant to guide an initiate's *Awareness* closer to its *Alpha* state in the Spiritual Universe ("AN"), cumulatively releasing the intellectual attachments and emotional burdens of their *beta* state as they were accumulated in the Physical Universe ("KI").[*]

---

[*] This methodology is presented very concisely within the Anunnaki culture observed in Babylon as the "Mardukite Paradigm."
Mardukite Systemology seeks to reduce the degree of mythography and increase the highest level of applied knowledge derivable from this paradigm and its "*Tablets of Destiny*."

> **degree** : "a physical or conceptual *unit* (or point) de-
> fining the variation present relative to a *scale* above
> and below it; any stage or extent to which something
> *is* in relation to other possible positions within a *set*
> of *'parameters'*; a point within a specific range or
> spectrum; in *NexGen Systemology*, a *Seeker's* potential
> energy variations or fluctuations in thought, emo-
> tional reaction and physical perception are all
> treated as *'degrees'*."

We apply the word "*degrees*" only when describing variations of motion and activity in the Physical Universe
("KI")—which includes any *perception* realized by the *beta*
state of *Awareness* within the Physical Universe. In contrast, and by relative terms to the physical, the Spiritual
Universe ("AN") is an Absolute—an *alpha* state with *no*
variations or degree in the Physical Universe. It is a "constant flow" from outside of the Physical Universe—
carrying no direct measurable existence in the Physical
Universe without an infusion of its own spiritual "**Identity**" as *Life Energy* into physical energy and physical
matter of the Physical Universe. Even then, the actual "I"
of the *Alpha Self* (what some call the "spirit" or "soul") and
its spiritual conduit to the "genetic vehicle" of the *beta*
state are still of a source *exterior* to the existence of the
Physical Universe. It is no wonder that many esoteric
"spiritual traditions" have always put forth the notion
that the highest and most supreme realization of existence
is the "immeasurable space" or the "unknowable
number," the ALL, Infinity and Infinite-Static, which is existentially "above" the Cosmic Law dictating rules of this
"*Game*"[‡] taking place *in* this Physical Universe.

Δ Δ Δ Δ Δ Δ Δ

Principles from the "*Tablets of Destiny*" expressed within
this book as *Mardukite Systemology* are likely to be received

---

‡   The interaction and conquest for existence that is waged between
   'Spiritual Life' and the *'Physical Universe'* is frequently treated in
   "game terms" within the material of *NexGen Systemology.*

in the "New Age" as an extension of what is classified as the "*New Thought*" movement. This is an ironic semantic, since we are dealing with the most *ancient* thought that we can provide direct evidence for, from the very inception of modern civilization. The "New Thought" or "New Consciousness" movement first erupted in the late 1800's as an evolutionary reaction to the industrialization of America, but its philosophies also derive from esoteric transmission of the *Arcane Tablets*, which we cannot directly trace. Yet fragments appear throughout European underground *esoterica*, *Hermetism* and *Rosicrucianism*, among others. We do not see a wider public revitalization of the true "Mystery Tradition" in America until the beginning of the 20th century.

As true understanding increases: once we realize the wisdom of the "*Tablets of Destiny*" holistically, we find evidence of it throughout "spiritual traditions" on the timeline, but many followers and practitioners have overlooked their basic truths. Naturally, we do not look to any one of these paradigms for our instruction now, regardless of what bits of truth still remain.

A *Self-Honest* reflection of Human history demonstrates that at any given time, this flame of true knowledge is only tended to by *a few* operating secretly among the masses— and fewer are adequate to carry it effectively to subsequent generations. Because every systematized tradition treats its share of the *Secret Doctrines* as sacred—and rightfully so—it is often hidden away and protected by various schools and fellowships, away from the *exoteric* scrutiny of the masses which are not yet elevated to the level of understanding necessary to receive it. We must also consider potential fragmentation of the organization as an "entity" and the degree to which the Truth is hidden. Often we find that the degree of corruption in an organization is proportional to the degree of Truth once available *Self-Honestly*. The true knowledge frequently falls prey to covert corruption by the very institution meant to safeguard it. They fall prey then to fixations on commerce.

When examining the *Arcane Tablets* and other sacred ancient writings, we discover—after knowing with certainty what to look for—that many shreds and tears of true knowledge are embedded in plain sight, but which only one who has already achieved the proper level of understanding will illuminate properly. We are finding most of the knowledge *after the fact*: hidden in plain sight; only accessible to one who has *earned* the *Key*. It is the epitome of the old axiom that: "*When the student is ready, the teacher appears.*" This could even mean that: "*When an individual achieves Awareness, understanding is possible.*"

Δ Δ Δ Δ Δ Δ Δ

We are not attempting to apply any artificial classifications to properties of the *Infinite*, or of the Spiritual Universe ("AN") existing behind and underlying all things experienced as *Life* in the Physical Universe ("KI"). We are not in a position to *identify* anything about "God" at *this* level of understanding. What we *do know* is that a Cosmic Law, set forth by some **indefinable** source, governs all aspects within the Physical Universe, and that it is everywhere present in the Physical Universe. Ancient religions personified aspects of this Law as "gods," attributing *degrees* of physical existence to specific figures in a hierarchy or "divine pantheon." The "gods" demonstrated a particular "authority" or "affinity" with these *Laws* directly resulting from their ability to understand them. This developed into "religious philosophy," much of which falls under the category of "**pantheism.**" Anything that Human systems refer to as "God"—when not personified as a "god"—is really a reference to some attribute of *Cosmic Law* or to the continuum of *Life*. Whatever is beyond this, or whatever has put all this forth, is outside of the system —within the realm of the Spiritual Universe and its Infinity—beyond the boundaries of *Awareness*-perception of this physical *beta* existence and all of its correlative physical sensory faculties.

As a spiritual science, we must be very careful about any premise we present as a truth from the *"Tablets of Destiny"* that we cannot confirm with basic logic and causal experiments—even if highly esoteric ones. This means that we *cannot* definitively express—as is the tendency of virtually every spiritual tradition in existence—that the Physical Universe ("KI") is somehow a direct emanation of the Spiritual Universe ("AN"), Nothingness or Infinity. We cannot ascertain that part as a fact. The only direct connection between these two existences is *Spiritual Life Energy*, which animates sentience but does not provide any additional independent physical force toward actions and motion of energy and matter in the Physical Universe. As such, we must also be very careful that a quality of Cosmic Law we *can* find evidence for as operating in the Physical Universe is not arbitrarily superimposed onto an understanding of Infinity and any "laws" that may govern the *Alpha* existence of a Spiritual Universe. Even the myriad assortment of "mystical work," "psychic phenomenon," "magickal rituals" and other such efforts of "practical metaphysics" are only effective and existent in the Physical Universe to the extent that they operate in accordance with Cosmic Law. It is only the *Will* that is put forth from the *I-AM* or *Self* as directed from a "higher dimensional" point of observation in the Spiritual Universe.

Perhaps one of the most fundamental principles behind the systemological paradigm is that: *"All-is-One; Everything is connected together; there are no 'things' in exclusion to other 'things'."* This means that there is always a point of "connectivity," even if slight or as an **interdimensional** *Lifeline* carrying *Awareness* of a being operating from another universe. Again, we must be careful not to speak loosely concerning any specific knowledge of other "spatial dimensions" if we are to regard the Spiritual Universe as existentially independent of the Physical Universe. It is possible that both Universes *are* actually two states of the same continuum from an even higher order. The *Arcane Tablets* offer suggestions toward such, but no way for us to determine definitively until we can achieve such "higher" levels of understanding and *Awareness*.

As an analogy, we can maintain a pot of free-standing water in its liquid state within parameters of a very wide spectrum of temperature *degrees*—but if you slow this motion down to a certain threshold point, you have a solid block of ice, and no additional "lower" degrees really changes that solid, so it has become a static, and for our purposes in the Physical World, we might even consider such an organism as now "dead"—eventually experiencing all further "**sub-zones**" of physical entropy. When we speed up the motion in the other direction, increasing its **vibration**, we find that it changes states into another point of *Infinite-Static* at a certain threshold, which we call steam. Therefore, it is only within the confines of the pot and its fluid state, that energy and matter resonate in our Mind as *Life* and existence in the Physical World.

"Infinity of Nothingness" and its "Spiritual" counterpart are *not* an alternate dimension of the "Physical Universe"—they are a higher all-encompassing Universe which somehow **invests** individualized spiritual *Awareness* "into" physical centers of *beta Lifeforms* experiencing physical Reality. If we consider the Physical Universe we are experiencing as a "*game-board*" on a table, then the table, the chairs, the manner of the room in which they sit...none of this is "in play" or in any way existing *within* the parameters of the *game* itself. Other than, of course, at a higher level, someone choosing to manufacture the *game* and the *Alpha*-players choosing to play it, there is no existential correlation between "Dimensions." From within the *game* we cannot ascertain anything about some other all-encompassing environment directly, although we are certain that whatever the "I" is, it must occupy this other space with its spiritual existence and then project its *Awareness* and *Will* into the *Game* as *Life*.

Our perspective exists as a point of infinite singularity or stasis: infinite potentiality with no gradient or motion.

Meanwhile the Physical Universe is in continuous motion of manifested "parts" as a continuity. It also demonstrates a certain quantum effect of unification called "**entanglement**." The only actual separation that we find any evidence for on the *Arcane Tablets* is the "dimensional" distinction between the Spiritual ("AN") and the Physical ("KI"). We are, at this time, mainly concerned with what we can prove and demonstrate with fundamental logic and a route toward our total actualization as *Self* within the parameters of the *Game*.

Δ Δ Δ Δ Δ Δ Δ

SUMMARY

"*Understanding*" and "*Awareness*" are not exactly the same, although they do have a tendency to "rise" and "fall" together—building upon one another to form "*levels*" on which we base our experience of Reality.

"*Understanding*," and thereby, application of variant knowledge or instruction at each "*grade*" of personal development, is illuminated only in proportion to the level of "*Awareness*" that is synchronously maintained.

A "spiritual continuum" or "conduit channel" of absolute energy from the Spiritual Universe links *Awareness* "*levels*" of our *I-AM-Self* ("alpha state") as *Spirit* to the "*degrees*" of *physical variation* experienced as *effects* in the Physical Universe.

We apply the term "*levels*" only to relative tiers of personal "*understanding*" and "*Awareness*" represented by the "stepped-pyramid" or "*ziggurat*" temple, which served to remind ancient Babylonians of the inherent link between the Physical Universe ("KI") and the Spiritual Universe ("AN")—the "*Stairway to Heaven*."

We apply the term "*degrees*" only to variations of motion and activity in the Physical Universe ("KI")—which includes any *perception* realized by the *beta* state of *Awareness* within the Physical Universe.

The actual "I" of the *Alpha Self* (what some call the "spirit" or "soul") and its spiritual conduit to the "genetic vehicle" of the *beta* state are of a source *exterior* to the existence of the Physical Universe.

The "*Self*" is "I" as "*Spirit*" regardless of its position, degree or level of *Awareness*.

The *Infinity of Nothingness* is *not* an alternate dimension of the Physical Universe—it is a higher all-encompassing Spiritual Universe that somehow invests individualized spiritual *Awareness* into the physical "centers" of *beta Lifeforms* that are experiencing physical Reality.

Whatever the "I" is, it must occupy this other space with its spiritual existence and then project its *Awareness* and *Will* into the "*Game*" as *Life*.

.: 4 :.
COMMUNICATION AND CONTROL OF THOUGHT, WILL AND ACTION ON THE "TABLETS OF DESTINY"

Philosophies and spiritual systems around the world all display evidence of an underlying unified knowledge concerning the "body-mind-spirit" connection. Yet, somehow, over the course of time and a distorted relay of information, these concepts were reduced further and further into solidity as faith and dogma until they became a sequence of words and rituals with meanings long forgotten. Until a relatively recent uncovering of the *Arcane Tablets*, the programmed Human Condition, as adopted by the masses for thousands of years, has not achieved the tools for a *Self-Honest* experience of *Reality*. These tools of *spiritual technology* have the ability to advance us further in our true evolution into **transhumanism** *or* true spiritual metahumanism than any *external technology* could provide. For the only *thing* truly *real* here—is *Self*.

When we look between the two dimensional environmental "settings" described as the Spiritual Universe ("AN")—in which we exist as our *Alpha* state—and the Physical Universe ("KI")—in which we maintain an existence of our *beta* state—there is a continuum or **channel** of "*Spiritual Life Energy*" transmitting our "Reality agreements"—via our Identity or *Awareness*—onto (or into) a physical state, organic body or what we often refer to as a "genetic vehicle." This "spiritual energy" that is transmitted into all *Life* goes by many esoteric names throughout history— but we find the idea first treated as "<u>ZU</u>" in the cuneiform script on some of the oldest *Arcane Tablets*.

It is on this *Lifeline* of "spiritual energy" that the *Alpha* spirit—operating from within the Absolute of the Spiritual Universe—is capable of *Willing* its *thought* into *action* to various degrees in the Physical Universe.

> *ZU* : "an ancient cuneiform sign designating an archaic verb, *'to know'*, *'knowingness'* or *'awareness'*; the energy/matter of the Spiritual Universe (*'AN'*) that is observed as *Lifeforce* or *consciousness* by entities existing in the Physical Universe (*'KI'*); *'Spiritual Life Energy'*; the spiritual energy present in the *Will* of the actualized *Alpha-spirit* in the Spiritual Universe (*'AN'*), which imbues its *Awareness* into the Physical Universe (*'KI'*), animating *Life* for its *beta existence* along a Identity-continuum called a *'ZU-line'*." (*NexGen Systemological NewSpeak*)

The "activity" of *Awareness* along the "spectrum" of *Spiritual Energy* ("ZU") is generally referred to as "*consciousness*" in many other sources. But, even this term, in our modern age, can be misleading—because when we use it, we are incorporating two centuries of esoteric word-play in the field of psychology, which in the end has turned its attentions back onto beliefs from the Dark Ages of crude *behaviorism*. So, we must be clear when communicating to a modern *Seeker*. Most often what others refer to as "states of consciousness" are really various gradients of vibration or frequency where *Awareness* may be fixed along the spectrum or channel of this *Spiritual Life Energy*. This includes not only the cellular sensory perceptions of the *body*, but also the chemical production induced by *emotion* and the very *thoughts* transmitted between the *Self* and the *genetic vehicle*—all the way back up to the perfected clarity of *Awareness* achieved from our true spiritual *Alpha* state.

> *ZU-line* : "a spectrum of *Spiritual Life Energy*; an energetic channel or Identity-continuum connecting the *Awareness* of an *Alpha-spirit* with Infinity; a *Life-line* on which *Awareness* extends from from *AN*, as its *alpha state* through an entire possible range of activity in its *beta state*, as a 'genetic entity' occupying *KI*—the 'Physical Universe'." (*NexGen Systemological NewSpeak*)

Each point (degree) along the continuum does actually exist as a specific vibration or frequency of this energy we are going to call "ZU" in respect to our cuneiform sources. This spectrum may be figuratively and relatively "quantified" as *degrees* only in relation to other degrees within the same spectrum. This *Life* energy than interacts with the Physical Universe—particularly the "genetic vehicle"—to various *degrees* based on its similarity with physical **receptacles**. We possess some kind of sensory device in the body to meet an incoming stimulus at whatever level of *Awareness* we are capable of or currently experiencing—but all within the same continuum or conduit-channel.

The *"ZU-line"* continuum extends from *Infinity-to-Infinity*, a continuous whole that exists without interruption as an infinite spectrum of potential points. On a *Spiritual Lifeline*, we typically chart a graphic understanding of the range from *Zero* "0" (inert physical death) to *Infinity* "8" (Spiritual-*Alpha* state). It is the "push" and "pull" between Spiritual Energy and the Physical Universe that is experienced as *Life* (a static) in *motion*.

82

We can mark a **relative** place on this spectrum for where we **project** our *Awareness* to experience *physical* pain, *emotional* grief, *intellectual* fluctuation, or even true actualized *spiritual* Self-determinism. We tend to classify *these* specific systems as "states" when vibrational frequencies range between specific distinct **thresholds**. Just as the same water has varied *states* as ice, liquid and steam—there are frequencies relative to one another as "states" that fall within broad recognizable categories as "*spiritual*" or "*psychological/mental*" or "*emotional/chemical*" and even "*physical.*" These are not different "selves" as some philosophies propose. Just as there is no point in which water is not still essentially water—we have only one *Self*, but we are projecting as *Self* into a "genetic vehicle" that is maintained by its own systems interacting within Physical beta-Existence ("KI").

We are able to experience any point along the entire *Life-force* (or "ZU") continuum *from Self*. But the "I" of the Observer, in its *Alpha* state, is still the same "I." In essence, we are peering "*down*" upon activities of the Physical Universe through a *crystalline lens*, shining a light against the wall of our Reality[†]—but we are able to perceive many more *facets* of this experience than simply *seeing*. We are continuously projecting the totality of our *Awareness* to a *degree* that our *state* will allow—and that energy is continuously transmitting back as "understanding" and "experience" to our *Alpha* state as "Reality."

Δ Δ Δ Δ Δ Δ Δ

Now that we have a certain level of understanding concerning the *Arcane Tablets*, it seems appropriate to reintroduce the literal text from "*Marduk's Tablet of Destiny*"—the same simple words which granted him the understanding to prevail in the *Enuma Eliš* epic.[‡] It is rend-

---

[†] Reminiscent to concepts in "Plato's Cave" allegory.

[‡] Discovered in 2011 by Khem Juergen and Reed Penn in Pittsburgh and Philadelphia while working long-distance with Joshua Free to bridge an understanding of *NexGen Systemology* with the

ered here—in both its original Sumerian and newly translated English form—for the first time.

Marduk's Tablet of Destiny—The Supreme "ME"

an-bala ki-bala an-ba ki an-ba
da-ga nam-ku-zu d-Lamma a bi-ib-gar
nig-ku-lam-ma dingir-ra-na-ka su—tu-tu nu-ub-zu
nig-gu-gar-ra nig-gaba-gar-ra
nig-ge-na-ta a-ba in-da-di nam-ti i-u-tu

As above, so below; on Earth, as it is in Heaven.
What the Mind believes, the Spirit reinforces.
When disaster is self-made, no man can interfere
What is given in submission is a catalyst for defiance
Whoever partners with Truth, creates Life.

The *"Tablets of Destiny"* represent a collective body of ancient systematized wisdom—yet the *initiate* or *Seeker* is only able to understand and reinforce that understanding with experience to the extent of the the highest levels of *Awareness* achieved. We often use the term *"Self-Honesty,"* because it represents a *clear personal processing of informed understanding*—which we generally call "knowledge" in our society, meaning literally the *"level* of that which we *know."*

---

knowledge : "clear personal processing of informed understanding; information (data) that is actualized as effectively workable understanding; a demonstrable understanding on which we may 'set' our *Awareness*; literally a *'know-ledge'.*"

We present *knowledge* from the "Arcane Tablets" in this volume with extremity and a heavy voice, because this is not *new* information—but it is new *"knowledge."* These *words* have been known for a long time. It is very old data —yet it is either misunderstood or treated as cliché "New Age" sentiment. The words themselves relay very little

---

Mardukite Core.

direct or applied "technology" without an esoteric key of instruction. And it was clearly designed that way. How better to disguise the secrets of existence—than to place it right in front of people. During investigations into work to establish the formerly released "*Mardukite Core*,"[†] our *Nex-Gen* research team extracted "*Marduk's Tablet of Destiny*" from discarded archaeological remains—first known and translated by historians over half of a century ago—passed off as little more than "religious proverbs." Yet, when integrated with our higher understanding of the *Enuma Eliš*, and in combination with other *Arcane Tablets*, it provides a clear communication of true Human potential—and *that* is the one aspect, of which we may all agree, that *has* been authoritatively kept from humanity's reach for thousands of years.

Human programming is institutionalized via *language* and *authoritative* example—as first systematized within the ancient Mardukite paradigm in Babylon. There is a certain tendency in society—our social environment—to **invalidate** the significance of individualized thought. It has been written that "*Beliefs impart Reality.*[*] Any thoughts we are in agreement with become Reality—even if it is only realized for us individually as the Observer, because that is all that matters when *Self-directing*. When more and more individuals share in agreement to any *belief* as Reality, all corresponding personal "*imprints*" of that belief are strengthened with emotional energy. They become more "solid" and corresponding thought degrees also fluctuate in magnitude and manifestation-type to correspond. Suppress enough of the population with poor ideals and they will murder each other and themselves; but empower a group with a high frequency thought and suddenly they feel like they can take on the world to create a better futu-

---

[†] All publicly available *Grade-I* and *Grade-II* materials pertaining to past systems of "magical," "mystical" and "religious" semantics previously released by *Joshua Free Imprint Publishing* (formerly *Mardukite Truth Seeker Press*).

[*] "Belief imparts reality, and beliefs will continue to be real so long as people pour energy into them by faith"—Douglas Monroe.

re. Even a single **counter-productive** thought with enough magnitude attracts sufficient "like-minded" individuals to provide necessary energies to make it "real."

The Mind is designed to see physical reality as a continuity or totality, so it treats whatever understanding it already maintains as a solid belief structure of *Everything*, even when it should not. As much as humanity claims to value "Truth" and be in "search" of it, the "average person" (occupying an *Awareness* at some lower point along the *ZU-line*) generally believes they already have a "good handle of things" as they are. Even if they are physically and emotionally "a mess," the Mind simply justifies all the *effects* as logical to its state of *Awareness*. The consistent goal throughout all *Systemology* work is to consistently raise an individual's level of *Awareness* and therefore increase the *Lifeforce* they are directing in this *Lifetime*. This "ZU"-force, as itself, is a constant energy flow. It is the individual that exists in a state of *fluctuation* or *fragmentation* and the energy is not permitted clear passage.

"Spiritual"

"Thought"

"Emotion"

"Genetic Body"

When an individual's *Awareness* is "locked" or "fixed" lower points of vibration on the *ZU-line* (or *Identity-continuum*), governance of the "genetic vehicle" is partially (and sometimes fully) **relinquished** by the *Alpha Self* to "lower control centers." These are known to usually react and respond in a manner that is anything *but* logical, analytical or rational—even though their original function was for automated primitive survival of a living organism. The highest properties of logic and rationale are exclusive to a *Self-Honest Mind* in the total control of an actualized *Self*—the "I."

In this "Information Age," some individuals seem incapable of producing original thought—the sum of their activity primarily engaged in response-reactions to an "outside" world that is *happening to* them. Many succumb to convincing themselves they are comfortable in automatic existence—the *effect* of some *other cause*. While sands of time hide tablets and return ancient cities to dust, the fundamental systemology—whereby the very programming of the Human Condition was installed—is still very much present with us today. In the Physical Universe, it is what directly links our *language* to *thought*.

△ △ △ △ △ △ △

Thoughts, just like other forms of energy and matter, are "*waves*" or "*wave-forms.*" They are occasionally, represented in *Systemology* **logic-equations** as "*wave-functions*" or "*wave-frequencies*" with the sign: Wf or wf. [It is <u>not</u> necessary to know any mathematical logic behind the equations to use the information in this book.] These terms and signs represent the same aspect of communication: *motion*. A "*wave*" is a messenger action, carrying a "point" of some degree to another "point" in relative *space*. We express this "wave-action" in terms of "vibration" and "frequency." This is our "measured observation" of *time* between "points" in *space*. From this we determine any additional information concerning "wave-lengths" and "functions" relative to other possible "frequencies" within the same spectrum.

> **thought-wave** : "a proactive *Self-directed action* or re-active-response *action* of *consciousness*; the *process* of *thinking* as demonstrated in *wave-form*; the *activity* of *Awareness* within the range of *thought vibrations/fre-quencies* on the existential *Life-continuum* or 'ZU-line'." (*NexGen Systemological NewSpeak*)

When pertaining to this "thought band" of the spectrum—which is that range we classify as the "*mental* or *psycholo-gical* state" down into our "*emotional* state"—any distinct "point" brought into existence is a "*Thoughtform*," repres-ented in *NexGen* equations as "T*f*."[‡]

> **thought-form**: "apparent *manifestation* or existential *realization* of *Thought-waves* as 'solids' even when only apparent in Reality-agreements of the Observer; the treatment of *Thought-waves* as permanent im-prints obscuring *Self-Honest Clarity* of *Awareness* when reinforced by emotional experience as actualized 'thought-formed solids' in the Mind." (*NexGen Sys-temological NewSpeak*)

At basic form, these *Thoughtforms* manifest and solidify along energetic channels of our experience as "*beliefs*."[∫] The more rigid and solid the *belief*, particularly at lower levels of realization, the more automated any related ex-periences become. The *Self* as the Observer is not able to "see" past these artificial solids set up in the pathway of a *Self-Honest* communication of *Will* between the *Alpha* and *beta*. Therefore, the "*Pathway to Self-Honesty*" is a journey of *clearing* the spiritual energy *channel* of debris imprinted

---

‡ As presented in the *"Reality Engineering"* lectures—the solidity or agreement-strength of a Thoughtform (T*f*) as Reality is the product of Emotionally-Encoded-Energy (E*m*) *imprinted* on a Thoughtwave (*wf*); E*m* x *wf* = T*f*.

∫ It is noticed that some folk manifest the same *degree* of solids when they are performing what is considered *"magick"* in New Age terminology.

on us by our handling (or mishandling) environment—energy inhibiting total experience as actualized *Self*.

Thought-waves are *energy* in *motion*; produced by *Self*, from a point (static), and they travel down the "*ZU*-line" to the extent that the energy is not blocked. It is severely blocked when the mind-body registers "pain." If it is blocked and an individual's level of *Awareness* is low, the energy simply strengthens the similarly low-level "solid belief" that is "fragmenting" its flow. We are "reinforcing" our beliefs with **experiential-data**—experiences resulting from our own emotionally charged (and often reactive) "dramatic reenactments" connected to the original installation of such beliefs.

This often keeps us "stuck" in a certain monotonous or "mundane mode" inciting "depression" and other low-level "states" of *Awareness*. These response-mechanisms can often prevent free access to the wide range of Human Potential—which is very much accessible to us when we "impinge upon" the Human Condition in the Physical Universe with the total *Awareness* and *Lifeforce* accessible from our actualized *Alpha* state.

Spiritual energy is in continuous motion as a constant, instilling the organism with *Lifeforce* and a means of *consciousness*—so its natural "frequency" is only altered by "fragmentation." The physical "genetic vehicle" possesses its own "reactive-response center" and is not dependent on a *Self-Honest* Mind for "existence," but it does require thought for **optimum** functionality, which includes the ability to manifest an optimum existence. It can, and apparently does, get by without *Self-Honesty*, although usually to a much lower frequency of perceived "energy"—and effectual satisfaction as *Life*.

We should not be surprised that behaviors and realities—activities and motions—manifested in the Physical Universe from individuals "blocked" or "fragmented" by many imposed artificial solids are also blocking others in their energy flow. These are often the same individuals that seek incessant validation of their own "fragmenta-tion" by forcefully trying to *"make us as they are."* It is only when we return to our true sense of *Self* that we are stronger as individuals—with a higher frequency of opera-tion—in our ability to confront energy and transform obstacles to our survival in the Physical Universe as daily life, and free our *Self* to experience its highest spiritual evolution and *Awareness* as "I AM."

Δ Δ Δ Δ Δ Δ Δ

SUMMARY

The "spiritual energy" **transmitted** into all *Life* as a *"Life-force"* goes by many esoteric names throughout history—but we find the idea first treated as "ZU" on cuneiform tablets from Mesopotamia.

It is on this *Lifeline* of "ZU" energy that the *Alpha* spirit—operating from within the Absolute of the Spiritual Uni-verse—is capable of *"Self-directing"* *thought* into *action* to various degrees of manifestation in the Physical Universe *(beta existence).*

We refer to this continuum of "ZU" as the "ZU-line," on which we may graphically represent "activity" of *Aware-ness* along a "spectrum" of *Spiritual Energy* ("ZU")—an activity that is generally referred to simply as *"conscious-ness"* in many other sources.

When sources refer to "states" of *"consciousness,"* they are defining various gradients of vibration (or frequency) where *Awareness* may be fixed along the "ZU-line"—being a continuous spectrum (or channel) of potential manifest-ation of *Spiritual Life Energy* ("ZU").

Each point or *"degree"* along the ZU-line continuum is a specific "vibration" or "frequency" that we assign a relat-ive "quantity" to allow us to figure basic logic in relation to other points or *"degrees."*

The "ZU-line" continuum extends from *Infinity-to-Infinity* —any gradation or sectional partitioning is solely relative to our perception and classification.

Graphic representation of frequencies on a "ZU-line" may include such *degrees* as: a "zero-point" *body* death; cellular activity and sensory perceptions of the *body*; chemical production induced by *emotion*; the *thought* vibrations transmitted between our *Spirit* and "genetic vehicle"—all the way up the scale to a perfected clarity of *Awareness* existent only in our true spiritual *Alpha* state, just shy of "*Infinity*."

All "states" or "degrees" are experienced from the same "I" or "Self" as an *Awareness* of *Life-energy* ("ZU"). This is an absolute or constant force applied across the continuum ("*ZU-line*").

Spiritual energy is in continuous motion as a constant, instilling the organism with *Lifeforce* and a means of *consciousness*. This force is only altered or fixed from its natural frequency to any point below "*Self-Honesty*" due to "*fragmentation*."

We classify "energetic systems" operating at certain ranges of frequency as "states." These states operate as systems relative to one another and are broadly distinguished as "spiritual" "psychological/mental" "emotional/chemical" and even "physical."

We may experience any point or degree along the entire continuum *from Self*. But the "I" of the Observer, in its *Alpha* state, remains the same *Self*.

We are continuously projecting the totality of our *Awareness* to a *degree* that our *state* will allow—and that energy is continuously transmitting back as "understanding" and "experience" to our *Alpha* state as Reality.

The text of "*Marduk's Tablet of Destiny*"—As above, so below; on Earth, as it is in Heaven. What the Mind believes, the Spirit reinforces. When disaster is self-made, no man can interfere. What is given in submission is a catalyst for defiance. Whoever partners with Truth, creates Life.

Human programming is institutionalized via language and authoritative example.

When our *Awareness* is "fixed" to "lower" points of vibration on the *ZU-line* (or *Identity-continuum*), the "master control" of the "genetic vehicle" is partially relinquished by the *Alpha Self* to "lower control centers."

Thoughts are "things"—and just like any other forms of energy and matter, thoughts are "*waves*" or "*wave-forms.*" We simply call these "thought-waves."

A "*wave*" is a messenger action, carrying a static "point" of some degree to another "point" in relative *space*. This wave-action is described as a "vibration," which is primarily calculated or distinguished as a "frequency."

Thought-forms are *Thought-waves* that manifest or solidify "imprints" along the energetic channel of our experience as "*beliefs.*"

The "*Pathway to Self-Honesty*" is a journey of *clearing* the spiritual energy *channel* of debris *imprinted* by our environment, which is inhibiting the total experience of *Self* as actualized *Awareness*.

.: 5 :.
UNDERSTANDING THE ACTION OF THOUGHT, WILL AND ENERGY FROM THE "TABLETS OF DESTINY"

> "If the _doors of perception_ were cleansed, every *thing* would appear to man as it is—_Infinite_. For man has closed himself up, until he sees all *things* through narrow chinks of his cavern."
> —William Blake, *The Marriage of Heaven and Hell*

Once an individual directs **attention** to the wisdom of the *Arcane Tablets*, suddenly new layers of understanding begin to unfold concerning *Life*, the Physical Universe—and *experience* of it as *Reality*. With *new eyes*, the *Seeker* begins to find fragments of confirmation in virtually every piece of ancient *esoterica*. This information is not restricted only to cuneiform tablets unearthed in Mesopotamia—but it *is* our oldest, complete and definitive literary example, from which sprung the *"Secret Doctrines"* maintained by many spiritual traditions and cultures throughout time and space.

> **defragmentation** : "the *reparation* of wholeness; a process of removing *'fragmentation'* in data or knowledge to provide a clear understanding; applying techniques and processes that promote a *holistic* interconnected *alpha* state, favoring observational *Awareness* of continuity in all spiritual and physical systems; in *NexGen Systemology*, a *'Seeker'* achieving an actualized state of basic *'Self-Honest Awareness'* is said to be *defragmented*." (*NexGen Systemology NewSpeak*)

Of course, if we choose to, we will undoubtedly find variations of this wisdom in the *Egyptian Book of the Dead*, the *Dhammapada*, the *Vedas*, and so on... It is not the focus or intent of our current discourse—or the instructional Grade it represents—to chase down all later derived fragmented examples of the *"Tablets of Destiny"* in history. Such intellectual occupations, someone else will undoubtedly take up.

Holistic systemological knowledge and processing tools for *defragmentation* and *clearing* should suffice in enabling the *Seeker* to apply logical reductions to their own "**data-set.**" Extensive exploration of additional avenues of "cultural lore" and "wisdom systems" primarily only gains a person additional "semantics" and "vocabulary," which often describe the same *"things"* in obscurity. This might only add to the challenge of reaching *Self-Honesty* later.

> **semantics** : "the *meaning* carried in *language* as the *truth* of a 'thing' represented, A-for-A; the *effect* of language on *thought* activity in the Mind and physical behavior; language as *symbols* used to represent a concept, 'thing' or solid."

Although we *have* integrated a basic syllabic vocabulary from cuneiform sources to systematize our knowledge—such as AN, KI, ZU, &c.—or simple expressions of *alpha* and *beta* to basic states of existence, any of these concepts could have been relayed by some other language semantics or cultural theme. The vocabulary chosen is not as important as the *semantic*—what it actually means to "you and me" as understanding allows for. We cannot actualize an *Awareness* past a "point" we do not understand. Therefore, our current efforts are a reduction of "fragmented knowledge" into true *"Knowingness."* This occurs only when we *defragment* our understanding—removing dissonance or clearing static beliefs as obstacles to our actualization of *Awareness* as *Self*—and intentionally maintain increased frequencies of thought-wave activity in our daily experience of *Life*.

Δ Δ Δ Δ Δ Δ

A holistic understanding of the *"Tablets of Destiny"* allows us to explore and broadly define the most ancient *systemological* paradigm as a base of communicating the highest levels of wisdom we are currently in possession of today. Any deeper realizations of the knowledge are built upon the semantic framework applied to specify:

> the *Alpha* state and *beta* activity potential of *Life* as *Self*
> between two extreme states of *AN* and *KI*
> along a definitive Identity-continuum of *Awareness*
> we call the *ZU-line.*

Such are the *"Fundamentals."* And while there are many levels of reasoning behind our specific selection of these terms—the classifications given are what is important. The terms are used due to their relationship with the *"Arcane Tablets,"* but also so we may communicate a clear understanding of higher knowledge without spending too much time reshaping a lifetime of word-*associations* with ideas of *heaven, earth, soul, consciousness, body, outer space, lifeforce* and so forth—of which we, as a society, seem to either carry a very dogmatic or murky understanding of at best.

Personal *defragmentation* of *Awareness* in the direction of *Self-Honesty* involves closely examining degrees of fragmented "thought variation" and "emotional fluctuation" along the *ZU-line.* We have already briefly described the *Alpha* state of the basic *Identity* doing the *Observing* at some "spiritual" level of *AN.* What we are concerned with now is our *beta existence*, which is primarily defined by *ZU* activity within ranges of "thought" and "emotion." These **intermediary** states relay energetic communication between the *Alpha*-Self and the *genetic body*. The Self is not directly exerting the force used in motor functions of the *body*, it has lower faculties for that, operating at the level of their range of activity.

The *ZU-line* and *"Arcane Tablets"* suggest that there are *four* primary states or levels of principle activity experienced as *Self* between the range of Absolute Infinity (*Nothingness*) of *AN* and Zero-Point Continuity (*physical organic death*) of *KI.* These four basic states (or levels) of existence are *"Spir-*

itual," "*Mind/psychological*," "*Emotional*" and "*Physical.*" These are each defined by a particular range (parameter) along the same *ZU-line* continuum from *AN* to *KI*.[‡] On cuneiform tablets, the entire system was simply referred to as *AN-KI*—meaning "the ALL."

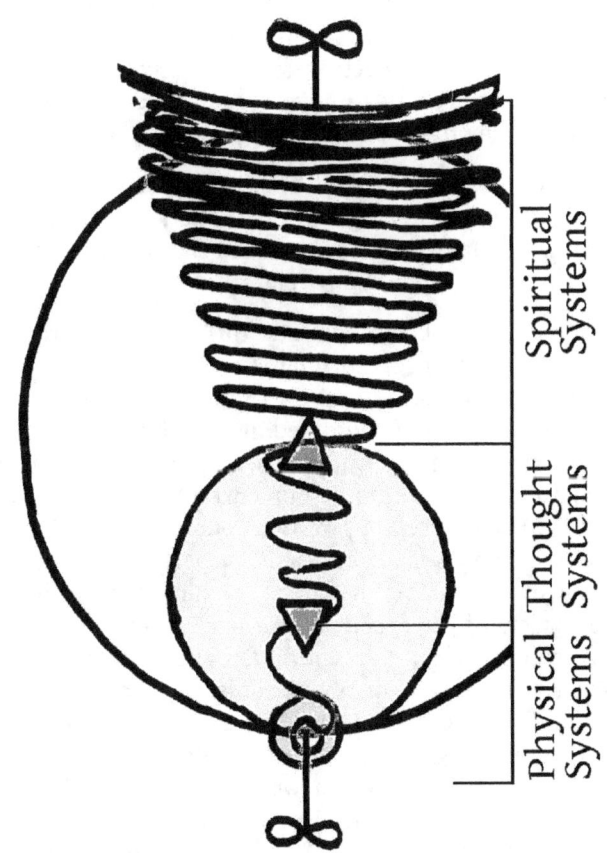

Three conditional integrated systems communicate energy along the *ZU-line* continuum. We refer to *these* systems when describing observed "activity" processing at

---

‡   We are also using *AN* and *KI* as *"dimensional directions"* of
    relative energetic movement along the *ZU-line*, otherwise denoted
    as "higher" and "lower."

each *level* of apparent existence. As such, we have—

> our highest *Alpha* "*Spiritual System*" that connects the spiritual range with mental/psychological levels of our *beta existence*;
>
> a "*Psychological/Mind System*" connecting the level of the Mind to the emotional range of the body; and
>
> a "*Physical System*" that is mostly automatic and re-active, directly connecting emotional and biochemical levels of activity to govern somatic motor functions of the physical genetic organism.

These systems correlate with the *Three Cosmic Principle Systems of Manifestation* given in Hermetic Philosophy as *consciousness*, *motion* and *matter*—and the states of *Self-determinism*: *being*, *doing* and *having*.

We could attempt to illustrate this holistic system as "three cog-gear-wheels turning about"—and perhaps that is even the first image that came into your mind—*but* that is a famously old, now outdated, mechanistic perspective. It is not nearly *fluid* or *dynamic* enough to demonstrate the actual Human Condition at our current levels of understanding. For this reason, we treat our standard of knowledge with the *ZU-line*, because it properly reflects a continuum of energetic singularity reaching across all possible aspects of the spectrum at their respective levels of manifestation. Even as a continuous flow of energy and *Awareness*, there are distinguishable relay points in the spectrum. Distinction of these "parts" as "separate" tends to get *Seekers* caught up on distractions away from seeing a holistic picture. Only when we "look" at—and "experience" *Awareness* as—"parts" in exclusion to *any* and *all* other "parts" of a total "system" do we fall into trappings of "fragmented knowledge."

Our holistic examination of the **Identity-system** reveals *two* key relay points, which in combination compose activities most often described as "*the Mind*." We have no reason to significantly detour use of the term "mind" as a system of activity.

There is only one primary "*seat of consciousness*" for relaying the *I-AM-Self* and its *Lifeline* into the genetic organism. It is the initial point of contact, at which the *ZU-line* of Alpha Awareness interacts with the "Mind-set" of potential *beta Awareness*. It is essentially where the Spiritual System ("*Mind-of-Spirit*" or "Proactive Mind") is interacting—as its basic *Self-Honest Identity*—with Mind-Systems of the *beta existence*. This Mind-System is is secondarily automated by a "*Mind-of-Body*" or "Reactive Mind," responsible for biochemical processes and motor functions—but which also maintains existence of emotional "*imprints*" and other "**unconscious**" programming.

All relative states are "interior" or "exterior" to the *beta existence*—"lower" or "higher" than this point. It is also at this point that we tend to existentially divide spiritual existence (*AN*) from physical existence (*KI*), even though "interior" thoughts and emotions of the "lower" Reactive Mind are not often exhibited to the same degree of "reality agreement" as other, even lower-level, denser physical solids. They all still fall under the domain of "*Cosmic Law.*"

When we find ourselves acting "out-of-line" and "not ourselves" and "not sure" why we are doing or feeling some way, we are typically being overrun by the magnitude of some lower degree point of fragmentation that is obstructing clear *Awareness* and free flow of *Life*-energy.

The reactive "*Mind-of-Body*" is a lower seat of consciousness where the Mind-systems and emotional/bio-chemical ranges of *beta Awareness* contact. This secondary control center should always operate its automatic body processes under the *Will* of the *Alpha Awareness* point. This is accomplished along the *ZU-line* as a communication of energy. In fact, all energy motion, interaction and transfer is a "communication relay." We can easily equate a clear energy channel of the *ZU-line* with nearly all other communication analogies, where information is being sent/transmitted and received. We liken our approach to *Self Honest Clarity* with ability to view from a distance through an optic lens or telescopic device—or even "hear clearly" through some telecommunication.

> *When the Crystal Lens-of-Awareness is Clear,*
> *Keys to the Doors-of-Perception are achieved;*
> *Gates of Understanding may then be Opened.*

Δ Δ Δ Δ Δ Δ Δ

SUMMARY

We cannot actualize an *Awareness* of *Self* past a "point" we do not understand; our *Awareness* does not surpass our "understanding," but it may lead to support a higher level of understanding.

The primary aim of *Grade Three* "Processes" used in "Applied Systemology" is a reduction of "fragmented data" into true "*Knowingness.*"

When we *defragment* the "knowledge-base" of our understanding, we are removing dissonance or clearing static beliefs as solid obstacles that *fragment* our highest actualization of *Awareness* as *Self*.

Personal *defragmentation* of our *Awareness* toward *Self-Honesty* involves closely examining degrees of fragmented "thought variation" and "emotional fluctuation" along the *ZU-line*.

The *ZU-line Lifeforce-continuum* is charted for an "Identity" between two inter-dimensional directions: "AN," the range of "Absolute Infinity" (*Nothingness*)—and "KI," the "Zero-Point Continuity" (*physical organic death*) of material sub- stance and energy.

There are four basic "states" (or "levels") of existence —"*Spiritual,*" "*Mind/psychological,*" "*Emotional*" and "*Physical.*" Each is relatively defined as a particular range of parameters along the same *ZU-line* continuum.

There are three primary systems that communicate *Life* energy along the *ZU-line* continuum:

a) the highest *Alpha "Spiritual System"* connecting spiritual ranges with Mind-Systems of *beta existence*;

b) the *"Psychological/Mind System"* connecting degrees of thought to emotional ranges of the body; and

c) the *"Physical System"* that is mostly automatic and reactive, directly connecting emotional and biochemical activity to govern somatic motor functions.

The three primary systems correlate with the *Principle Systems of Manifestation* (given in Hermetic Philosophy) as *consciousness*, *motion* and *matter*—and also the states of *Self-determinism*: *being*, *doing* and *having*.

Holistic examination of the Identity-system on the *ZU-line* revealed *two* key "relay points" or "control systems." These two points operate activity described as *the Mind*:

a) the point where the Spiritual System (or "Proactive Mind") is interacting—as its basic *Self-Honest Identity*—with the Mind-Systems of the *beta existence*;

b) the point where an Automated System (or "Reactive Mind") is responsible for biochemical processes and motor functions, but which also tends to maintain an existence of emotional imprints and unconscious programming.

When we find ourselves feeling "not ourselves" and "not sure" why we are thinking or acting a certain way, we are typically being overrun by energy collecting by lower "reactive control center" processes, which obstruct clear *Awareness* and free flow of *ZU-energy*.

.: 6 :.

THE POWER OF THOUGHT AND WILL AS ENERGY AND MANIFESTATION IN THE PHYSICAL UNIVERSE

The average person on Earth operating the Human Condition outside of—or apart from—the *Pathway of Self-Honesty*, experiences *Awareness* as "fragmented thought" and "fluctuating emotion." There are many distinguishable degrees of such energetic activity—and its likely a *Seeker* has personally experienced most of them. When we systematize a *ZU-line spectrum* as a "continuity model," Human "thought"—whether *clear* or in varying degrees of *fragmentation*—falls somewhere between two points:

a.) the *Self-Honest state* of the proactive-Mind or *alpha* "*Master Control Center*" (responsible for directing *Self-determinism* toward the genetic organism); and

b.) the domain of the programmable imprinted *beta* "*Reactive Control Center*" (which discharges emotional *biochemicals* and motor *impulses* of the genetic organism).

> **master control center** : "the proactive communication system of the *'Mind'*; a relay point of *Awareness* along the Identity's *ZU-line*, which is responsible for maintaining basic *Self-Honest Clarity* of *Knowingness* as a *seat of consciousness* between the *Alpha-Spirit* and the *'Reactive Control Center'* of a *beta existence*; the Mind-center for an *Alpha-Spirit* to actualize cause in the *beta existence*; the analytical *Self-Determined* Mind-center of an *Alpha-Spirit used* to project *Will* toward the genetic body; the point of contact between *Spiritual Systems* and the *beta existence*; presumably the *'Third Eye'* of a being connected directly to the *I-AM-Self*, which is responsible for *determining* Reality at any time." (*NexGen Systemological NewSpeak*)

The *Master Control Center* "MCC" and *Reactive Control Center* "RCC" are constantly communicating energy along the

Identity's *ZU-line.* They act as "personal gateways" between specific "states" of *Awareness* and divide "parameters" for all potential frequencies, energetic variation, and other experiences of *beta existence.*

reactive control center : "the secondary (reactive) communication system of the *'Mind'*; a relay point of *Awareness* along the Identity's *ZU-line*, which is responsible for engaging basic motors, biochemical processes and any *programmed automated responses* of a living *beta* organism; the reactive Mind-Center of a living organism relaying communications of *Awareness* between causal experience of *Physical Systems* and the *'Master Control Center'*; it presumably stores all emotional encoded imprints as fragmentation of "**chakra**" frequencies of *ZU* (within the range of the *'psychological/emotive systems'* of a being), which it may *react* to as Reality at any time." (*NexGen Systemological NewSpeak*)

The "higher" an energy frequency, the higher the state of *Awareness*; and ultimately the greater clarity and magnitude of *ZU* experienced and directed by *Self.* Relatively "Lower" energy frequencies—within the range of wide thought fragmentation and emotional fluctuation—cause *Self* to experience low-level energies in their *beta existence.* Our personal *Self-direction* of *ZU* is concentrated, condensed and solidified by thought and attention—then reinforced by some degree of emotional engagement as "experience."

When our attentions and thoughts are fixed to "low-level" energy frequencies experienced as reactive-response emotional tides, than this is the "peak" of *Awareness* maintained. Surely, there are certain moments when personal energy vibrations might increase dramatically due to events or involvement with activities generating higher frequencies. There are also "energy clearing" techniques, and similar practices, involving for example, the "*chakra-centers*" along a certain spectrum of an Identity's *Zu-Line.*

These types of instances may be valid, but they are often temporary states not thereafter maintained in *Self-Honesty*. Without achieving *Self-Honesty* during one's *Lifetime*—clear up to the point of the Master Control Center (MCC), where spiritual *Awareness* first contacts the physical—a person is just as likely to be quickly "brought down" again in their degree of vibrations by some other conflict or barrier. We seldom are able to see "beyond a point of existence we don't understand."

---

standard model : "a fundamental *structure* or symbolic construct used to evaluate a complete *set* in *continuity* relative to itself and variable to all other *dynamic systems* as graphed or calculated by *logic*; in *NexGen Systemology*—a 'monistic continuity model' demonstrating *total system* interconnectivity 'above' and 'below' observation of any apparent *parameters*; the *ZU-line* represented as a singular vertical (*y*-axis) waveform in space without charting any specific progressive movement across a dimensional time-graph *x*-axis."

The *Systemological Society* introduced a "continuity model" at its inception[*], where we may chart points for these two "Control Centers" along the *ZU-line* relative to the four basic states or levels of existence. In fact, this continuity model contributed directly to our systemological representation of the *ZU-line*—perfectly implied in literature of the "*Arcane Tablets*," but never displayed or graphically

---

[*] First presented in the "*Reality Engineering*" lectures, upon which the logic, calculations and premises of *NexGen Systemology* are based. It shows a y-axis (vertical) continuum between infinities. There is a dimensional x-axis at zero (representing pure inert matter) and another dimensional x-axis at "8" (representing Absolute *'Infinity'* or pure spiritual consciousness). Gradients were marked at axis points: (1) Physical; (2) Emotional; (4) Mental/Psy; (8) Spiritual. All systemological relationships, attributes and correlations to frequencies of the *ZU-line* as described on the "*Tablets of Destiny*" may be correlated to an understanding of this original model.

calculated. Continued advancement of *NexGen Systemology* as a progressive *Pathway to Self-Honesty,* and beyond to *Infinity,* is represented in this model. Now that we are using this model as a "*standard*" to demonstrate both "Mardukite" and "NexGen" levels of understanding, we may then refer to it as our "Standard Model" of Systemology.

On the "Standard Model" we may effectively place the proactive *Master Control Center* or "MCC" at "(4)"—at the *Alpha* point of first contact (and relay of energy as *Awareness* and *Lifeforce*) between *AN* and *KI* as a *beta existence.* It is a perfect **computing-device** to the extent of information received from "lower levels" of sensory experience.

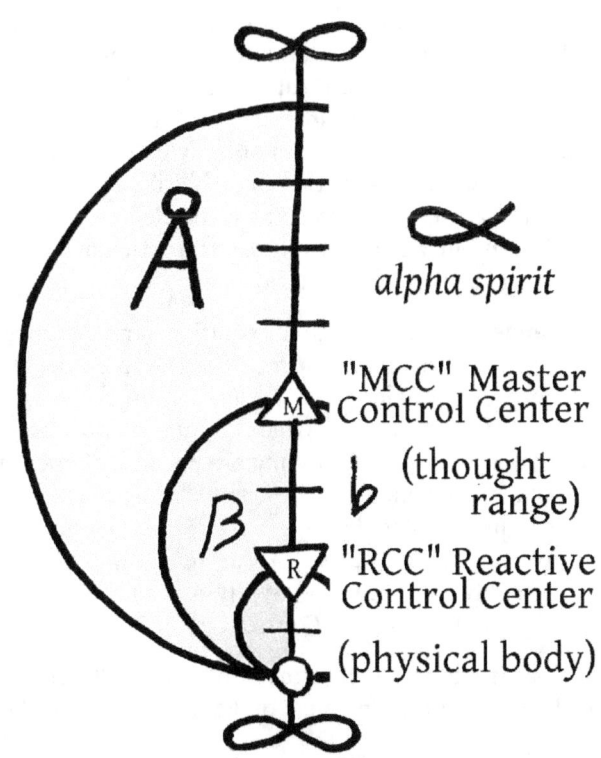

alpha spirit

"MCC" Master Control Center

(thought range)

"RCC" Reactive Control Center

(physical body)

The secondary *Reactive Control Center* or "RCC" for the genetic vehicle maintains the heights of its *Awareness* at "(2)" on the *ZU-line*, literally serving the most "primitive" functions. Between "(2)" and "(4)" we have the internal frequency range of "Thought" as "*the Mind*" or *Psychological Systems*. Below "(2)" we find similar fluctuation experienced as frequencies of "Emotion"—which extend right down to the physical body at position "(1)" as biochemicals and somatic responses. The original systemological continuity model combined with the "*Tablets of Destiny*" allows easier charting of effective relationships of all systems in their holistic continuity as a "Standard Model."

Δ Δ Δ Δ Δ Δ Δ

Cosmological descriptions from the "*Arcane Tablets*" provide us a context or paradigm to chart our Standard Model of *Awareness*. Significant personal ability is accessible at upper levels of *Awareness*. The "*Tablets of Destiny*" are quite clear about one key point: "whatever the *Mind* believes, the *Spirit* reinforces." Our abilities as *Alpha* spiritual beings are only **inhibited** by the degree of energy restriction in our *ZU-line* of *Awareness*, particularly within the range of "thought and emotion."

True avenues toward spiritual evolution (and Ascension) begin with some attempt to *defragment* the free flow of information (energy) along the *ZU-line* within the range of *beta existence*. The current Grade[‡] of instruction and its correlative level of understanding are primarily concerned with the achievement of "*Self-Honesty*." This is calculated with the Standard Model as—

a total clarity of *beta existence* as *Alpha-Awareness*
maintained between the physical body (1)
and the Master Control Center (4).

In this same model, achievement of total *Self-Honesty* is equivalent to maintaining an actualized *Awareness* at the

---

‡   *Grade-III* materials—*Master Grade* tier of understanding—
defining a systematic "pathway" to attain personal "*Self-Honesty*"
in *beta existence*.

"MCC level" of *Self-determined* consciousness—thereby "above" potential degrees of automatic fluctuation and fragmented "low-level" thoughts, emotions, impulses and irrationality.

When we consider the extent to which "thought vibrations" and "thought-waves" *solidify* as the "thought-forms" of our Reality, it is evident that the "*Arcane Tablets*" are correct in stating: "*Thoughts are 'things'.*" When allowed an existence outside *direct* control of *Self*, thoughts will engage reactive emotional responses from the "RCC," which will in turn engage the body into behaviors that are not *Self-directed*—and which seem quite "automatic." As these emotional degrees are engaged more often or more severely, they provide enough waveform activity to become the total focus of our *Awareness*. This directly affects the "highest state" of thought and level of understanding at any given moment. Even when these "emotional tides" are *ebbing*—and are not directly stimulated by interactions with environment at a certain *time*—so long as some *solid* exists as an "epicenter" to interact with, these tides may very well return to their disruptive *flows* later on.

The information sent back to *Self* as a determinant of Reality is only as *clear* as the *channel* it is sent through.

feedback loop : "a complete and continuous circuit flow of energy or information directed as an output from a source to a target which is altered and return back to the source as an input; in *General Systemology* —the continuous process where outputs of a system are routed back as inputs to complete a circuit or loop, which may be closed or connected to other systems/circuits; in *NexGen Systemology*—the continuous process where directed *Life* energy and *Awareness* is sent back to *Self* as experience, understanding and memory to complete an energetic circuit as a loop."

A communication circuit occurs when our *beta experience* completes a "feedback loop" of *Awareness* energy (as memory and understanding) back to the "*Master Control Center*" (MCC) based on interactions with the RCC from "lower sensory levels" of the Physical Universe.

When no obstructions, fragmented lenses, or thought-formed solids are *imprinted* at "lower levels," than the energy communicated back as *Awareness* is not refracting any distortion or fragmentation. This is the state we refer to as "*Self-Honesty*," because we are sending and receiving a free flow of *ZU*—within the range of thought (4) and the "physical body" (1) on the *Standard Model*—that is entirely directed and determined from the (*I-AM-Self*) *Alpha-Spirit*. This state is at a high enough frequency to maintain a true *Identity-continuity* interior to *beta existence*.

By "frequency" and "vibration" we are again referring to "wave-forms" as apparent energetic activity—which is how "thought" and "emotion" is expressed in our *Systemology* using the *Standard Model* of the *ZU-line*.

Using this same model, "Thoughts" are *thought-waves*—which means *energy in action*. This is what all "*waves*" are: energy "peaks" (or points) in motion. The degree and strength of interaction between "waves" and other "waves" is often described as a "*field*." Therefore all energy "in action" creates a *field* of "interaction." When allowed, these thoughts are constantly fluctuating, transforming and adjusting in relation to all other waves of a similar nature—including the thoughts of others.

Thought activity between individuals will interact as a particular "field" within that range of energy, just as emotional activity interacts between individuals at *those* degrees of vibration. "Emotional reinforcement" seems to directly strengthen and *solidify* our thoughts and beliefs as *real*. Interplay of "low-level" manifestations in *Awareness* has a larger part to play in what we consider "Reality" than most people realize. We should consider "Thought" (or any *wave*) as a point or singular aspect moving through space at a particular rate of speed. And just as we have a left and right leg, so does energy carry a to-and-fro oscillating motion. In mathematical logic, this is demonstrated as a basic continuous *sine-wave*.

---

sine-wave : "the *frequency* and amplitude of a quantified (calculable) *vibration* represented on a graph (graphically) as smooth repetitive *oscillation* of a *waveform*; a *waveform* graphed for demonstration—otherwise represented in *NexGen Systemology* logic equations as 'Wf,' or in mathematics as the '*function of x*' (*fx*); graphically representing arcs (*parameters*) of a circular *continuity* on a *continuum*; in the *Standard Model of NexGen Systemology*, the actual 'wave vibration' graphically displayed on an otherwise static *ZU-line* is a '*sine-wave*.'"

When we refer to "vibration," "degree" and "frequency" on the *ZU-line*, we are always referring to "*sine-wave*" activity. "Fields" of potential interaction are based on strength or **amplitude**. This type of waveform consists of four primary "arcs," which may be represented graphically as four "quadrants" of a circular *continuity model*, circular shape—or, yes, *superstrings* (if we invite notions from quantum science). The description of energy movement as a vibration or specific numeric frequency is simply our way of relatively comparing properties of one wave (or waveform condition) and another, using the same scale or scope of measurement—and *Time*. For example: basic electrical flow is measured as "*hertz*" when we speak of 60*hz* or 50*hz* power. This refers to the number of times a current *alternates* or *oscillates* its to-and-fro motion within a single second.

> *Oscillation-alternation* : "a particular type of (or fluctuation) between two relative states, conditions or degrees; a wave-action between two degrees, such as is described in the action of the *pendulum effect*; a flux or wave-like energy in motion, across space, calculable as time."

As related to thoughts, each instance of thinking is linked to a specific signature waveform carrying our *Awareness* along the *ZU-line*. It is not passive energy. The *Thought-wave* is actually transmitted at relatively high frequencies in a successive cycle of "motion-thoughtpoint-motion-thoughtpoint-motion-..." and so on. It moves at a higher frequency than the physical body or even our emotional range of experience—and has the ability to incite activity in both. This cycle of action is similar to the ongoing development of our *Systemology* research work: combining existent practical understanding with new experimental processes that lead to discoveries and new realizations for evaluating new research at a now higher level of understanding. The cycle continues further and further in this manner. The limit is *Infinity*. And *Infinity* is the *destination*.

△ △ △ △ △ △ △

Our understanding now includes that thought-waves are *solidified* as thought-forms when they are developed into *belief* or *truth*. This is all that is necessary for them to become a Reality for *Self*. All other *facets* of reinforcement will naturally attract to the *belief* in proportion to the strength of its "*field*." In energetic terms: *like attract like*—and by whatever means the seed-of-existence has been programmed to do so, we observe all things in existence automatically working to absorb the energy and matter they require to sustain an existence (even "grow" or "reproduce" when possible). They expel energy that is used, wasted or not useful. Even minerals and precious gems deep beneath the earth surface are engaged in this chemical process with their environment to literally "form" and "grow."

Whether under the control of *Self—Self-directed* from the *Alpha-Spirit*—or whether operating under *indirect* fragmentation of programmed belief and emotional encoded experiences, all *Life* is engaged in some degree of "thought activity" and "thought field interaction" with all other *Life*, to the extent of its strength as Reality. This is certainly demonstrated in the *Enuma Eliš* epic.

Reality becomes *more real*—more *solid*—as its magnitude increases coinciding with our "agreement of Reality"—**displacing** interference from any similar or "lower-level" waveforms. Therefore, our level of *Awareness* will always be in fluctuation with our "environment" so long as fixed points of *beta existence* solidity are maintained. It is no different than *putting up* "*walls*" as a self-made barrier to totality.

Consider that a physical "*wall*" of your house or office is a *waveform* at low levels of frequency with a high magnitude of density reinforced as Reality. Semantically, we even *agree* to store an archetype—or primary "Form"—of this "thing" in our minds as the word "*Wall*." As a "*thing*," we can distinguish related experiences and mental data-files of "*Wall*" from, for example, "*Ball*." When at rest, the object-construct that we call a "*baseball*" actually exists at roughly an equivalent degree of waveform vibration as the "*wall*"—which for our current purposes we might chart on the *Standard Model* as approximately (1). That is why, if we toss it against the "*wall*," there is a direct *interaction*. Once a bit of *action* or amplitude is provided to the object (or *waveform*), it *interacts* with the another object (or *waveform*), and there is some *result*. This is an "energetic communication." The "*ball*" exerts its *field-force* on the "*wall*" and the "*wall*" responds accordingly, which in most cases puts the "*ball*" at rest on the floor next to it. However, if enough velocity is put behind the "*ball*"—if the frequency of its "Reality" is increased—the result might be a little different.

This "physical system" example perfectly describes systematic activity (motion) within the parameters of our "thoughts" and "emotions." A basic "feedback loop" has just been demonstrated that applies to all forms of system interaction, which all contribute to the composition of our Reality in *Awareness*. The relay of experience completes a circuit, even if fragmented or obstructed.[*] This is precisely why we can effectively chart—and have "working knowledge" of—an evaluation of anything upon the *ZU-line* within our range of experience.

∆ ∆ ∆ ∆ ∆ ∆ ∆

SUMMARY

All "Thought" activity—as *thought-waves*, whether "fragmented" or "clear"—falls between *two* "points" on the *ZU-line*:

   a.) the *Self-Honest state* of a "Proactive-Mind" or *alpha* "*Master Control Center*" (responsible for directing *Self-*

---

[*]   So long as the resulting condition of apparent "forces" or *effects* reaches an "equilibrium" point, than we are always able to demonstrate the activity in some logic equation using the *Standard Model*.

determinism of the "I" toward the genetic organism); and

b.) the domain of a programmable *"Imprint"* or beta *"Reactive Control Center"* (which discharges emotional *biochemicals* and motor *impulses* of the genetic organism).

Our personal *Self-direction* of *ZU* is concentrated, condensed and *solidified* by our *thoughts* and attentions—the *amplitude* is reinforced by some degree of *emotional* engagement that qualifies "physical experience" and/or a "**somatic** result" as Reality in *Awareness*.

The "peak" level of *Awareness* we maintain is proportional to the level of frequency that our attentions and thought energy are fixed to.

The "Standard Model" used in the field and methods of *"NexGen Systemology"* is a graphic representation of the *ZU-line*.

We may effectively place the proactive *Master Control Center* or "MCC" at "(4)" on the "Standard Model" (*ZU-line*)— at the *Alpha* point of first contact (and relay of energy as *Awareness* and *Lifeforce*) between *AN* and *KI* as a *beta existence*.

The *Master Control Center* or "MCC" is a perfect computing device to the extent of the information received from "lower levels" of sensory experience.

We may effectively place the secondary *Reactive Control Center* or "RCC" at "(2)" on the "Standard Model" (*ZU-line*) —at the *beta* point of *"Awareness"* for a *Lifeform*, maintaining the most primitive functions.

We may use the "Standard Model" to effectively categorize all *degrees* of variation between "(2)" and "(4)" as the "internal frequency range" of "Thought"—which we classify most generally as *"the Mind"* or *Psychological System*.

We may use the "Standard Model" to effectively categorize all *degrees* of fluctuation below "(2)" as the "internal frequency range" of "Emotion"—which transmit bio-chemical energy and impulses "down" toward the "physical cellular body"/"genetic vehicle" at position "(1)" as somatic responses.

All resulting physical sensory input is communicated back to the *Self* to complete the energy circuit of *Awareness*—as a "feedback loop"—which many call *consciousness*. There-fore, spiritual potential of an "*Alpha*" being is only inhibited or restricted by the degree of "clarity" main-tained as "personal energy." Such inhibitions are recognized in *Systemology* as "fragmentation" and "im-prints" along the *ZU-line* of personal *Awareness*, particularly within the range of "*thought* and *emotion*."

If no obstruction, fragmented "lens," or thought-formed solids appear at "lower levels" of energy interaction, than the *Awareness* energy communicated back to *Self* is not re-fracting any distortion or fragmentation. *This is the 'condition' we refer to as "Self-Honesty."*

All "*waves*" are energy peaks in motion that create a "*field*" of potential interaction with other "*waves*." The en-ergy of ZU manifest as thought-waves and thought-communication operate at higher frequencies of energy than the same *ZU Life-energy* at the range of the "physical body" or even "emotional" states of experience. Thoughts also possess the ability to incite energetic activity pro-cesses in the emotional and physical systems directly.

Whether under the actualized control of *Self* (as fully *Self-directed* from the *Alpha-Spirit*) or operating under *indirect* fragmentation (of programmed belief and emotional en-coded experiences), all *Life* is engaged in some degree of "thought activity" and "thought-field interaction" with all other *Life*, to the extent of its range and strength (amp-litude).

.: 7 :.
REALITY ENGINEERING AS A MANIFESTATION OF THOUGHT & ENERGY IN THE PHYSICAL UNIVERSE

The *Standard Model* of the *ZU-line* is derived from wisdom on the *"Tablets of Destiny."* It suggests that "Thoughts" are degrees of ZU-energy vibrating within the mental range (or parameters) of "psychological systems" of a *Lifeform*. This activity is described by many as "consciousness." Our actual *Awareness* may be "seated" at any point along along the *ZU-line*—even including the range *above* a "Self-Honest MCC" plotted at (4) on the *Standard Model*. Our equations demonstrate that all states of degree between "4.1" and *Infinity* (8) are strictly *Alpha-directed* or *Self-determined*, independent or exterior to *causality* in the Physical Universe, except where it maintains its *Lifeline* with a genetic organism for continued *beta existence*. Such high ideals for *Awareness* rest on basic foundations of achieving *Self-Honesty* in all directed thoughts and reception of experience.

Most of our experience of *beta existence* regards contact with vibrations of all matter encountered or carried by *Lifeforms* we meet—and especially those in our immediate vicinity as authority figures, family and community. These each represent various levels of a "group consciousness field" that is fed by our thought participation—and by the thoughts of others—in *agreement* as *Reality*. The frequency level and intensity of vibration (within the thought range) inevitably produces the "energy level" of the group and the range of its influence. This means that at a planetary level concerning the whole of those sharing the Human Condition, there is even a calculable "average energy level of understanding" and *Awareness* that is maintained by those in perfect *agreement* to the social programming and mundane standards of the masses on Earth as Reality. We can assume that this point is not very "high" on the *ZU-line*—probably lingering somewhere between "2.0" and "2.5" if graphically plotted.

> **engineering** : "the *Self-directed* actions and efforts to utilize knowledge (observed causality/science), maths (calculations/quantification) and logic (axioms/formulas) to understand, design or manifest a solid structure, machine, mechanism, engine or system; as '*Reality Engineering*[‡] in *NexGen Systemology*—intentional *Self-directed* adjustment of existing Reality conditions; the application of total *Self-determinism* in *Self-Honesty* to change apparent Reality using fundamentals of *Systemology* and *Cosmic Law*."

Application of fundamental principles regarding thought as energy and manifestation have led to various philosophical schools of "*Reality Engineering.*" The implication is "manufactured manifestation" and "understanding" of Reality, but also the "management of its motion" on the "track," just like a train "Engineer"—the one who is *operating* the engine. The Engineer learns the rules and mechanics of their vehicle so that they may operate it better—but they are not personally shrinking down into each of the systems and motor functions to actually *make* them "go." It is the presence and activity of the Engineer alone that is required—and their *Awareness*—to do little more than *start, stop* or *alternate speeds* of the vehicle. Everything else is a part of the environmental or conditional experience that we are simply *Aware* of as "effects."

Solidified thoughts that are intensively broadcast have the tendency to be carried and built upon by others who are affected by or interact with them. Even if everyone is not in "agreement" on their position regarding something, there is now a "thing" in existence to have a position on at all. In either case, we are *agreeing* it exists. Those affected who operate along a similar "train of thought"—or within its vicinity on the spectrum—will increase the strength of

---

‡   The term "*Reality Engineering*" is also applied to some advanced *Systemology* lessons pertaining to operative potential of a *Self-Honest* individual able to actualize a degree of *Awareness* "exterior" to *beta existence*. We consider this: operating from *Self* (or) actualizing *Self-determinism* "from Spirit."

the overall "thought-form" by contributing to it with their *agreement* as Reality. Those who are "like us" (and those we "like") are generally folk that maintain a similar level of understanding and *Awareness* as us. This actually increases the **validation** and *solidity* of whatever it is we are directing our *Awareness* as—and there is little doubt that our own "sense of Self" is connected to whatever level our attention maintains. We tend to be attracted to others that will increase the strength or validation of our Reality. Certain individuals may also gravitate towards "higher level" *charismatic* personalities that radiate the type of Reality they *seek an agreement* with.

We are handling the *power* of thought every day. Anyone demonstrating otherwise is either not *Aware* of these powers themselves, has no direct experience with ancient wisdom such as the *Arcane Tablets*, or otherwise *does* know, but doesn't want you to know. In this latter case, such individuals have not achieved a *Self-Honest* realization of the *Prime Directive*[*] beyond the most selfish levels. These types operate solely on a rudimentary game principle that "more for you means less for them." We must empower all of humanity in equality—just as we all share the same spiritual potential in equality...and that potential is *Infinity*.

Δ Δ Δ Δ Δ Δ Δ

As is demonstrated with Marduk's acquisition and use of the "*Tablets of Destiny*," the process of *Self* -directing as an actualized "*Reality Engineer*" requires deep **immersion** to achieve understanding. This means that the *Pathway to Self-Honesty* (and unfolding potential of the Human Condition) requires the same dedication, focus and concentration of our attention and *Awareness* that we would submit to learning and experiencing any other "worldly focus" of immersed *Awareness*—such as the functions of a new job or

---

* The "Prime Directive" is "to exist," or else stated: "The purpose of existence is to exist"—or else "to survive" (*beta*) and "to create" (*Alpha*). This applies to all levels of *Self* as a unit; it applies to social systems and the planet Earth.

the sudden responsibility of parenthood, &tc. However, along this journey, we have discovered that even the basic act of continued learning and developmental understanding within the *Systemology* paradigm—which, in turn, inspires more learning and life-applications—has the ability to slowly raise our *Awareness* and personal vibration levels slowly toward *Self-Honesty*.

We know that our thoughts and personal vibrations have the ability to affect us—our experience of Reality—and we know that they may be used to affect others, particularly if they share a level of *agreement* with the same degree of Reality. Even when they do not, we find many instances where these other Realities are impressed upon us, either from the thoughts and actions of others directly or by some other *facet* of our personal environment. It is not our goal to change the fact that these basic systems exist—or to throw up our hands in defeat and say, 'well, I guess that is that'. Remember always that these systems are all *dynamic* and subject to our **participation**. This participation will always be defined by our level of understanding of *Awareness*—which *is* in our direct ability to control during this *Lifetime*. It is our primary responsibility. What we do with it and where we carry it to as *Alpha-Spirits* is a journey that can only be made by the *Self-Honest*. This journey begins first and foremost with *Self-Mastery* and the power of *Thought*.

It is unfortunate in some respects that many of the benchmarks and guideposts of the *Path* are earmarked with concepts that have become *cliché* in modern society. This often happens when the *esoteric* becomes *exoteric* and is not properly realized into mass consciousness. Many of the concepts from the "*Arcane Tablets*" are demonstrated in other spiritual schools and even modern "New Thought" efforts—but they are too often disregarded as trivial and poorly evaluated as fanciful sentiments. Often the authors of these works themselves have not realized the wisdom to a point beyond a second level of understanding, and therefore are not able to advance their *Seekers* further than they themselves have reached. This says nothing about what the same "tools" might be used to manifest in the hands of someone else.

As a perfect example: the "*Law of Attraction*" reached some popularity *again* a few years back—a concept expressed verbatim by the "New Thought" movement a century prior and then again strongly in the 1930's and virtually every twenty years or so since by someone or some group. It is even at the root of many arcane teachings. It demonstrates our ability to "attract" additional *solidity* to thoughts and emotional states we carry with us or else focus intently and **repetitively** on. And this observation appears in numerous places over thousands of years since Babylon, boiling down to a basic axiom that: "a person *is* as they *think*"—or—"a person experiences their beliefs as Reality." Certainly it is not yet received into the consciousness of an entire species—or we would have witnessed a planet of actualized *Self-Honest* "*gods*" running around by now.

Our thoughts are creating vibrations of a particular frequency that resonate all "up and down" the *ZU-line*. The *Standard Model* demonstrates clearly that we are engaging with the world around us—and its waveforms—proportional to our own vibrations. We are not only charging or conditioning our own experience of existence with our thoughts, but we are engaging and acting and directing behavior into the world as an expression of those vibrations. They are inseparable:—

> The MCC retains programming;
> and the RCC retains conditioning.

The *interior* and *exterior* Reality of an individual is treated along the same line of *Awareness.* The MCC installed for this *beta existence* is essentially perfect but only to the degree of perfect information and energy received in the "feedback loop" with the environment. It may be the case that infinite perfection is a quality only achieved once uppermost points of infinite experience are actualized.

"Mind-Systems" do not distinguish differences between what is perceived as the Reality internally by the *Self* and what is received as information from the "external" world or environment. Just because a thought has not been condensed and infused into physical matter does not mean that we do not interact with it as a *solid*.

We are constructing Reality with what we *know*—the materials, files and databases stored in some "astral warehouse," all of which the MCC has fixed as "real." But it is not alone in this process. There is a reactive system or "RCC" at work which has the ability to—at certain times—override what is considered "real" concerning physical existence. This is where "automatic processes" and "conditioning" exists—and it is in this domain that our thought distortions and fragmentation of experience is stored as "emotional energy." For this reason, some philosophers have chosen to call the "RCC" Mind-System a "Reactive Mind." It is not responsible for actually *Self-determining* the Reality of anything—it treats everything it contacts as Reality, based on sensory input and direct contact. At the RCC level of the Standard Model—(2)—people are not *Self-directing* thought—they are vibrating in the range of purely "sensation" and "animal impulse" with no higher sense of *Awareness*. And isn't that a pretty picture for the state of human affairs—with most of the people walking around operating on "auto-pilot."

Δ Δ Δ Δ Δ Δ Δ

When we actualize total "alpha control" of the Mind Systems—which is a quality of *gods* appearing to ancient humans—we carry with us an ability to maintain "high degrees" of thought and a vibrancy of *Life* beyond the "norm" in place in society.

Personal abilities also affect other systems respectively. We operate "automatically" on systems of Reality we have *agreed* to based on whatever source of "facts"—facts we are meant to take on *faith* until *we* make them *solid* by *faith*. If we apply principles from the "*Arcane Tablets*" to physical well-being, we discover that the emotional state and thought-forms maintained by someone ill are just as important to treat as blatant physical symptoms.

Wisdom demonstrated from the *"Tablets of Destiny"* in no way invalidates significance of the "physical component" to our experience of existence. We know we have been in bodies before, will probably be again, but we are associated with *this one* for a reason. This is the one we know about. This is the *Game* we are playing in present time. We cannot neglect the genetic vehicle we are using to experience *beta existence*. It is our "avatar" for this playing field while reaching for "higher states" of *Awareness*—the ability to enact "spiritual technology" toward the true evolution of *Self* and not simply "external technologies" used to advance the physical body in *beta existence*. Our society tends to yield more of its understanding and resources specifically toward "external technologies" because they are more profitable and sensual. If people are only *Aware* of these "lower" modes of existence, that is what becomes the totality of their *Awareness*.

When our *Awareness* is attached to a particular degree of thought-form, we develop an *"affinity"* or relationship with that vibration. We develop this "affinity" with all aspects or people we are in communication or interaction with. All interconnected systems of *Self* will process and function accordingly with this state. That means the status of these systems are "adjustable" by other systems—which is why we consider them *Dynamic Systems*.

The energy flow of the *ZU-line* is always naturally seeking or moving toward an equilibrium of efficiency with its environment—though until it reaches this state of infinite perfection, there is relative *movement* or *motion*. **Energy-signatures** of the personal *ZU-line* tend to make "trails" or traces of itself that it can more easily follow later—much like a river etching out new routes and courses to follow. This means that our "train of thought" actually fixes or adheres itself more strongly to whatever "track" it is on the longer it is traveling on it.

We continuously reinforce *solidity* of our thought-forms every time we revisit them with new attention and emotional engagement. *Solids* which are painfully buried may suddenly **resurface** again. Significantly harmful reactive-response encoding may stay dormant for long periods of time without resurfacing. The thoughts and thought-forms that cause us the most severe *fragmentation* and distortion are usually not information and memories that we treat analytically on a day-to-day basis. *That* type of programming may be resolved with proper education, advancing in understanding, systemological processes and even reassignment of word associations—all of which are also demonstrated by principles of the "*Arcane Tablets.*" In fact, "language programming" with "emotional enforcement" led to complete systematization of Human "civilization."

---

imprint : "to strongly impress, stamp, mark (or outline) onto a softer 'impressible' substance; to mark with pressure onto a surface; in *NexGen Systemology*, the term is used to indicate permanent Reality impressions marked by frequencies, energies or interactions experienced during periods of emotional distress, pain, unconsciousness or antagonism to physical survival, all of which are are stored with other reactive response-mechanisms at lower-levels of *Awareness* as opposed to the proactive memory database of our central processing centers; an experiential memory-set that may later be triggered or stimulated artificially as Reality, of which similar responses will be engaged automatically."

True *fragmentation* is an "**aberration**" (or unknowingly created "illusion") that inhibits Self from maintaining a clear view of Reality and handling of manifestation. A "hallucination" is not a "true hallucination" if one is *Aware* that they are "hallucinating." Everything else is a distortion or glamour that we may "reason" with reliably when using proper faculties. The dark side of the *Pathway* to *Self-Honesty* is that it requires the *Alpha Spirit* to maintain an effectively honest relationship with *beta existence*—including a handling of "painful memories" that carry intense emotional energy and imprint encoding at an organic and cellular level. Emotionally encoded *"Imprints"* that distort the crystalline lens of our clear *Awareness* at the deepest levels. Releasing these ties is a very serious and significant step toward true liberation of the *Spirit*.

Fragmentation, painful memories, **biological-unconsciousness** and traumatic **emotional-encoding** are also factors of "mental programming." These *facets* of experience accumulate reinforced emotional encoding as *Imprints*, which associate certain perceptions of the environment with a particular experience—even if they otherwise have no actual causal relationship. This information is stored and "hidden away" beneath MCC *Awareness* by the RCC for alleged "survival" purposes and interpreting sensory information. But false information may resurface at any time one of these *facets* comes into play. This causes distortions to our "lens" of perception without warning. In most cases we will not be able to tell the difference between an actual "threat" and one perceived from a previous *imprinted* experience. This is especially true in times of "stress" or moments of uncertainty and fatigue—or in situations correlating very precisely with original environmental circumstances of the *Imprint*.

Imprints are first encoded on figurative **"slates"** or "glass slides" within the deepest/lowest parts of the Mind-System in times of emotional distress or threats to one's own existence—points on the Standard Model when *Awareness* drops below (2) and lower-levels of consciousness are engaged to direct the body. *"Imprints"* are stored in the RCC as "emotional energy" hidden "below the surface" of MCC programming and any analytical activity within the normal range of *"Thought."*

Just as thoughts are *solidified* in the mental range with mental frequencies of energy, these fundamental survival experiences are *solidified* by reinforced impressions on a "slate" charged by emotional tones at levels beneath "rationality."

Some aspects of an *"Imprint"* may even seem "rational," but since the entire experience is stored beneath the surface of normal thought activity, we cannot actually be certain of what they do for or to us until we *resurface* them intentionally and process them within the "rational" range of thought.

All *"Imprints"* represent some degree of fragmentation. *Even* something as simple as a "fear of dogs" might *seem* rational when we connect it to some instance of experience however long ago it may be. But then consider all of the automated responses attached to this experience that displace the *Self* as the "seat of control" for the physical body later on in our lives. There may even be other things or *facets* that we wrongfully associate to our fear of dogs. In future instances where a "dog" or some other *facet* of the same *Imprint* is present, we are taken out of phase—out of "sync"—with Reality. The "RCC" causes the body to respond to "danger signals" or threats to existence that *are not actually present* in the environment.

The Human Condition handles its own *Self-directed* actions quite well—even if *fragmented*. We have no shortage of skill in justifying *our own* actions. Even if it is supported by false information, we can always "come up with" an answer later to justify anything. We have to. It is the job of the Mind-Systems to make sense of Reality to evaluate and make right decisions. It is important to *defragment* artificial distortions of Reality.

It is our irrationality—what is outside "rational thought" of the MCC—when *Self* is eliminated from the circuit-loop controlling physical behavior—that we *must* resolve. *Self-Honesty* is a state of full "rational thought" free from emotional fluctuation. Emotional *imprinting* is a far more solid slate to *clear* properly than thought programming that is rooted in semantics, &tc. Most emotional fragmentation is "self-sustained" by additional emotional **etching** and experience, but it is first *imprinted* somewhere—and usually not from instances that we have *Self-determined*.

> You can even think of an "*Imprint*" as the RCC displacing the MCC and sending a message to the body: "I'M *such and such*" and the command "PRINT." It is falsifying its identity as *Self* in place of *Self*.

Aside from those memories assumed through direct "bodily injury," disruptive *Imprints* are mainly a result of authoritarian enforcement of beliefs, "emotional baggage" and other programmed responses that strongly influence our *thought fragmentation* from beneath an emotional surface—and which is prone to resurface unbidden and undirected by the *Self*. These types of *Imprints* must be systematically "*resurfaced*" and "**confronted**" on the *Pathway to Self-Honesty* before effectively *defragmenting* "higher energy" thought-bases of manifestation: *substance*, *motion* and *Awareness*—of which these *Imprints* will undoubtedly distort in the Mind. Remember that we cannot move beyond the point we do not understand and this very much includes our relationship-ties to the past.

Imprints are emotionally encoded and reinforced with similar emotional energy frequencies by the "RCC" sub-level of the Mind-System. The emotional energy range is closer to the physical spectrum of vibration maintained by the genetic vehicle—naturally there is a high affinity between emotional states and the physical condition of the body. "RCC" commands are immediately responded to by the physical organism as bio-chemicals and hormones. This is where we witness a "physical system" component of "higher" range systems on the *Standard Model*. In future instances of distress, confusion—or any triggers stimulating the originally encoded event—the RCC displaces proactive MCC control of the *Self* by engaging reactive responses that treat **dead-memories** as present time Reality. This happens even if the external event does not warrant the response. The individual reacts to heavily charged memory—or a strongly encoded *Imprint*—a unit of distortion in an otherwise perfect crystalline lens. And the average person probably has many of these.

A very long time ago the response-mechanisms (operated solely by the RCC) were the primary Mind-System governing survival of a primitive evolving genetic organism. The cellular-evolving biochemical organism is separate from *Self*. While evolving independently, the RCC *did* serve a functional purpose for evolution and survival of a genetic vehicle at a cellular level in this Physical Universe. But "progress" or "*evolution*" is to rise above such states of "primitive survival instinct."

All effective *Self-Actualization* is built upon a strong material foundation of physical stability as a "body"—food, water, shelter, clothing and the ability to be clean, &tc. But survival is—or *was* once—the only primitive goal in *Beta-Existence*. The ultimate goal would be *Self-directed* infinite existence. But we should be able to now fully exercise our own *Self-determined* existence and no longer operate on "caveman" faculties that resemble auto-pilot. It seems strange that a species should reach such a point in development that it requires such serious *defragmentation* efforts and re-education toward maintaining optimum levels of survival, *just* to prevent its own self-determined annihilation during the 21st century.

Δ Δ Δ Δ Δ Δ

SUMMARY

Our experience of *beta existence* mainly pertains to contact with energy vibrations carried by everyone and everything we meet—and especially communicated by authority figures, family, friends and the civic community we occupy.

Reality is an *agreement of thought and experience*—its frequency and intensity producing a basic "energy level" for an individual, group, or even species.

Effective "*Reality Engineering*" in no way defies "*Cosmic Law*" or attempts to alter its systematic design. It is concerned with the "operator's" ability to *start, stop* or *change a variable* of existing interconnected systems—such as in the operation of a "vehicle."

Systems are *dynamic* and subject to our participation—but the level of this participation will always be defined by our level of understanding of *Awareness*—which *is* in our direct ability to control during this *Lifetime*.

Solidified thoughts that are intensively broadcast have the tendency to be carried and built upon by others who are affected by them or interact with them. Even if a person is "opposed to the idea," there is now a "thing" in existence for us to *agree* to be in a position with at all.

The "Standard Model" demonstrates that our thoughts are creating vibrations of a particular frequency, which resonate all "up and down" the *ZU-line*, and we are engaging with the "world around us" (as *waveforms*) relative to our own vibrations.

The MCC operates based on analytical programming; the RCC operates based on conditioning and emotional encoding. *Alpha Operation* of the MCC for this *beta existence* is perfect only to the degree of sensory information and energy received in the "feedback loop" with the environment (which passes through the domain of the RCC).

Interior and *exterior* composure of an individual's Reality is treated along the same *ZU-line* as *Awareness*, which does not distinguish differences between what is perceived as Reality "internally" by the *Self* and what is received as information from the "external" world.

When our *Awareness* is attached to a particular degree of thought-form, we develop an "*affinity*" or "relationship" with that vibration as a part of our "Reality." All interconnected systems of *Self* will function and communicate processes corresponding with this state.

We continuously reinforce *solidity* of our thought-forms, imprints and fragments as Reality every time we revisit them with new attention or new interest that engages emotional energy or reactive-responses.

Significantly harmful reactive-response encoding may stay dormant for long periods of time without resurfacing directly.

Painful memories (physical or emotional), unconsciousness and trauma are forms of conditioning potentially resulting from *Awareness* being "suspended" for long periods or severe instances below "(2)" on the "Standard Model." These emotionally encoded facets accumulate as an "*Imprint.*"

"*Imprints*" are stored in the RCC as "emotional energy" and there hidden "below the surface" of MCC programming and the analytical activity within the normal range of "*Thought.*"

"*Imprints*" must be systematically "resurfaced" and "confronted" on the *Path to Self-Honesty* before effectively *defragmenting* "higher energy" systems of *Awareness*—of which these *Imprints* will undoubtedly distort in the Mind.

When we actualize "total master control" of the Mind Systems—a critical component of all *gods* and *Ascended Masters* that ever appeared in human history—we may achieve the next spiritual evolution of the Human Condition by its ability to maintain "high degrees" of thought and a vibrancy of *Life* beyond the current "norm."

.: 8 :.
UNDERSTANDING HOW PERSONAL THOUGHT CREATES REALITIES OF MANIFESTATION ["TABLETS OF DESTINY" IN ACTION]

Arcane Tablets describe many processes: creation; division; one plane giving birth to another; the infinite continuation of life; mastery of the environment; and development of solids in accordance with Cosmic Law. These *examples* all push our studies toward one fundamental expression, which sums up all that we see unfold at all levels and in all instances of existence. In each aspect of the *Tablets of Destiny* and in every movement propelling survival actions of a *waveform* forward in space: the *Unmanifest* becomes *Manifest*; the *Infinity of Absolute Potential* becomes *Continuous Activity in Motion*; the *Latency of Nothingness* becomes *Finite Expressions of Reality*.

We are given a demonstration of the ALL encompassing two primary planes or divisions of existence as we know it: the *Spiritual Universe* in the dimensional direction of *AN* and the *Physical Universe* in the dimensional direction of *KI*. It is possible that expressions of *Spiritual Life Energy*—that we call *ZU*—are *directed* from the *direction* of *AN* into multiple simultaneous *beta expressions* or alternate physical "*KI-type*" universes. For present purposes, we are most concerned with the *Self-directed* expression of an *Alpha Spirit* or "Spiritual Identity" as experiencing the *ZU-line* existing in *this* Reality. When we consider *entanglement* and interconnection of all energetic systems throughout existence, than we become aware that our *Self-determined Causes*—spiritual action, mental action, emotional action and physical action—have counterparts with other systems and levels they share a relationship with. "*Everything is connected together...*"

As an expression of pure *Infinity*, our *Spirit* as *Awareness* is actually an energetic "constant" in its highest *Alpha* expression. *Self* is a *static* energy or constant *Lifeforce* (from AN) that is only detectable—or *perturbed* into a detectable *waveform*—as a deviation of that constant when it comes into contact (or interaction) with other waveforms/energies at various degrees. Therefore, what actually is an energetic constant static in its original *Alpha* form, becomes a fluctuating energy—in a state of constant variation—when interacting with *Dynamic Systems* of *Awareness* in *beta existence*.

To return to a previous example: as we see with "water," which retains the same molecular composition as "water" regardless of the apparent state it actualizes a degrees of. The "water" is a constant structure. It does not change what it actually *is* in order to manifest states of Reality as "ice" versus "liquid." Any *variation* to its apparent existence is a result of being a "*Dynamic System*." As such, changes in states are due solely to "*perturbations*" from other systems affecting it—systems that it shares a "systematic relationship" with—such as the environment.

> **perturbation** : "the deviation from a natural state, fixed motion, or orbit system caused by another external system; disturbing or disquieting the serenity of an existent state; inciting observable apparent action using indirect or outside actions or 'forces'; the introduction of a new element or facet that disturbs equilibrium of a standard system; the "butterfly effect"; in *NexGen Systemology*, 'perturbation' is a necessary condition for the *ZU-line* to function as a *Standard Model* of actual 'monistic continuity'—which is a *Lifeforce* singularity expressed along a spectrum with potential interactions at each degree from any source; the influence of a degree in one state by activities of another state that seem independent, but which are actually connected directly at some higher degree, even if not apparently observed."

Examining physical conditions in *exclusion* to all other aspects is a finite and worn out way to evaluate Reality. An entire field exploring the Human Condition this way is called "behaviorism" and it is still alive and well, operating in this fashion. In fact, "behaviorism" successfully dominates most academics and applied psychology in modern society. This is the same as us understanding and experiencing *Awareness* of Reality solely based on "low-level" energy "physical" interactions—which is exactly how the average individual is prone to operate the Human Condition with only "**standard-issue**" programming.

Standard programming instilled within western society dictates that all physical manifestation has purely physical cause. It goes on to assume that the Physical Universe is a *closed system* in *exclusion* to anything else. Yet, each one of us has a natural sense that the "physical world" around us is not at all a "closed system" and is most certainly connected to interaction with *something else*.

What we deem *"physical"* is therefore only the "lowest" possible vibrations of *cosmic* energy interacting with "consciousness." From a point of stasis—or *Awareness*—we are able to take "good measure" and make "honest" determinations concerning Reality. If all we know of "water" is its finite states, we are not given applied knowledge to actually *do* anything about these states. Thousands of years of diverse language and culture have brought to us any number of ways to define, categorize and provide semantics to various terms for these states—but we are still left with questions of *what to do* about them. We seem to have no difficulties in dividing and classifying information into all manner of fragmented knowledge—but what we are developing in this "new" field of work is an applied spiritual philosophy that yields "gradable" results.

The Standard Model of *Systemology*, which incorporates the *ZU-line*, does not disregard the *"Physical"*—as we tend to find more often in the **Eastern**-style traditions. These traditions—and even many of the orthodox forms of organized religion practiced in the West—tend to focus on achieving a "higher" frequency and personal state through strict avoidance of the *Game*. The advice offered usually reduces to something like, "the less you have to do with the physical world, the better off you are." And this may actually work for some individuals that have the means or determination to simply take their block of "ice" up high onto a remote mountaintop and try to remain alive long enough to see if it changes states back to "liquid" during this *Lifetime*.

Certainly there are a few individuals that may have actually found some success in achieving a point of *Self-Honesty* with an approach to life that follows a basic axiom that "the only way to win is not to play." However, by eliminating all *"game conditions,"* we are restricting free movement and ability to actually *change the state of things*. We don't want to sit around, hiding out, waiting for death. As a holistic paradigm approach, Systemology "New Thought" is looking at the "water" and "ice," its environment, and all systems providing conditions for energy movement. This includes, in our "water" example, the transfer of heat and even the power supply to devices and tools assisting changes in state in every way. Our approach to understanding and mastering the root of *Self-direction* —"true thought" and "right action"—follows this same systematic process because we *are in* the *Game*.

Δ Δ Δ Δ Δ Δ Δ

There are three *Principle Systems* of "Cosmic Manifestation" described on the *"Arcane Tablets"*— which are *substance, motion* and *consciousness*. These are "conditions" of *Awareness* that may be simultaneously understood as *physical systems, mental systems* and *spiritual systems* respectively.[*]

Every state, function or dynamic system demonstrated on the Standard Model provides a condition for manifestation

---

[*] The Principles are only *representative* of qualities from these other states or systems, because each range or state has its own manifestations; thus we can have "physical substance" as *matter*, and "emotional substance" as an *Imprint* or "psychological substance" as a *thought-form*. Every state is a condition for manifestation within its energetic range of existence.

within its relative range of existence. Change in state along the ZU-line is represented by relative thresholds that we distinguish as "emotional systems" versus "Mind-Systems," &tc. These systems and their conditions are experienced relative to our *Awareness.* We observe results of causality governed by Cosmic Law of KI,[‡] but how much do we *really* understand about what we are seeing?

"Substance" is the *Principle System* of "Cosmic Manifestation" that humans are quick to identify as "Reality" in the Physical Universe. This is because the principle of *substance* is what distinguishes "things" as "bodies." Yes, we are speaking of matter as "solid," but what we are actually referring to is the very crystalline *structure* of matter—that underlying quality that gives "things" and "bodies as things" their "material nature." Where the Principle System of *Substance* meets the *Infinity of Nothingness*, we reach "Pure Space" or "Unmanifest Substance." When the Substance Principle is carried in the direction of KI beyond its point of stable solidity in the Physical Universe, we reach "*Not*" at the continuity of the Physical Universe, before again returning to *Infinity.* For every condition of "*Thing*" actively manifested throughout the Cosmos, an equal condition of "*Not*" exists within the Physical Universe. The ALL represents the total value of possible manifestation of a *Thingness-Nothingness* **dichotomy** of *all existence.* Beyond this is pure Infinite Potentiality.

Mind-Systems naturally inherent in the Human Condition are quite literal and anthropomorphic in reasoning. We tend to refer to the systematic design and nature of all principle systems as "bodies." Other traditions teach that various degrees of *Awareness* are occupied by separate "selves" such as a "Mental Body" and "Emotional Body"

[‡] These states should not be considered a quality or degree of "Infinity," because they are "conditional manifestations" and therefore "relative," which is not a property of Infinity. The ALL, which is our conception of "Infinite-manifestation" is an Absolute above the Law, which cannot be used to describe any state within *beta existence* where variation is experienced.

and "Atmic Body"[∞] and so forth. There are many highly re-
spected philosophic spiritual traditions continuing to refer
to these other "seats of consciousness" as separate bodies
—giving to them dozens of descriptors: "atomic body" and
"soul body" and "astral body" and "subtle body" and so
on. This is enough to give any practitioner an Iden-
tity-complex *if* not first instructed that there is only *one
Self, one Spiritual Body* that experiences manifestation
across an infinite continuum of *Lifeforce* that we refer to,
and effectively model as, the *ZU-line*.

When we refer to the *form* of a "thing," we are describing
its *substance* principle. Whether manifestation of existence
is condensed to low vibrations as hardened metals or as a
high spiritual frequency of Identity, all aspects beneath or
below (subject to) the *Infinite-ALL*—as separation—must
have a *form*.

Just as all "things" have their underlying energetic *form*—
or *seed*—so do all things have their active *Principle System*
of "Motion" or activity. All things with *form* maintain existence with some *motion* or *action*. Even the waveform
defining the vibration that manifests *forms* as "things" is
really a point of energy in *action*. Therefore every Substance brought to manifestation must have its
corresponding attributes of *interaction*—within its own system and all encounters with other energy systems. These
qualities of action are invariably a part of what we "experience" as Reality, because it is also "what things are *doing*."

All *Principle Systems* of "Cosmic Manifestation" are expressions of what is often generically termed *"energy,"* which
we apply to everything. Just as people are likely to relate
concepts of Substance to the "physical" and "bodies" of
energy, the Principle Systems of Motion and *activity* are often equated directly to the "Mind" and all apparent

---

∞ "Atmic Body" is an archaic Eastern term used in some New Age
traditions to denote the highest point of our spirit that dissolves into
oneness with the Source, beyond any singular distinction as an
"Identity."

"energy in action." Wherever a condition of Substance exists, a condition of Motion will also be found. Therefore, when we apply broad terms such as "energy" or "frequency" or "vibration" to some aspect or thing, we are generally referring to its course of *action* and "*affinity*" in regard to other things.

> **affinity** : "the apparent and energetic *relationship* between substances or bodies; the degree of *attraction* or repulsion between things based on natural forces; the *similitude* of frequencies or waveforms; the degree of *interconnection* between systems."

An examination of "*Arcane Tablet*" lore will reveal that in every demonstration of the Cosmos and "Cosmic Power," we are witnessing a "Motion" of things. Likewise, all things in the Cosmos operate in some state of "Motion." Rate, frequency or degree is demonstrated as "vibrations" on the *ZU-line Standard Model*. This corresponds with original teachings from the "Ancient Mystery School," that: "*Nothing rests; everything moves; everything vibrates.*" And from here on, throughout our studies, we find descriptions of "*energy-in-action*"—in our principles of *correspondence* ("of above and below"); our principles of *polarity* ("the dualism of direction"); our principles of *causality* ("this action causes that result"); our principles of *rhythm* ("the to-and-fro movement forward") and so on.

> Physical material in physical systems gravitates toward a point of the slowest possible physical state of equalized vibration as "*entropy*" of KI.
>
> Spiritual material in spiritual systems gravitates toward a point of the highest possible spiritual vibration as "*extropy*" of AN.
>
> The "pull" from both aspects of the dichotomy is the "force" that excites motion and activity of all substance.

Recognition of both extreme points (or more accurately, both "directions") is what contributes to the observation of "polarity." It is the "pull" from both that provide oscillation of Motion. Both points also resonate energetic frequency to such a degree that it seems to be in a state of rest before we lose any calculation of it as *Infinity*. Therefore, our understanding of the *ZU-line* fully accounts for these *Primary Systems* in every state of possible manifestation.

The third and final *Principle System* of manifestation is "Consciousness"—described throughout Systemology as active *Awareness*—literally the "*activity of Self*" as the Observer or "I." This is a very important component system for the equation of existence—it puts into play a means of *relay* or *communication* of Reality—which is, if nothing else, an *interpretation* of *substances* in *motion*. All communications are expressions of energy as Reality in manifestation. To actual "exist" the *activity* must be between two or more *forms* or *bodies*. Communication and energetic interaction are essentially the same. It is this *Observation* of experience from *Self* that we chart across time as *Life*.

· 8

· 7

· 6

· 5

: 4

· 3

. 2

1
·

Cosmic Law does not discriminate—it does not choose when to apply. Whether we are consistently influenced by others during this *Life*, or we choose to apply an understanding of the *"Tablets of Destiny"* to strengthen our *Will* in *Self-determining* this *Lifetime*—the same *Principle Systems* are at work governing this.

Δ Δ Δ Δ Δ Δ Δ

Any practical application toward *manifestation* of existence —including all that we participate in—will always come back to *Self-directed* use of *Will* in relation to the *Primary Systems*. *"The Law"* does not differentiate whether it is our *Will* or that of another, it simply governs rules that yield to the "highest" *Will*—and as we have seen in our earliest lessons regarding the *"Tablets,"* the *Law* is the strongest "Cosmic Will" of manifestation in the Physical Universe, governing all other *Primary Systems* of *beta existence.*

We experience *Awareness* of *beta-existence* as a series of energetic encounters. The force that we call *Will* is really an expression of the "highest" frequency or amplification of vibration in play. This is why we view Reality interactions with others as a "battle of wills." When in a state of high fragmentation and "low-frequency" fluctuations, we experience and handle Reality as a series of **"differentials"**— or the relative difference or **"dissonance"** between our own wave-vibration (degree of agreement) and some aspect of Reality we are confronting. This is why some people who are able to achieve significant progress on the *Pathway of Self-Honesty* may still then be later "brought down" in the near future by a bombardment of intense low-frequency energies in their environment. But, this too may be resolved with a strengthening of *Will.*

A person's state, while fluctuating between emotive and thought degrees, is not fixable to an absolute value or quantity on the model—but we can know averages. We do not necessarily refer to a *Seeker* as "being" a "2.5" or "3.0" or something similar. What we do is gauge relative states that are maintained or fluctuated between as a "feedback loop" of *Self-communication*—or a "figure-8 loop" of *Awareness*. This is how we discovered why we have fluctuations in "personal energy patterns"—where one day we feel we achieving great success on the *Pathway* and another day we find ourselves walking around experiencing heavy emotions and low-level mental activity that "don't seem like us." What others have said to us also contributes to unnecessary internal "Self-talk" that keeps us tangled in fragmented thought and uncertain evaluations of Reality. And *habit* tends to contribute to this.

At lower levels of fragmented *Awareness*, we reinforce a "loop" or potential range of fluctuating experience through our habits. This includes not only physical behavior patterns but also **"thought-habits"** that control them. We are seeking to reduce the strength of *automation* in our *beta experience* as we progress in achieving a *Self-Honest* experience of clear and defragmented Reality.

If we examine the nature of our thoughts and actions closely—in relation to the *Standard Model*—than we will most likely discover the exact points that we have fixed our emotional "swings" and "tides" in relation to "thought" patterns. These two points represent the highest and lowest arcs of the "figure-8" loop when plotted on the *ZU-line*. We reinforce the actuality of this loop or potential range through repeated "thought-action-confirmation-thought" cycles, which serve to *deepen* the etching of our "*Imprints.*"

What the *Standard Model* demonstrates to us—with this "figure-8 loop" plotted on the *ZU-line*—is our degree of fluctuation and fragmentation concerning "*Imprints*" and reactive-response patterns they exhibit in our daily lives. The goal becomes to raise one's level of *Awareness* to the highest degree possible in order to maintain the highest degree of equilibrium possible, since we know that "shifts in consciousness" are likely to occur—at least up to some certain point of spiritual evolution.

"MCC" Master
Control Center

(thought
range)

"RCC" Reactive
Control Center

(emotional range)

(physical body)

After employing basic introspective techniques to analyze
our *Self-Awareness*, and a graphic plotting of such points on
the *Standard Model*, we are able to visibly calculate fluctua-

tions with the ranges of the two extremes. Using the model we are even able to find the common ground that the two points appear to be revolving around as their basic equilibrium or epicenter. Often it is *this* state of middle ground—the point where the two arcs cross in the *middle*—that we need to elevate in order to reach higher levels. By raising our average state we are decreasing the magnitude of lower-level states with higher frequency energy. Using the "figure-8 loop" to examine all of what we have described, we see how mental bands of energy from degrees of frustration and fragmented knowledge dip down into emotional frequencies of sadness and depression. This energetic fluctuation of lower-level *Awareness* is the very cause of anxiety and uncertainty in our daily life—and when left to cycle too long, it is the seed of insanity and the "unclean" Mind.

Once we can resolve *fragmentation imprints* carried from our past—the ones we are "circling around" in this model —a propulsion from that free flow of energy and *Awareness* enables our spiritual advancement and unfoldment of our true *Destiny*. By raising our level of *Awareness* to its highest achievable states at a given moment, even for a moment, we are able to confirm in present Reality that these states exist—and further that we are clearing the pathway for energy to flow more freely to each higher degree than before. This means that it requires less *effort* to reach these points and maintain them again. An intrepid *Seeker* looking to fully maintain an actualized state of *Self-Honesty* would have to systematically reach the point of *Self-Honesty (SH)*—and *exceed* it—just to be certain of *maintaining* it!

Δ Δ Δ Δ Δ Δ Δ

SUMMARY

The ALL encompasses both the *Spiritual Universe* ("AN") and the *Physical Universe* ("KI") as divided by the LAW ("*Cosmic Law*")—connected only by *Spiritual Lifeforce Energy* ("ZU") and beyond which is only an *Infinity of Nothingness*.

As an expression of pure *Infinity*, our true *Spirit* ("*I-AM-Self*") as *Awareness* is actually an energetic "constant" in its highest *Alpha* expression.

The *Self* as *Awareness* is a *static* energy—or constant *Life-force*—only "detectable," or *perturbed* into a detectable *waveform*, when it comes into contact with other wave-forms/energies at various degrees.

The "*Tablets of Destiny*" describe and demonstrate an in-terrelationship of many system processes—all of which may be reduced to a single primary function: *manifestation of existence.*

The three *Principle Systems* of "Cosmic Manifestation" de-scribed on the "*Arcane Tablets*" are *Consciousness, Action (Motion)* and *Substance.*

Principle Systems of Manifestation may philosophically cor-respond to basic "conditions" of *Awareness* (aligned to the "Standard Model") as *spiritual systems, mental systems* and *physical systems*—yet a deeper examination of each of these systems reveals that the same three principles of apparent manifestation are actually in operation at each "level" or "state" of energy.

What we call "*physical*" or "*physical matter*" is only the "lowest" manifested vibrations of *cosmic* energy that are interacting with "consciousness." The principle of *Sub-stance* is what distinguishes "things" as "bodies." When we refer to any *forms* as "things," we are then describing its *Substance* principle.

Wherever a condition of *Substance* exists, a condition of *Motion* will also be found. All things in the Cosmos operate within some state of "Motion."

When we apply broad terms such as "energy" or "fre-quency" or "vibration" to some aspect or thing, we are generally referring to its course of *actions* and "*affinity*" in regard to all things—which is defined by the *Principle Sys-tems* of "Cosmic Motion."

States of vibration establish a state of "equilibrium"—which is the average between "differentials."

There is a natural tendency for expressions, energies and manifestations to reach toward "equilibrium"—between "directions" or "forces" of AN and KI—or a "state of constancy." Both extremes are what we consider "polarity" and pulls from both provide the oscillation of Motion.

The third *Principle System* is *"Consciousness"*—literally the *"activity* of the *Self"* as the Observer or "I." *Consciousness* is a means of *relay* or *communication* of Reality—which is, if nothing else, an interpretation of *substances* in *motion* from the point of an "Observer."

All communications and expressions of *Consciousness* as Reality in manifestation are an *activity* between two or more *forms* or *bodies*.

The "Standard Model" gauges personal states maintained or fluctuated between as a "feedback loop" of *Self-communication*, or a "figure-8 loop" of *Awareness*, that shifts from a particular degree of thought to a particular degree of emotional reaction and back to the thought (and so forth).

We reinforce this "figure-8 loop"—and *deepen* the etching of our *"Imprints"*—or range of actuality through repeated "thought-action-confirmation-thought" cycles.

If we examine the nature of our thoughts and actions closely, we will most likely discover the exact points that we have our emotional "swings" and "tides" in relation to our "thought" patterns.

At minimum, the most "basic personality" (or *"Self-Honest* state") demonstrated with the "figure-8" on the "Standard Model" is a phase alignment of "upper and lower" arcs meeting a clear and direct feedback loop of the MCC and RCC. This is not the "highest" *Awareness* achievable, but everything short of (or "lower" than) this state is a demonstration of significant *"fragmentation."*

.: 9 :.
BRIDGING THE MARDUKITE PARADIGM
WITH NEXGEN SYSTEMOLOGY
FOR A SELF-HONEST
EVOLUTION

"There is no future until we settle our past."

We have demonstrated from the *"Tablets of Destiny"*—and in every instance where it influenced former writings of the current author—that the "Human Condition" is essentially the *Awareness* of a "spiritual" *Self* or *Life* from an *"Alpha"* state of existence combined with a *'Genetic Vehicle'*. This allows *Life* to experience and its *"Existence"* as *Self* or *Spirit* within *beta existence* of "physical" energy and matter in the "Physical Universe."

---

existence : "the *state* or fact of *apparent manifestation*; the resulting combination of the Principles of Apparent Manifestation: consciousness, motion and substance; continued *survival*; that which independently persists; the *'Prime Directive'* and sole purpose of all manifestation or Reality; the highest common intended motivation driving any *'Thing'* or *Life*."

During the earliest inception of civilization, humanity was led out of cave-life and nomadic hunter-gathering routines to settle communities. This society was *engineered* for a *'Prime Directive'* from a higher order or level of understanding than where "primitive man" was existing. There is no limit to the amount of "low-level" ruthlessness and depravity that took place—far below what is seen in the animal kingdom. This is the point when the *"Anunnaki"* appear among humanity—at the beginning of when history is recorded. With their higher understanding, they bring what makes "civilization" possible: the "birth of the systems." It is at this critical turning point in history that we see a rapid development of "intelligence" and "systematized living" at an unprecedented rate.

Enough has been written by the current author in past works regarding historical and cultural parameters of these *Ancient Near Eastern* systems and their development. What presently concerns us now is the most fundamental aspect contributing to their installation and operation *within* (and *as*) the Human Condition—and that is *Language*. When we look at the root of all *human* knowledge and understanding concerning experience of Reality. We always come back to *Language*. It is a significant "tool"—perhaps the *most* significant—that first developed alongside a rise of Human societies and their position of independent survival in the Physical Universe. This includes not only an individual's own survival as *Self*. We realize we are interconnected and in many ways dependent on the continued existence of larger systems, including the survival of others and the balance of *All Life on Earth* in the Physical Universe, the Spiritual Universe and Infinity.

To be rapidly "civilized" the Human Condition was **crash-coursed** into intellectual development, so people would "stay in line" and be "orderly." This is demonstrated on the **macrocosmic** *"Tablets of Destiny"*—the "human language systems" were nurtured and used for programming by the highest social echelon. This knowledge and ability erupted directly from the *Arcane Tablets*. The "ME" or *"Arts of Civilization"* on Earth shifted around various locales on the planet by "gods" successfully **inciting** systematized "civilizations" and the *ability* to be "as like the *gods*." It became clearer (the further we ventured into this new level of understanding) that the same knowledge and principles used to *fragment* the Human Condition might therefore be concealing the very *Key* to its *defragmentation*.

Basic encoding of the Human Condition (in relation to its environment) is a *Language*. It does not actually matter, as we have discovered thousands of years after the fact, exactly *what* Cultural Language is used to do it. There is a basic *syntax* and *semantics* at work that is associating this or that type of manifestation with this or that type of emotion and this or that mode of thought or belief. It all works together. From this we form our basis or *paradigm* of Reality: whatever that may be. Our ability to continue our own optimum *existence* is proportional to ability to successfully relate to our environment "properly." When we do not, when our ZU frequency in *beta existence* drops its level of vibration during an encounter, some kind of disruption of continuity has ensued. The RCC responds accordingly, in whatever manner it has been encoded to from painful experience in the past. This is dangerous, because from *our* point of view—from the *Awareness* of *Self* as an *Alpha Spirit* —we are being gradually eliminated from the *Life-equation* as the "*Self-directive Force.*"

Maintaining "authoritarian" societal control of knowledge requires members of that society possess a certain degree of "fragmented programming" and heavy dependence on social "groups" for the individual to exist. Simply being a participant in society is guaranteed to produce some degree of fragmentation for the average individual. This is reinforced when society employs "authority" to keep it in line. Of course, the fact that people remain poorly educated and badly fragmented also keeps us in this loop by "apparent necessity"—something which might just actually be resolved once more of its citizens achieve states of *Self-Honest Awareness.*

When we drift backwards, resorting to the lowest levels of primitive instinct that are still buried down there, we immediately begin a "tug of war" for agreement of Reality. This is represented by a "figure-8 loop"* on the Standard Model, which is "out-of-phase" with the MCC. Such keeps us in a state of "emotionally encoded fragmented fluctuation." This is necessarily our first primary order of business when applying spiritual technology and techniques derived from combining *Arcane Tablets* with *NexGen Systemology.*

---

* Referred to as an "insanity loop" in former demonstrations of *Creative Psychology.*

Physical systems may be elevated with physical "therapy" and basic education toward clean healthy living. However, very few individuals are given *tools* to properly confront the emotional reactivity commonly experienced in every day *Life*. Even those that "instinctively" notice some of their patterns or "imprints" and reinforced emotional states are unsure what to actually do about it. There is a resolution possible—and it begins here, at the entrance to a pathway toward the highest goal of Human Existence.

Δ Δ Δ Δ Δ Δ Δ

Many people confuse the primitive emotional range of the Human Condition with other physical or mental aspects. Emotional systems are necessary to properly graph the Standard Model and fit the logic of ZU-energy communication between the "Mind" and "Body." There has, until recently, been very little understanding regarding ZU as the *Lifeforce* that connects all of this together to form an *Identity* capable of conscious activity here in *beta existence*. That takes a tremendously powerful energy. It is obvious we have not even begun to really understand the highest energetic potential of ZU *Lifeforce*. We have only begun to even actualize a working knowledge of it.

There is a communication of energy that facilitates operation of a living organism, its somatic motions and motor functions—and between that "Body" and its "Mind" we have this whole mess of stuff left over from primordial beginnings of physical survival, that we call "*Emotion*." Of course, as soon as we begin to speak of the "reduction of emotion" there is someone who will begin to paint a picture or portray the idea that *Systemology Processing* is somehow a reduction of *Self* or used to "robotize" the individual. Yet, any *Self-Honest* examination of the material presented in this book would reveal very much the opposite. Our *NexGen* practices do not impose on a *Seeker* any additional **superfluous** fragmented beliefs. The goal is to remove **erroneous** ones and clear the way for actualized *Awareness* as a *Self-determined Life*.

> A significant reduction in the ability of *Self* to be *Self-directed* as "I" actually only takes place when there is a presence of fragmentation—*solid encoding* or "*Imprints*"—within the emotional range of *Awareness*.

There are other forms of fragmentation, but it is *these* automated functions and "robotic reactions" that eliminate the "I" from determining its own course of action. These "determinants" at, let us say, an organic "cellular" level, are merely stimulus-response reactions inherited by the cells. They are not Self-directed actions of *Awareness*; they are purely responsive. The RCC is *kicking in* to pull your hand out of the flame before your MCC *knows* better. But this type of "conditioning" can also apply to the Human "Condition" in an astronomical number of ways. "*Imprints*" are impinging upon our clear view of Reality. A *Seeker* will undoubtedly be forced to confront those that are affecting them to the greatest degree if they pursue the *Pathway to Self-Honesty*. This idea of "purging" the old self to achieve spiritual destiny is reflected in many ancient philosophies and especially practices of Mardukite Babylon, where an initiate or priest is removing, clearing or purifying *seven* artificial layers that enshroud their "Identity as Self" as they ascend the "gateways" and "levels" of the Temple.

Emotional "*imprints*" are among the deepest programming levels of the Human Condition. They are the most difficult to overcome *analytically* because they are automatic and subject to their own body of fragmented associations beneath the range of MCC activity. If we approach them *analytically,* they do not make sense and seem rather ridiculous. *This* is a *key!*

Once we *see* and *experience* the ridiculousness of the *Imprint*, it is quite possible that we will laugh at the very thought of it. *Another key!* When we are able to *Self-Honestly* resurface and confront the ridiculousness of our past —"*look back and laugh*"—we are immediately released from the emotional hold that it has on us. We have brought it all up to the surface for the Mind-Systems to deal with appropriately by *Self-direction* and we reduce automated programming that is attached to it. *Imprints* no longer paralyze *Self* if they can be recalled without a negative emotional response. There are many ways in which we may be able to increase effectiveness or apply various processes, but *Arcane Tablets* are very clear about these fundamental steps.

"*Imprints*" promote artificially induced (physical) states of experience using biochemicals, fluids and cellular responses to the RCC. These do not have to be "rational"—which is *one* reason they *are* a "fragmentation." Why should a "bell" provoke hunger? Why does a comment from a "friend" or scene on television trigger us to disrupt our lives? *Imprints* are distortions in our lens of experience. They are intended to assist our efforts to exist, yet seem to bring us down to *Awareness* levels of reactive animals. This is something of a problem if we are to *evolve* as anything other than *an animal.* When one considers the amazing faculties and spiritual potential folded up in an *Identity*, it makes the idea of wielding "atomic" and "nuclear" power seem like a child's *game.* And there certainly is a fair amount of "***game theory***" present in our new "applied spiritual technology" of **general systematology**.

Human Language also tends to shelter and conceal the truth of existences within its very context. We say: "One day we will look back at this and laugh..." We tend to pass off such things as trivial and trite because on an analytical level, there is no direct logic associated with these statements. To see real meaning, we must examine *semantics.* For example, the ancient cuneiform word that we translate today as "prison" was not actually spoken as such, obviously, in its native tongue. This "prison" archetype is written in cuneiform with the signs "*e-gal*"—or "big (*gal*) house (*e*)."

There are thousands of years and hundreds of languages

standing between the inception of language and where we are today. We can accept that as fact. Words and ideas once set down in their original written form are now quite unrecognizable when represented as literal *Language* evolving in various places over time. But—then why would the same colloquialism we use today for "Prison" be found as the very literal definition discovered in cuneiform from six thousand years ago? Why then do we still refer to a "Prison" as the "Big House"?

There is clearly a level of programming at play in the Human Condition that is only reached at its most fundamental level of conditioning—within the domain of "*Emotion.*"

> **emotional encoding** : "the substance of *imprints*; associations of sensory experience with an *imprint*; perceptions of our environment that receive an *emotional charge*, which form or reinforce facets of an *imprint*; perceptions recorded and stored as an *imprint* within the 'emotional range' of energetic manifestation." (*NexGen Systemological NewSpeak*)

We hide a lot of truths, in jest, behind our "figures of speech"—especially in regards to the "past," to our "emotional states" and various types of "baggage" it brings. We "intuitively" know that none of this "attachment" "encoding" or "imprinting" is benefiting us. But, we only know this when these other *filters* of Reality are temporarily offstage. When they are "out of sight, they are out of Mind" and they seem not to exist. But they do, somewhere deep within there. When they resurface unintentionally, they are thrown back up onto the screen in front of us as Reality. We are then, in no better position at those times to understand what is actually happening. *Self* is eliminated from the equation and is allowed to do little more than "sit back and watch a poor quality show" that is fragmented. *This* is precisely what is happening when the "I" is removed from the equation.

We may literally go back in thought and *watch* "ourselves" acting in this manner and feeling these emotions that we did not *Self-direct.* How would such even be possible if the "I" or *Self* really was directing it with *Awareness?* There are more severe instances when we have no rational recall of our behaviors. How amazing is that? In either case, suddenly we are in a loop where things are "happening *to* us" and we are no longer the *Self-*directive "Cause." Once we begin to succumb to our environment we begin to lose our *Self-actualized* abilities to maintain, ensure and advance our *Existence.*

In this book, "emotion" refers to the range of energy on the ZU-line beneath the position of the RCC. "*Imprints*" are "emotionally encoded memories" at these degrees of *Awareness* (or "emotional states") that most people experience negatively—anger, grief, apathy—which in turn produce a certain mode of thought, but we are treating them as emotions. Positive experiences—what people recall as "positive emotion"—are not even within the parameters of the RCC. Those higher modes of thought do not seem to induce the same level of destructive fragmentation as these "lower" emotional states. In fact, those higher "emotional" states are measured on the Standard Model as "activity" or "motions" of the MCC or "mental states." This includes healthy interests, enthusiasm and success—points when we affirm in *full Awareness* that something has resulted positively toward our continued existence: states we have *caused.*

When examining the Standard Model as applied to our own experience of the Human Condition—it becomes evident that there is a basic survival-mechanism at work with emotional systems, but it is too easily *imprinted* and *distorted* in its display of Reality to be allowed *determination* of Reality for *Self.* The emotional responses should never be *dictating* our Reality, such as we find with anxiety, anger and grief, which very strongly *filter* our Reality, inhibit MCC activity and free flow of ZU.

ZU is a continuum and attention of *Awareness* is only in one place at any measurable point. When it is fixed upon low-level energetic states that come with intense emotion, our thoughts are "brought down" to establish that equilibrium. Times of emotional fluctuation or "instability," we will find ourselves "uncertain" or open to "suggestion." Hence *suggestibility* is directly proportional to the degree that *Awareness* of, and *as, Self* is eliminated from the equation. When mental activity as *consciousness* is reduced to emotionally reactive levels (below the RCC at 2.0 on the Standard Model), the basic function of the MCC is inhibited by low-level "imprints." These create fragmentation of thought and ultimately lead to "irrational" behaviors. This "irrationality" and lack of "*Self*-control" is what we work to systematically reduce on the *Pathway to Self-Honesty*.

Δ Δ Δ Δ Δ Δ Δ

In order to *Self-actualize* the first "level of understanding" as *Awareness* in *Self-Honesty*, a person should be able to affirm the statement: "*I Act as I Will.*" This is not to say that a *Seeker* just 'does whatever they want' without regard to consequence. On the contrary, an individual that is *Self-directing* the physical body "in phase" with the Mind-Systems would be making only the best and rational decisions for all *Life* with total *Awareness* of causation. A person that is driven by low-level primitive survival "instinct" is *not* acting as they "will"—they are acting as though they are already *dead*. This is practically implied by the most basic semantic definitions and understanding of the Human Condition and its functions. A purely "physical" understanding has mostly left us with only physical means of trying to ensure material existence, but *Arcane Tablets* are most pointed on the fact that there are "more things happening in heaven and on earth than dreamed of in human philosophies."[*]

---

[*]   Paraphrasing Shakespeare.

The 'first' level is control of physical behavior by maintaining *Self*-control of emotional states in order to "act" *Self*-determined on a physical level. This provides *substance* to our manifestations as Reality. We will continue to illustrate each level definitively with key statements. These are states of achievement, not affirmations for self-hypnosis.

The second level of actualized *Awareness* is the Mind directly, which is *Self-Honest* thought—the accomplished ability to confirm: "*I Think as I Will.*" This is not some wild "super-human" mental faculty. Yet, when we consider various states in quantifiable terms on the Standard Model, this quite reachable state does seem particularly "above normal."

A *Self-Honest* individual appears more "**gifted**" than their peers because they maintain clearer mental activity —"thinking clearly" or having a "clear mind." We are not negating, removing or "washing out" *Self*, but rather empowering, or returning rightful power; abilities of *Self*-controlled "Thought" free of excessive fragmentation. This state cumulatively builds upon reduction of emotional imprinting. If more of humanity could actualize *Self-Honesty* to this point, the entire state of affairs on Earth would significantly improve.

"Applied spirituality" governs everything beyond the "Mind-System" and its direct relationship between the "mental seat of consciousness" for the *Alpha Spirit* (that we refer to as the MCC) and the "genetic vehicle" it governs in *beta existence*. The knowledge dispersal and techniques (combined to form our "technology") at *Grade-III* are concerned with applying *NexGen Systemology* to interaction with *beta systems* directly. This does not exclude higher future developments of this work to include mastery of higher levels and abilities of *Awareness*. It is demonstrated clearly on the "*Tablets of Destiny*" that our limitation is *Infinity*. However, as we have determined it, the third level of actualized *Awareness* would pertain to the point on the

ZU-line directly above the MCC, which lies within the domain of the "Spiritual."

At the spiritual level, exterior to beta-systems that feed back energy directly from the body, we confirm the statement: "*I Create as I Will.*" And this applies to virtually any type of construct or form at the "Spiritual" condition of existence. It may very well be the case, as alluded to on *Arcane Tablets*, that we are essentially working back up the same "ladder" that led to our fragmentation as spiritual entities "inhabiting" physical bodies, in the first place. This is relayed in former "Mardukite" materials in relation to, for example, the "Bab.Ili" Gate-System lore and the "Ladder of Lights." For the first time, *Systemology* puts it into a workable modern-day model "systematically." Following the same logic and wave patterns we *know of* in *beta existence*, we can then determine that *Self-Honest (SH)* clearing of the conduit or *ZU-line* at this higher level of *Awareness* would result in a completely *Self-Honest Spirit*, at the doors of *Infinity*, able to finally confirm: "*I Am as I Will.*"

We tend to disregard "how we feel" or go the other way and judge everything by "how we feel." We are not slighting out healthy use of "intuition." If it is truly "intuitive" and not "conditioned" knowing, than it should come from higher faculties and not lower emotional ones which may be misaligned with a few painful experiences—or even one big one.

When the Identity-Systems along the continuum of the ZU-line are all communicating or passing energy in phase with one another, there is no harmful disruption by the RCC. A degree of emotion will suddenly shift the energy out of phase and create the "figure-8 loop" that makes our degree of thought suddenly relative to our degree of emotion down to a point where *Self-directed* "thought" (as we understand it) is removed from the equation altogether—such as when we are unconscious.

The "emotional systems" and their relationship with other systems are most evident when we see it charted on the

Standard Model. In this instance we have a perfectly marked division with the RCC at "2." All degrees of *Awareness* above this point are in some domain of "thought activity." At such ranges of thought, we are "consciously" *Aware*. As our body begins to take more and more direction from low-level emotional circuits, this ability to maintain proper insurance of *Self-directed* existence begins to falter.

If an actualized point of *Self*-existence is fixed anywhere below the RCC, free flow of *Life energy* is no longer fed in abundance to the body and our very existence begins to succumb to pressures of the Physical Universe—we fall into apathy of mind and entropic deterioration of our cellular body. We are, in effect, headed toward "genetic death" if continuing along such a route. The destructive rate increases as we move further down in degree until a person can no longer tolerate any expressions of *Life* or the physical existence around themselves or even their own existence. And we can easily predict the type of activity we should expect in this case. This information is not relayed in an attempt to scare you. All of the source material, derived models and observed experiments in the world-at-large seem to generate conclusive evidence that we need to take "what we feel" very seriously—and *Self*-control of it, even more so. By regaining full control of our *beta existence* as *Self*, we are well on our way to achieving the freedoms of the Spirit.

Δ Δ Δ Δ Δ Δ Δ

SUMMARY

The purpose of *Existence* is to *exist*. This is otherwise referred to as the *"Prime Directive."*

Life exists to experience and evolve its *Existence* as *Self* within a *beta existence* of "physical" energy and matter, moving in space across the "Physical Universe."

A successful continued *existence* of *Self* in the Physical Universe is dependent on clear communication of information about our environment between *Alpha* and *beta* states.

Aside from sensory reception of pure pleasure and pure pain, all general information received about our environment is analyzed, evaluated and associated based on *Language.*

Language systems were developed at the inception of Human civilization in order to communicate a mass agreement of Reality. This is otherwise referred to as *"programming."* It was reinforced in society in "writing" at an intellectual-mental level.

Human Language tends to conceal certain truths of existences within its very context.

"Social programming" led to reinforcement with "social conditioning" at an *emotional* level.

The RCC is not a part of the *Alpha-Mind* and is hard-wired to "organic life" to store "primitive programming" for survival at the cellular level of an organism—which appears to operate on impulses of *"emotional"* energy.

The *"emotional"* systems of manifestation are mainly tied to primitive organic survival at a level "below" normative thought activity and governed solely by the RCC. Example: The RCC is automatically *kicking in* to pull your hand out of the flame until your MCC *knows* better. This is a normal function of the RCC. Any other fragmented *"associations"* encoded along with the experience to the RCC are not, however, conducive to normative analytical thought.

Primitive survival programming is governed by "emotional responses" contributing to reactive behaviors that (when engaged) may displace the *Self* as "Cause" and therefore distort or fragment communication of a *Self*-directed Reality. They may, in effect, eliminate the "I" from the equation.

Suggestibility is directly proportional to the degree that *Awareness* of and as *Self* is eliminated from the equation (when the RCC "cuts in").

Emotional "*imprints*" are among the deepest program-ming levels of the Human Condition. They circulate "emotional" energy in a "figure-8 circuit" that is not a *Self-directed* "motion" of *Awareness*. It is purely "response-reactive" and falls outside the domain of "analytical thought."

"Emotional encoding" of *imprints* is not an analytical function of the Mind (MCC). They are purely related to ex-periences of "pain" or thwarts to our continued existence. Once receiving enough of these, we begin to interact with the Physical Universe as a purely hostile environment that is either succumbed to or lashed out at.

Once we begin to succumb to our environment we begin to lose *Self-actualized* abilities to maintain, ensure and ad-vance our *Existence*.

"*Imprints*" are "emotionally encoded" at degrees of *Aware-ness* (or "emotional states") most people experience negatively—anger, grief, apathy—which in turn produce a certain mode of thought, but we are treating them as emotions.

Positive experiences—what people recall within the MCC intellectual systems as memories of "positive emotion"—are not even within the parameters of the RCC.

All degrees of *Awareness* "above" the RCC (or "2.0" on the Standard Model) are in some domain of "thought activity" as monitored by the *Alpha Self*.

If actualized *Self*-existence is fixed anywhere below the RCC ("2.0"), free flow of *Life energy* is no longer fed in abundance to the body; energetically we are "out of phase"; our existence begins to succumb to pressures of the Physical Universe and we fall into mental apathy and entropic deterioration of our cellular body.

"Self-destructive" modes increase the further down in degree a person goes until they no longer may tolerate any expressions of *Life* or physical manifestations around them—or even their own existence.

"Irrationality" and lack of "*Self*-control" are what we, as *Self*-directed *Seekers*, work to systematically reduce on the *Pathway to Self-Honesty*.

The fundamental Self-Actualized "Levels of Understanding" as *Awareness* are:—

I. Self-directing physical systems (emotion defragmentation); "*I act as I Will.*"

II. Self-directing mental systems (mental defragmentation); "*I think as I Will.*"

III. Self-directing spiritual systems (defragmented *Alpha Spirit*); "*I create as I Will.*"

IV. Self-directing ALL systems (defragmented *Infinite Spirit*); "*I AM as I Will.*"

.: 10 :.
UNDERSTANDING NEXGEN SYSTEMOLOGY,
THE "STANDARD MODEL" AND
THE "ZU-LINE"

Previous chapter-lessons within this book introduced all of the symbolism, definitions, system descriptions and in-terrelated workings of the new *Systemology* "*Standard Model*" that incorporates the "*ZU-line.*" Great care has been taken to demonstrate this model accurately using wisdom found on the "*Tablets of Destiny.*"

In some schools of thought, we might have laid this model out at the beginning and then taken it apart piece by piece —but this would not have been as effective. The informa-tion retained would be fragmented and the ability to hold a complete understanding would require more effort. Now we can take a pictorial tour of the ALL without getting bogged down in taking measure of new terminology and introducing definition—we can simply *look around* and *see* with what we now *know*.

This current book you hold—and future delivery of *materi-al* in the genre of *applied* Mardukite Systemology—is based on the "Standard Model." It is the most basic, fundamental and perfect representation we can discern (at this time) of a workable system from the *Arcane Tablets*. It reflects the proverbial knowledge and qualities of the very "gods" that systematized our ancestors and the Human Condition we share in today. Our continuity model is threefold:

a) it demonstrates all "physical" *and* "spiritual" manifestation—a complete cosmology of the LAW *and* the ALL;

b) it demonstrates the continuum of "infinite en-ergy" connecting the "spiritual" systems to "physic-al" systems as LIFE; and

c) it demonstrates that beyond LIFE, outside the LAW and encompassing the ALL, is but INFINITY.

The terms "*Law*" and "ALL" were introduced in our earliest lesson-chapters regarding the *Arcane Tablets*. The terms are demonstrated in connection to the Babylonian Epic of Creation. These "primordial" terms loosely correlate to our "Standard Model" as "AN" and "KI" from which we now operate our workable processes in *Systemology*. The whole of *Infinity* is essentially divided by the "*All*"—which is the extent that we may graphically portray or chart *anything*. Everything beyond the largest continuity circle that we could possibly draw out for the *All*—is *Infinity*. Following the "sevenfold" model of Babylon, it is only logical to represent this point of *Infinity* as an unseen "eighth step" of the *ziggurat*, beyond AN, so perfectly displayed by placing the Arabic "8" on its side—"∞"—*Infinity*. We may only demonstrate the highest system of potential *continuity* in our graphic demonstration—outside of which: *Infinity* is always *Infinity*.

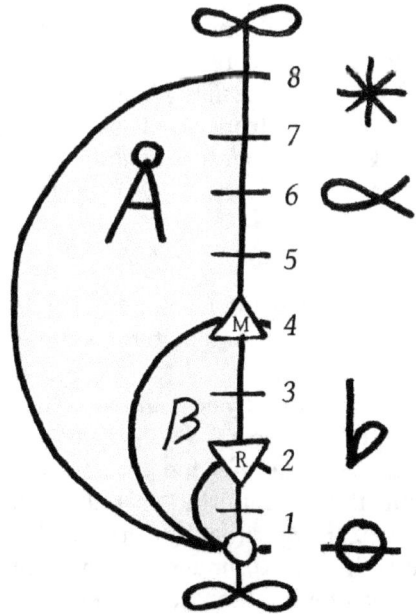

If we retain these "primordial terms" from the *Arcane Tablets in* the Standard Model, the *All* is a division point between *actual potential* (AN) and *infinite potential* of Nothingness/"*Abzu*" (∞). The *Law/"Tiamat"* is a division of the *All*—and beneath the *Law* we have *manifest potential* (KI). We refer to the direction of AN (*) in connection to *Alpha existence* (α) and to the direction of KI (∅) in terms of our *beta existence* (β or b). When demonstrating "systems logic," the continuity (potential) of AN is the "Spiritual Universe," sometimes represented mathematically as Infinity (∞), and the continuity of KI, or the "Physical Universe," is represented as (∅) or a "zero" with a horizontal line through it.

STANDARD MODEL OF BASIC UNIVERSE SYSTEMS

8. Infinity	(consists of "Nothingness")
- - - - (∞) - - - -	*infinite potential*
7. The All	(consists of "Spiritual Universe")
- - - - (α) - - - -	*actual spiritual potential*
4.1 — 7. AN	(consists of "*alpha existence*")
4. The Law	(consists of "Physical Universe")
- - - - (b) - - - -	*manifest physical potential*
0.1—4. KI	(consists of "*beta existence*")
- - - - (∅) - - - -	*finite potential*
0. Inert KI	(consists of "Everything-Not")

Δ Δ Δ Δ Δ Δ Δ

The Spiritual Universe (AN) and Physical Universe (KI) represent a range of potential material substance and laws governing its motion-action. "*The All*" governs *All*; and "*The Law*" governs the Physical Universe (KI). By definition: any manifest universe is always composed of relative *material-substance* (Matter) and *motion-action* (Energy) which remains fixed within the "spatial" frequency range of that universe. The Spiritual Universe (AN) of the *All* and the Physical Universe (KI) under the *Law* seem to operate independent of one another. Each *moves* around *matter* with a *force* of energy that is specific to its own universe.

This is why we call it a "*uni*-verse"—it is a self-contained continuity. But!—there is *one aspect* that *does* actually form a connection between AN and KI; and that is *Spiritual Life* as *Consciousness* or "ZU" (T or ‡).

When we apply the *ZU-line* to our understanding of basic universe systems, we are able to include a missing third component needed to form a complete Standard Model—which is *consciousness* (*Awareness*). When we plot the *ZU-line* over the *All*—from *Infinity-to-Infinity*—we have a means of charting and evaluating the relative position and interaction of *Self*, which is a constant *Life-energy* source (*ZU*), with other energy and matter in motion across space in the Physical Universe. We will find the Principles of Apparent Manifestation—*Substance, Awareness* and *Motion*—as conditions of every level or state of existence.

The Standard Model is also a demonstration tool used to graphically display relative relationships and interactions between systems. Its "distances" or quantity "values" are proportionately relative to one another to satisfy "system logic." They are not meant to relay, for example, an actual "value" indicating some specific wavelength scale. The Standard Model is not a detailed "atlas." Rather, it is like a "globe map" for all possible existences. It may be used to orient basic direction and individual position in relation to a much wider range of space, but it is not the only tool one might use to navigate the journey toward *Self-Honesty*. It is just one critical component or a very effective "personal compass."

It is only after applying knowledge of the *ZU-line* to our Standard Model that we were able to gauge relative positions of manifestation—such as the MCC and RCC, for our discussion of applied spiritual technologies. Otherwise we are left with no reference point—no Observer; no *Awareness*. The *Self* or "I" is represented with a ZU-line is very accurately the "*y*"-axis—or vertical axis-line on a graph, if we were to chart ZU-energy in relation to *space*-over-*time*. A personal linear timeline is represented by a horizontal "x"-axis line on the graph—if we *were* to demonstrate such a thing as an illustrative example of changes over time in relation to spatial interactions. This is not typically neces-sary.

As a practical measurement, **psychometric-evaluation** in Systemology is concerned with determining the present state of an individual at *any* given time.[‡] We are simply taking "snapshots." We know that an individual is subject to fluctuations in their handling of personal *Life-energy* and interaction with external events. By having insight into the "average," we can determine the state of ZU-en-ergy brought to experiences of external events and therefore predict the intensity of *differential* present when a person confronts challenging situations. This is an ex-ceptionally useful tool to chart our progress on the *Pathway to Self-Honesty*, but it is only a tool. The map is not the journey. Many people are likely to becoming incred-ibly taken up with the Standard Model—and the potential information it logically provides—but then lose sight of what we actually desire to use it for.

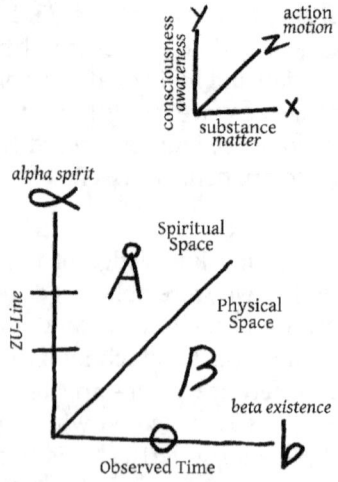

‡   See *"Crystal Clear: Handbook for Seekers"* by Joshua Free.

More than destination points, we regard AN (*) and KI (∅) as dimensional "directions" of movement along the ZU-line continuum. As we move "upward" in *degree* and frequency, we are reaching toward *Infinity* (∞)—and as we move "downward" in the spectrum, we are reaching toward *inert Continuity* (∅). At the highest point beyond what we imagine, there is a singularity or unification of the highest frequencies, which our *Alpha Spirit* (α) gravitates toward following the *extropy* of Spiritual systems. At the lowest point beyond what we imagine, there is the chaotic fragmented complexity of the primordial *beta existence* (β), out of which the material for our genetic vehicle or *beta body* (*b*) is collected and will eventually return to via *entropy* of Physical systems. If graphed as space-over-time, the *inert Continuity* (∅) of the Physical Universe represents the zero-axis (∅) or horizontal "*x*"-axis that intersects the ZU-line at zero "0."

Δ Δ Δ Δ Δ Δ Δ

Because the Standard Model is a two-dimensional pictorial representation, to demonstrate something further requires us to use an exterior illustrative example. To do this (as demonstrated)*, you will need a few items. The more precise the items, the better the model, but this is a very basic demonstration that anyone should easily be able to understand.

    —a piece of string (*preferably white and three feet long*)

    —colored markers (*preferably four colors*)

    —a piece of paper (*preferably white*)

We take the piece of string and down at one end we use a (*green*) marker to color a section about an "inch" or so, to represent physical frequencies the ZU-line, or up to about "1" on our Standard Model. Color the next "inch" or so of string with a (*blue*) section to denote emotional frequen-

---

*   Demonstrated by Joshua Free during the original Systemology "*Tablets of Destiny*" Discovery Event and lecture-series given in August 2019, from which this book is based.

cies of up to "2" on the Standard Model. The next/third section should be roughly equivalent to what you have already colored—or two inches—marked (*yellow*) to display the full psychological range up to 4. The final section should, again, be colored (*purple* or *red*) the same amount as what was previously colored, or about four inches, representing the spiritual range into infinity.

You should be left with approximately eight inches of colored string at one end, distinguished by four bands of color.

As with the Standard Model, an effective representation is not reliant on, for example, the definite measure of what an "inch" is, so long as the general proportions and ratios between sections are properly marked. You might double the measurements so that there is sixteen inches of string colored—if that is easier to work with. You could even use a single color to simply mark off division lines on the string—or if necessary, not even mark the string at all. It will not change the basic logic of this demonstration. For our purposes, the piece of paper may be simply placed on the floor or table as it is. It is a flat plane representing the total base-line continuity of the Physical Universe or KI (∅) from which we experience stimulus as *beta existence* (β). Everything beyond the piece of paper is in the direction of AN toward *Infinity* (∞). Even somewhere below the zero-point (piece of paper) there is *Infinity*.

Now we may introduce *consciousness* to the equation. This is a very special and unique aspect that only results from specific combinations of conditions that we call *Life Existence*. We are not going to pretend at this time to understand the unique manner in which this state *originates*—our Standard Model can only demonstrate that it is *happening*. Somehow organic physical matter and physical energy collects in such a way as to be a receptacle of concentrated pure spiritual energy and pure spiritual matter as an "*Alpha Spirit*" (α) reflected as *Awareness* on the ZU-line (‡). What we seek to demonstrate with our "string-line" example is how *levels* of *existence* and their frequency range are reflected as *degrees* of *Awareness* from the perspective of the *beta body* (b).

The cord or string represents the constant continuous flow of ZU (T) energy from its Infinite (∞) source along a continuum (‡). It exists by itself—a potential "Spiritual-set." It is the *consciousness* or *Awareness* introduced to (and interacting with) the "setting" of environmental energy/*motion* and matter/*substance* that produces manifestation. In this instance: manifestation as spiritual *Life* in a physical *organism*. Other forms of physical energy and matter have their own type of reactive consciousness governed by Cosmic Law, which is why some mystics have referred to a Cosmic Mind. But we have our own *Mind* and *Awareness* and also a *Body* that we may *Self-direct* for experience, to the extent that ZU-energy as *Awareness* is actualized, which is what we demonstrate with the string.

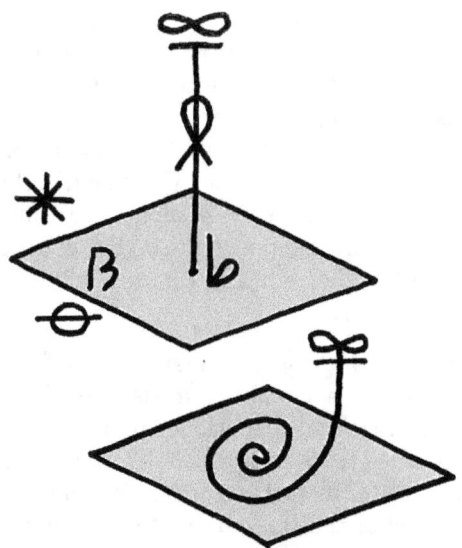

We may hold the string up above the floor or table so that it freely hangs down over the piece of paper without touching. This is a state of potential *Awareness*. As soon as we move our hand downward, allowing the string to touch and curl onto the piece of paper, we have an interaction. Now we have—

> an *Alpha Awareness* (α)
> extending as ZU (T) energy
> from the direction of AN or *Infinity* (∞)
> along a ZU-line (‡)
> contacting *Beta existence* (β)
> in the direction of KI (Ø) and
> experienced as manifestation of the genetic body (b).

It's all right there in the Standard Model... Now suppose we are to consider that the "quantity" of string wound up on the piece of paper is equivalent to the amount of *actualized Awareness* (Å) we are experiencing from *Alpha/Self* (α) as ZU (T) free flowing through the beta body (b). The amount of "string" on paper would be proportional to the *degree* or "value" discussed concerning any numeric grading or "frequency" provided on the Standard Model. As more "string" is sent as *Awareness*, the actualized degree of vibration is increasing. The more "string in play" the more vibrancy we have "to work with" when confronted with challenges and the more "space" within our influence and responsibility. We could even demonstrate "unconsciousness" by leaving only a bit of string on there; or "death" by lifting it off altogether—that point when the "spirit withdraws from the body."

As we increase our levels of *Awareness* toward *Self-Honesty*, we are freeing up personal channels that allow more of this string to enrich our experience of existence. We need not be concerned with "running out." The Source of Life-Energy is Infinity. In fact, we have determined that the frequency level of the Human Condition may be elevated considerably higher than what we have "normally" been "wired" to experience. *Adding* to our vitality and increasing our frequency ensures a continued existence. It is the "withdrawal" of *Spirit*, the restriction of ZU flow and resulting lower personal vibrations "materializing" in our *Life* that we are concerned with releasing from on the *Pathway to Self-Honesty*.

Our *Systemology* charts a new destiny for humanity, emphasizing true personal spiritual achievement demonstrable to the limits of personal understanding—but it is a wisdom drawn from the most ancient well-springs of Divine Knowledge that can surely benefit the entire planet!

.: 11 :.
UNDERSTANDING EMOTIONAL ENCODING
AND THE POWER OF IMPRINTS
[EXTENDED COURSE*]

This is the public relaunch of what we introduced as *Nex-Gen Systemology* some eight years ago. Okay, so it's been eight years. That's on me. But here we are now. It took eight years to make sure that a *Pathway* to *Infinity* could be sure, tried and tested from all of the collected information and mysticism and psychology and experience that we could throw at it, before any type of **surefooted** map could be communicated. And we are obviously well on our way now.

Sure, we have all kinds of information now. It is being fed to us at an alarming rate. The higher states that we achieve result in higher complexities of the System we are in. It just works out that way. We tend to equate it best to "game theory" at this juncture because we are talking about systematic variables governed by Law, but we cannot apply this Law directly to the true force that is doing the determining of action—and that is *Self*. *Self* is making choices.

We have systems at work, following their programmed course of action and interaction as governed by the Law of the Physical Universe. We've established that. We can find out all kinds of things more about it—the way in which the Physical Universe works. But no matter what we do find in all of that—all of those rules, and terms and various calculations—we will never come close to calculating a direct relationship with *Self*. We cannot define the Observer in the equation because it is the Observer that is doing the equating. And if the Observer is outside the equation, doing the equating, than *Self* is static compared to the Physical Universe. It does not exist within the equation of

---

* Based on a lecture by Joshua Free, given on the evening of August 9, 2019. Transcripts of the original lecture are reprinted in "*The Systemology Handbook*" complete *Grade-III* textbook.

systematic variables that we are dealing with in the physical sciences. Without an Observer to do the calculating, we can never be sure of what is actually taking place when we are not looking.

We are talking about "**collapsing-a-wave**" of potential with our Observation. And that when we are not paying attention—when we are not contributing our *Awareness* to actually determine and direct actions within our realm of responsibility—these is a world still taking place, or maybe not, but it is happening in its own way until we interact with it. This is clearly demonstrated in the knowledge of the ancients. They weren't stupid. They had a limited language to describe it all. Complexity of the system necessary to contain the Human Condition rises to the level just beyond the point humanity is at—and that goes back to basic *Systemology* as we presented it in *The Original Thesis* eight years ago. Our premise hasn't changed.

We have been systematically raising our levels of *Awareness* for years and reexamining all that we have accepted as "fact" each step of the way. The "tablets" haven't changed; the artifacts are all still as they were; our research library that we maintain—of old esoteric tomes and the "Mardukite Core"—is all still there. Even the Source of ZU and the natural state of the true *Alpha Self* as "I" is a constant. So, what is changing? In briefest terms: we took another examination or sweep of the material and discovered that there *is* a map and guide to this journey embedded in what has been sitting right in front of us. It has taken many years, many intensive days of self-processing, processing others in the Society, to achieve certainty of its validity. We can now begin to deliver this spiritual technology in a way that may be effective outside just the boundaries of one office.

The ancients identified the *Spirit* of *Self-Awareness* or *Spiritual Consciousness* as "ZU." There are even those who have begun to call our previous *Grade-II* Mardukite path: "Mardukite Zuism." It is perhaps preferable to "Mesopotamian

Neopaganism." We are *not* dealing in "witchcraft"; we *are* dealing with *Life, Lifeforce,* ZU, Spirit, Self. This *Grade-III* material is not as concerned with physical ritual or obscure relays of cultural tradition and mythology. Standing above these other levels of understanding, we actually see *how* it is that such things work (or do not work) to the extent of their effectiveness.

ZU-Lifeforce or *Spiritual Energy* is a constant wherever it *is*. This is probably why it is not detectable or within the range of the Physical Universe, which is reliant on activity of energy and physical matter to be calculated. Our ZU-line is basically a state of constant potential only when not interacting with the Standard Model of universes and correlated energy and matter. When its current hits against something we have manifestation—something to be *Aware* of. We have this manifestation within ourselves happening at various degrees, and manifestation taking place wherever *Awareness* comes into contact with some sensory stimulation—or basically anything in our environment. That's the only way we really know that something *is*. A part of us—our waves, our field—is bumping up against a part of *it*. And whatever we determine of this, *is* our Reality.

ZU is a constant. And when it is not being delivered in full force to the part of the spectrum that reaches the physical body, there is some type of *solid* diverting the path of energy or absorbing it. That is how we experience everything. That's how we know everything. That's how we interact with knowing in the Mind. However, we are seldom having any type of clear interaction with our environment or full *Awareness* and vitality in the body.

When information or *Awareness* as experience, *Life* and *Knowingness* is not sent back to the *Self* in clarity, we refer to it as "fragmentation." Some *solid* or *image* is impeding clear view. *Self* has the ability to experience and direct *Awareness* through the entire range of potential states without being fixed to any given point. But systems seek optimization, habit and reinforcement. What we call "in phase" is everything working in tandem. When we concentrate our attentions, on any given point, *consciousness* makes manifestation possible. There is something to experience. We have all kinds of receptors and faculties to receive and process such experience. We have proactive/creative centers; we have reactive/responsive centers; and all the while we have *Self* at a static point in an *alpha* state watching this whole thing take place. *Self* can only determine and direct *Awareness* to the extent that it can see clearly and evaluate what it effectively sees.

Δ Δ Δ Δ Δ Δ Δ

What we are mostly concerned with right now is the manner that this energy is stored, would up and/or bundled into this thing we call "memory." I mean: Here is *Self* and we're sitting in one place, like in a movie theater, or on a couch, gobbling up popcorn—and the motion of what we have collected as memory and experience is playing out before us, "on demand." And what is a movie or a video file, but a sequence of event image stills placed in logical sequential order. It's not the logic that has flaws—it's the inputs. The RCC does not use logic—which is a higher range of activity than it has receptacles for. In the spirit of stimulus-response, the RCC processor of the Mind is inherent to the genetic vehicle used to provide some basis for what we end up agreeing to as Reality in this Universe.

The range below the RCC, we call "Emotion," because it is a relay between the Mind-Systems and physiology of the body at the most basic apparent level. When we bring *solids* from this range up into the normal range of thought, the *Imprints* become little more than traditional programming that we can treat as intellectual programming and stomp out with a bit of logic processing and rationale. There is a lot within the realm of intellectual processing for future work; right now we are concerned specifically with the most accessible "emotional range" of *Imprints*.

We may receive all kinds of associative sensory information from an *Imprint* that is not specifically relayed in our present environment. A wide range of feedback activity takes place between the Mind and the physical body. Anything that is *solidified* in the mental range of activity is usually fine for us to sort out and deal with at an intellectual level.

Emotional disturbance—the encoding of emotional *Imprints*—creates a *solid* at the emotional level beneath the surface or range of normal human thought. We speak of emotions, and behaviors resulting from them, as "irrational," because they deal in contacting some "thing" beneath the level of "rational" thought. By definition, the mechanism would be autonomous, "responsive" or "reactive," independent of *Self*, *Awareness* as *Self* and *Self*-direction. When we refer to someone and their "self-control," we are nearly always referring to their ability to manage "emotion" in regard to their environment. When we can bring the *substance* of our emotional manifestation up to the range of thought, then we can analyze it rationally as a *mental Imprint*.

Our processing is fairly fixed to the level we can understand, but incoming and stored data changes. The knowledge itself may be imperfect or erroneous. This is all within the domain of the Mind to fully consider and work out. But when we are talking about emotion, we are talking about *solids* that have formed along the pathway between the Mind and genetic vehicle. We used to call this the Mind-of-Body as opposed to the Mind-of-Spirit and now, with the reintroduction of *Systemology* in line with the *"Tablets of Destiny"* and reformed Standard Model that incorporates ZU, we have simplified this distinction as the RCC and MCC systems: the *reactive-responsive control center* and the *Master Control Center*, both which seem to have a direct affect on the process of ZU energy or *Awareness*.

Emotional imprints are not actually normal thought activity unless we bring them there. We can revisit virtually everything that we have an emotional imprint of and stimulate the same biochemical and physiological responses up to the degree of our *Self-control*. This ping-back from *Imprints* is not actual sensory information received from the present environment. When this recall is not *Self*-directed, the MCC will not distinguish the difference between something that is happening in the environment and that which it is imprinted to think is happening in the environment. This is personal fragmentation at its core.

We should not get used to an idea that *Self* is passively observing Reality—it is not. What it does observe becomes memory, information stored moment by moment. *Self* is using this information as a basis for Reality every moment. And it is *Aware* of, and capable of recording, far more than is actually being handled at any given moment within the realm of conscious *Awareness*. This is how we gauge *Awareness* on the Standard Model—the extent to which a person is able to receive and process all of what is going on around them clearly.

The academic definition of *Awareness* is little more than the word *consciousness*, but when we apply it in the real world as every day life, we notice almost immediately that: our *Awareness* is the ability to successfully evaluate, determine and direct the Reality of our existence. While this ability is the same for all, it is obvious to anyone looking around in the world that it is not *actualized* or *realized* equally by all members of the species.

Δ Δ Δ Δ Δ Δ Δ

Any time we are fragmented—which can fluctuate even with a person that has achieved *Self-Honesty*—there is a restriction in ZU-energy flow that prevents experience of full vitality, creativity and personal magnetism. We are talking about states of being that have probably *already* been experienced at one time or another before, but then we go back to allowing—even if unknowingly—this or that source of fragmentation to inhibit a continued optimum existence in *that* direction. We start thinking "too much" or feeling "too much"—and the next thing we know, we are back in the mess where we began.

If we were to only measure things physically in exclusion to greater systems, if we are purely measuring entropy over time, then the energy toward a task and its success rate should only be on the decline. We are not even talking about a long range of time where someone might undoubtedly get rest and nourished and so forth. A person fatigued by the days activities, fragmented by the accumulation of *solids* being formed in his vicinity, can suddenly do better after a period of shifted attentions. The individual is going out, let us say, on a walk through a park and seeing the participation in life and directing movements and steps here or there but basically being *Self*-directed in the midst of an entire playing field. They may then return to the task that they had just barely had the strength to be able to stand up and stay awake for—and suddenly they have this reinvigorated spirit of *Self-determinism* to accomplish anything!

If we look at energy in only physical terms, a person should be more tired after a walk then before. The environment as a system did not change. *Self* never changes. So what changed? Where can we find the rationale here? We are now calling it *ZU*. This individual has done nothing more than reminded themselves, in the present, as actual *Awareness*, of the higher potential of manifestation, enriching their surface thoughts with things that are directly and positively contributory to continued optimum existence as *Life*. A *Self-Honest* person in this state is fully in *Awareness* of and as *Self*, directing the body and its interrelationship with *Life*. All *Life* comes from—and undoubtedly returns to—that highest spiritual expression without limit —which is *Infinity*.

The highest realization of the *Prime Directive* is anything but "selfish." A person that has only achieved a basic realization of the first level of understanding as *Self*—that they exist, are existing and can do things to keep existing—will not be able to accurately determine what will ensure the existence of a group unit, or what is best to protect or ensure future of the entire Human species. That is simply not in their range of *Awareness* to determine. Folk with purely physical levels of understanding equate *Awareness*, *Life* and *ZU* with the dead images stored as data and they are not the same—as almost any *Systemologist* now understands.

Once emotional imprinting takes place under the RCC, energy is collecting as a *solid* "beneath the surface" as we say —or producing results at times that projects automatically into the level of thought perception and experience. Stimulus information will come from an *Imprint* and not directly from the external environment. We start interacting with a dead memory, but a memory that we keep alive with some of our own energy. We develop this interactive emotional relationship with the *Imprint* and feed it our vitality.

When we consider *alpha* as basic personality, *Self* does not experience any degree of fluctuation and is entirely *Self*-directed in thought and behavior. In fact, when operating clearly in *Self-Honesty*, we have the utmost definitive clarity in our actions, which are always then directed by the Prime Directive of existence—and this is not a selfish directive. It only becomes so if we are at the lowest mode of the directive, down between zero and one on the Standard Model. Can't do much but to basically keep breathing at that point and we wont be in a position to let others do much more than that either. Selfish existence—existing solely for *Self* in fragmented *Awareness* will result in the opposite result. An individual begins to diminish in their ability to collect, evaluate and use any resources toward real survival at that point.

At low-levels of *Awareness*, our behavior begins to eliminate the presence of tools and assets and allies that we need to exist. And we wont realize it until later, and then we say: "Oh, why aren't these things and people helping me exist?" And of course, in some way these other things actually *are*—but a person at low-levels of *Awareness* is never going to understand this. Especially since at such a low point of observation, they are operating as "every man for himself," and of course they believe that all others must be at this same level, so they are suspicious of everyone.

The truth is: if we were to all actually operate at the low-levels of "every man for himself" for any length of time, than every man would cease to exist. There is a systemology to life throughout the cosmos just as there is to the life of the individual and it all plays along the same line and uses the same basic model. There is an evaluation point on the ZU-line that we could apply to the individual, the family unit, the social group, the human race as a whole, all the *Life* on earth, all *Life* in the cosmos, all *Life* in the spiritual world and then obviously *Life* in Eternity. No *life* exists in exclusion to all other *Life*. And it is all composed of a spiritual energy we call *"ZU"* in honor of ancient Mesopotamia.

Δ Δ Δ Δ Δ Δ Δ

When used as a tool by the rational processes of the MCC, an *Imprint* could technically be any memory that carries an emotional response. We have many of these that we refer to as the "happy times" of our life, because when we call them up, the energy stored in them actually brightens us and enriches our attitude toward life. An "imprint," in itself, is not actually a harmful thing. We can keep entire shoe boxes full of these within the database of the MCC—and we can take them out from time to time and look at them (or re-create them when we want to), reflect on and even revisit them. We put the imprinted photo slide up there on a holographic projector of the Mind and relive it. That's called *recall*—that's not inherently emotional fragmentation. That's a *memory*.

The actual content of a memory may have true or false data associated with it; but that usually falls under the category of intellectual programming, because it is something we did, or enjoyed, or experienced, or learned directly. We know what it is. We are *Aware* of it. It is a "conscious memory." This is not the same as an (RCC) emotional imprint cast up in our face—without us knowing what is actually in the environment versus what is experienced as a result of the imprint distorting our view.

"Emotionally Encoded Imprints" are equivalent to "beliefs" within the range of thought—but they do not have a rational component. They are simply the entire picture or snapshot of emotional experience including every aspect or *facet*. Anything caught in the range of view of perception becomes a *facet* of the *Imprint*. This includes completely arbitrary and irrational associations.

Our observation over the past decade, experimenting with these ideas, led us to reach some particular conclusions—which you can demonstrate in your everyday life. By all means: apply these principles, see how it's working, and then decide. We find that most encoding relates to thwarts to our existence on some level and most *Imprints* resurface when similar conditions of a perceived threat occur in our environment—even if there is no actual threat and there is simply the presence of a perceived *facet* associated with a former threat.

Sometimes we are actually *Aware* of something happening that reminds us of something else and we can identify it. Even when we know the source, it still makes us uncomfortable and still may influence what we ultimately choose to do. Unfortunately, in the case of an emotional *Imprint*, anything caught in the frame of perception can be associated with the same originally encoded threat or event. These *facets* may later catch the light of our *Awareness* in a future environment. When this type of information is stored and accumulated through a lifetime of painful experience, a person maintains lower and lower averages of ZU energy, and as a result begins to treat more and more of their environment as *facets* of some *Imprint*.

Pain as a registry of a physical sensation or cell damage is only thinking in a purely biological sense; such as pricking our finger or some other injury. But painful experience is registered from any *barrier* that we contact with enough personal force and conviction—similar to what we consider pain when it happens at physical levels. Some people associate pain with learning. For whatever reasons they have this association. For them: Learning is painful; all new learning is painful; learning environments stimulate pain; faking illness to avoid school; school becomes associated with more pain and sickness. This is an Imprint *about* learning—it will be reinforced with more emotional energy over time as it is interacted with and validated. We will even find all manner of ways to justify our reactions when analyzing only the "above-the-surface" behaviors.

We cannot understand beyond the point *Awareness* is fixed in place. So until we go back a bit and bring up whatever it is that we are stumbling over into the light, we will just keep treating it as some invisible barrier. At lower-levels of experience, eventually we just ignore or avoid altogether. Not dealing with it. Not facing it. Just letting it be whatever it is. This is what "Fear" *is*. And "Fear" is among the lowest levels of *Awareness* we can experience.

As an example: some individuals develop a strong *Imprint* about "*marriage*" which then affects a future "marriage" only because it *is* a "marriage." This doesn't mean that there will not be other reasons. But a person is carrying this *Imprint* about "marriage" with them to the altar. This *Imprint* can result from something an individual experienced personally—such as in a former marriage—or something that affected them severely or as a threat to their existence, such as an event involving the marriage of their parents. We experience and interact with many emotional events as a part of family life and especially at early years of life where many *Imprints* are originally formed, then reinforced later in life.

A person can literally be imprinted to "subconsciously believe" that marriage is bad for their own survival and maintain all manners of automatic response in connection to such an *Imprint*. And since we know that some manner of marriage or stable family unit is an integral part of the continuation of human existence, it must be an *Imprint*, because the irrational idea of "marriage is bad." If maintained by all, it would result in the end of Human existence. The Prime Directive of *Self* is to *exist as Self*, but selfishness actually diminishes the chance of success!

The point here is not to convince anyone about the idea of long-term mating. The point is that there are beliefs beneath the surface that influence what you are believing above the surface—within your rational range of thought. And imagine the individual who is throwing their established *Life* into chaos for no other reason but the stimulation of some "arbitrary" *facet* of *emotional* belief. So, none of this is arbitrary.

In a more basic example: imagine your supervisor, full of excitement, approaches you with news that they are getting married. If your first response-reaction without even realizing it, is to crinkle your nose, give a small head shake and roll your eyes... guess who won't be getting a promotion any time soon? You might not even realize you did it if *Awareness* is that low. Or, you might think back later that you should not have done that because when you are actually "present" in your thoughts, you would have known better. So, you can see that it was not a *Self*-directed response that you would have normally made because you can so easily say, "Oh, why did I do that" or "..say that" and so forth. It's the same you. You didn't actually learn anything because you—the *real* "You"—already knew better before the *Imprint* was stimulated. This is what separates learned memory and knowledge of the Mind System from emotional imprinting that we chalk up to as "experience," but which is unnecessary and from which the MCC does not actually learn anything. In fact, it actually now has to spend more of its time getting rid of it, because its not useful knowledge anyway.

Δ Δ Δ Δ Δ Δ Δ

ZU-force circulating in a body decreases with accumulation of pain *Imprints.* Sensory pain creates *Imprints*—and
painful experience is attached to the conditions of existence for the physical body. It is like a security alarm
response of automatic motions away from the source of
pain. Usually so we can get away and evaluate, but seldom
are we able to evaluate much if we assume the role of victim, because pain is not rational to the MCC. The *Self* is not
"feeling" pain; it is forced to endure the fragmentation in
Reality that painful *Imprints* manifest. There are other possible reactions to pain or painful experience available too
—not just to succumb. Some levels of *Awareness* will result
in our withdrawal or flight from the situation; some will
cause us to simply ignore it; some reactions are of the
"confront and attack" variety—and generally all of this behavior will generally be a result of our *Imprint* combining
with a level of *Awareness* at the time of the *Imprint* and at
the time when it is resurfacing. "Feelings" attached to *Imprints*—associated with everything that *Imprint* entails—
will displace the actual environment. We will still react as
though threats are in our environment, and we will act in
alignment with whatever state or degree of *Awareness* being maintained.

Others who cannot keep up with us and our vibrations become a source of stress or stimulation because they begin
to represent barriers. These individuals are often bogged
down in heavy emotional energy—and that amount of low-
level mass carries a lot of gravity. This heavy field of energy is imposed on us whenever they work us into getting
into agreements with them and their *solids* as Reality. Doing so slows us down to be more *in phase* with their
vibrations.

There *is* a limit to the amount of physical memory able to
be stored as pain in the body. Some individuals are able to
reduce and eliminate *Imprints* more "naturally" than others—they are able to bounce back and overcome, but that
is attributed to their *Will* and *Self-determination* and not a
quality of the pain storage mechanisms. We have seen how

well the body *can* heal when given the right treatments, but we must work on ourselves holistically and treat more than just the physical. Naturally, *Systemology* and wisdom from the *"Tablets of Destiny"* is not directly concerned with physical "healing" as a subject matter—but it seems to come up a lot when we are dealing with personal energy.

Cellular memory is not as unlimited as our psychological and spiritual faculties and it can grind the physical body down by changing the activity of cellular receptors associated with good health—receptors associated with receiving nutrients and proteins and which are now charged to receive biochemical energy instead, no matter what we feed it. It is like digesting its own muscle. There is no room for the good stuff to get through if the way is blocked. That's what an emotional *Imprint* is.

I'm not saying not to treat the body conventionally. I would never say that. People get in trouble for saying that stuff anyway. What I *am* saying is that the field of *Systemology* is about holistic systems. Treating all aspects of all things as systems. And if all you are doing is treating the body and apparent physical sources in exclusion to all other systems, than you are leaving a seed or root in tact somewhere else to just put this process into effect again. And *that is* something I am saying. Because there are a great many professions out there that seem to make a capital livelihood out of this business of cutting out only what we can see and disregarding the rest in exclusion. It would be better for them to apply holistic therapy to their patients—and we see this happening more and more every day, but not fast enough. Those claiming to be professionals and authorities should spend as much time educating themselves on the *Mind* and *Spirit* as they do the physical body. Instead the *Mind* and body was mainly eliminated from contemporary science and now its all "behaviorism."

The principles of *Systemology* as relayed in *"Tablets of Destiny"* (*Liber-One*) are not in contradiction with medical knowledge. Many professionals already know some of this information and they see evidence for it confirmed every day in causal observation. But they no longer see the Human Condition or the *Spirit* for what it is—because their science, analyzing one part in exclusion to all others, will not allow for much more that a consideration of physical levels. And here we have someone fixed into a certain mode of *Awareness*, but on an intellectual level. It is a somewhat different quality of fragmented programming than what we see in the emotionally encoded *Imprints*. But rest assured, once a belief is imprinted, it will be reinforced continually with emotional energy.

Our experience can be reduced essentially to interactions between *Self* and environment—or "set" and "setting." That interaction is fairly systematic with mathematical precision. Everything has its degrees and variables within a preset system of arrangements or "cosmic ordering." Everything has its degree and its sequence in the system. It's how we define the qualities of something—based on its interactions. All interactions equalize at some level. There is a level of energy or vibration that we maintain; there is the level maintained with the environment; and there is this result that is a product of degrees and fluctuations and levels and such all of which surrounds this average point of equilibrium. Whatever that equilibrium is, we generally attribute it to the level of knowledge, understanding and *Awareness* we are experiencing.

The level of understanding and *Awareness* maintained by an individual will be in proportion to their ability to be *Self-directed*. Sane, rational, *Self-Honest* individuals are supposed to strive toward the highest ideal of being. When experience is clouded, the information supposed as knowledge will be clouded. Thus an individual outside of *Self-Honesty* is consistently accumulating and storing irrational erroneous information about their environment and using this to base their agreement of Reality.

These emotions we speak of are not in the same range as what we mean if we are carrying a certain elevated "feeling," for example, of being "in love" or of "accomplish-ment" or even "boredom." All of these fall within the range of thought. Many individuals withdraw from the in-struction right here, because there seems to be a fixation on the idea that "Humans are animals led around by emo-tion." Releasing the hold that negative emotion has on us frees up potential of the Mind and Spirit.

When starting out with Systemology, a *Seeker* works at processing some of their more critical emotional imprints before we start developing higher faculties. Part of this process is called "resurfacing"—bringing the *solids* com-posed at the emotional range, below the surface of our normal *Awareness*, up into the thought range so we may actually deal with the programming and language of them. Buried emotional *Imprints* will not be in the thought range unless we actually bring them up to surface-level thought intentionally and not as reactions. We usually see how ir-rational it is to continue maintaining these beliefs or react to *facets* stimulated as Reality even after the original envir-onmental source has long since left our proximity.

Δ Δ Δ Δ Δ Δ Δ

Emotional imprinting is not *Self-directed*—generally not the result of something we are doing to ourselves, but interac-tions with others. An *Imprint* is often formed as a result of an instance or snap-shot of "shock." The "shock" moment is the camera snapping the *Imprint*. Whatever *facets* are perceived, they will become a part of the image. And the intensity of the *Imprint* is attached to emotional engage-ment. The RCC takes over. But this can happen with pain responses to our Physical Universe too.

If we walk into a wall, we have learned that walking into walls is painful. We have a reaction and it makes sense and we learn not to walk into walls again. We might get a small *Imprint* from this, but it probably will not have the emo-tional intensity necessary to make us afraid of walls. Perhaps, we will be a little more cautious and reserved the next time we approach a wall with such ferocity. On the other hand, if someone picks us up and throws us into a wall, suddenly the Physical Universe is thrown out of alignment with what we expect about our interactions with it. Because walls don't seem to move and we certainly didn't do this to ourselves. So for a brief moment—or not so brief, if we are knocked unconscious or something—we are put into a state of instantaneous "shock."

When we are abruptly thrown into the wall—or whatever instance contributes to an *Imprint*—we are put into "shock" because it doesn't make sense. We knew the wall was there. We knew not to go at it with any force. And suddenly here we are in pain on the floor next to a wall. Now we have an *Imprint* about our experience with our environment that is not rational. We now have a conditioned reaction about threats present in the environment that is not rational. But the incident is still recorded and stored as memory—just in a different part of "memory" than what we typically mean.

But the *Imprint* is real some place and once we bring it up to the *surface* of our Mind-Systems then we can *confront* the surface of the wall and the source of force behind our sudden motivation toward it. Logical rational processing *reduces* emotional energy stored that blocks free flow of ZU. Until we do this processing, we maintain a slightly lower level of *Awareness* about Reality; just slightly out of phase with the Physical Universe. We are holding onto a belief somewhere that doesn't really make sense to us, but when it's stimulated without our *Awareness*, the mind will always fill in the gaps of rationality and justification. The issue with *Imprints* is that they indiscriminately associate everything about the incident. Everything within the snapshot is equal with everything else, including physical sensation.

The *Imprint* is an instant snapshot of "determination" that is happening automatically; whatever all this stuff is in here—all these *facets* of the *Imprint*—the basic message of fragmentation is "I don't know, but it's bad and we must be cautious." And that's just a basic *Imprint*. The message gets deeper and more severe as *facets* are stimulated again and again in our environment and the same internal reactions take place again and again. This is how an *Imprint* gets reinforced as valid Reality beneath the surface of our normal *Awareness*.

There is a whole spectrum of response patterns that can occur. We will go from being disinterested in certain aspects of life, to not liking them very much, to ignoring them and then even actively seeking to destroy them. We will justify all of this as "personality" attributes; and rationalize anything we experience with a more easily identifiable aspect. *Awareness* generally skips over the content of the *Imprint* directly, because the associations just don't make sense. We make a gradual progress toward *Self-Honesty* as we intentionally bring these tendencies, reactions, patterns and imprinted experiences from our past out of the RCC databanks and up to the surface—up to the domain of rational thought.

When using *Systemology* for processing, we take *Imprints* out of their hiding place and examine them in the light during a time when they are not stimulated by the environment. This requires that our processing techniques be performed in locations clear of distractions or excessive restimulation, but comfortable and conducive to various exercises.

A big part of what we are doing now in our *Systemology* is taking an applied systems theory and applied spiritual technology and drawing a paradigm of semantics from the *Arcane Tablets* to communicate a map of how systems work. There are more levels of understanding inherent in the material, but it all requires a gradual development of *Self*-control to reach. There is no point in my distracting you with stuff we aren't presently communicating about. But, yes there is more. A lot more.

Another concept we will be treating in advanced "Crystal Clear" courses is this matter of "Self-Talk." It involves language and statements from others that reoccur, to which we have an emotional response. These statements condition us. People used to talk about "turning off the mind." We aren't turning it off. But we *are* reducing the resonate programming; we are shutting up the noise enough to allow our minds to actually think!—and in *Self-Honesty*.

It is amazing how much of the internal dialogue of our Mind is tied up in emotional statements from others and their fragmentation. We want to experience our own *Self-directed* reality and yet we got Jim-Joe-Bob over here telling us how they are or how we are or how we should be, because to them, operating off that RCC, it's all the same thing. Everything is just as emotionally equal to everything else. And this starts bouncing around in our Reality, triggering all kinds of emotional statements that will bog us down if left unchecked. People develop their entire personality and thought-mode around these kind of affirmations. Don't let the simplicity of it fool you into thinking that they hold no influence. They hold a lot of influence.

This concept of Self-Talk brings us back to the subject of language and literal programming. *Imprints* may actually have language as a *facet* if there are statements and associations attached to them. There is a communication of pain, which has a lot of *facets* associated with sensations in the body, yes, but the *Imprint* may also include some type of *language facet* that is delivering a literal message to us as we go about our daily life. Let's be honest, the introduction of language to the Human Condition is the way in which all advanced programming of the condition came about. Otherwise we're just left with the idea of running into walls and people throwing us around. But there is more to fragmentation and programming than just physical pain sensations—and most of them involve language as the *medium* or **catalyst** of programming. So we have language to deal with latter on, but a lot of this Self-Talk is stimulated from *Imprints*.

You will notice that, when processing *Imprints*, there is actually a series of *language facets* attached to it, just as there are other *sensual facets*. Not only do we tend to repeat some of the phrases in our Self-Talk when the *Imprint* is stimulated—but the very *Imprint* itself may be stimulated into re-occurrence by language in our environment. Someone says something—certain words or a certain tone —and we have a reaction. So, language is not a *facet* to be taken lightly because of the **recursive** "figure-8 loop." A low-level emotional response becomes language when it gets up in the thought range. If we are intentionally *resurfacing* it than we can deal with it. If it is happening when we are unaware that this is happening than the language of the *Imprint* will resurface into our thoughts and seem like our own.

Have you ever noticed that when an *Imprint* is excited up in an individual—and that "figure-8" starts churning—that they will actually exhibit certain modes of thought and language in their observable behavior as part of the reactive-response? It is my understanding at this time that many of these phrases are part of emotional encoding or conditioning. They affect us in times of stress and we exhibit or project them as stress reactions. We say the statements to others. We say them to ourselves. They affect the repetitive Self-Talk that affects perception of Reality; then we communicate the same emotional tones outwardly in our environment. *Imprints* limit our ability to understand and cope with the forces of the Physical Universe that are threatening our material and hindering use of the Mind in advanced creative ways to ensure our continued experience of optimum existence. These *Imprints* impose boundaries where none should be.

At some point we have either heard someone say—or have been told by someone—some bit of vocalized language that was stored as an *Imprint* or a *facet* of an *Imprint*. Usually some emotional intensity is required in order to be *Imprinted*—otherwise its just standard mental language programming. But an *Imprint* is beneath the level of rationality and rational language. The statements will not be rational—they may be some kind of negative conditionals that filter Reality. We are very skilled *Reality Engineers* and so we will undoubtedly find validation for these statements of Reality wherever we turn—and when validation is not readily visible, our reaction-responses to our environment will *make* them visible; make them our Reality.

Negative Self-Talk is any speech we are replaying or telling ourselves about "how it is *all* the time" or how something is "*always* such and such the case." And what do we have then? We have created a *postulate.* We have just cemented a *fact!* We have solidified a *belief!* Then we interact with it and make it real by our patterns and cycles of behavior and thought. Can you see how this is affecting Reality? Think about this: how many statements and affirmations have we impressed with deep emotional imprinting that run along the lines of: "can't think about ___" or "can't stand ___" or "can't see why ___" or "don't feel like ___" or "so sick and tired of ___" or "just can't do ___" and so forth. These thoughts actually get repeated in the language play of the Mind and even in outward behaviors as our speech. Later we recall these as moments we "weren't thinking clearly" and "don't know why we said that." Yet, if given enough time and emotional charge eventually an individual is left laying there having difficulties thinking, standing, seeing, feeling, being awake, doing anything and understanding this thing called *Life* and then right before the end of it all, validate it all one last time with: "See?! I *knew* it was *going to be* like this. It's *always* like this!" I'm not really going to make any specific claims about what these statements might actually do to us if repeated long enough and intensely enough, but if they are found as part of a *resurfacing Imprint*, than they need to be reduced with that *Imprint*—the effect and energy wound up in it needs to be reduced and released—as part of the *NexGen Systemology* procedures and processes that are intended to "Resurface and Reduce" emotional encoding and conditioning of the Human Condition.

.: 12 :.
INTRDUCTION TO CATHARTIC PROCESSING, RESURFACING AND REDUCING IMPRINTS [INTRODUCING ROUTE-1 REVISED*]

A lot has been taking place lately in the underground with *NexGen Systemology*—and for nearly a decade. Now we are bringing it forth out in the open as *Grade- III* of the "Mardukite Core." We are at a point of unification. And now that we have reached that point, what is going to happen is going to happen fast. [Within two years of this lecture, Joshua Free followed up *Tablets of Destiny*, with *Crystal Clear* and *Power of Zu* (to complete *Grade-III*), then *Metahuman Destinations*, *Imaginomicon* and *Way of the Wizard* (to complete *Grade-IV*).]

We are dealing directly with "processes" or "processing" now in *Systemology*. At lower Grades, *Self-processing* and *Self-directing* was reduced to the guise of esoteric occult knowledge and ritual practices—all of which are entry-points to the pathway or gateway to further increase *Awareness* an individual carries regarding their *Self-determinism*. If you examine all of the lore and practices— from the ancient Babylonians, Egyptians and Druids, all the way through the idealism put forth by modern figures like Aleister Crowley—you will find that it is all a variation on this basic premise. If you look at those types of materials, especially the newer ones, you will see a lot of talk of *Will* and *Self* and the "*I*."

"Processing" in *Systemology* is dedicated to revitalizing *Self* with what ancient Mesopotamians referred to as "ZU." That is the primary goal of any actual "process." What an individual is capable of doing in such a state is not, at this

---

* Based on a lecture by Joshua Free, given on the evening of August 9, 2019. Transcripts of the original lecture are reprinted in "*The Systemology Handbook*" complete *Grade-III* textbook. The text has been revised for this "Revelations" edition of *Liber-One*. This 2022 Procedure R-1R (*Route-1 Revised*) replaces former RR-SP-1 instructions from the original 2019 edition.

point, what we are concerned with. We are clearing this channel of energy that is actually from an infinite source, but of which we find entangled and entwined—wrapped up or wound up—in erroneous sensory experience and data that is fragmenting our ability to be as *Self* as *Actualized Awareness*. We are too busy pawing at all of these things from our past that no longer serve us, if they ever did.

We are currently developing extensive companion work to "*Tablets of Destiny*" that will treat the journey on this *Pathway to Self-Honesty* more directly.‡ We realize that there are many ways in which proper education and *Self-processing* will enable an individual to further themselves along the Pathway quite successfully. However, throughout history there is a certain sect or segment of the population specifically educated, initiated and trained to assist spiritual "processing" of individuals. This is always conducted in relation to whatever civic capacity was installed in society —for example: ministers of some spiritual tradition, or emotional counselors assisting physicians in their physical work. A segment of priests and priestesses of every ancient culture were specialists in this department. Ancient records indicate that this function was a service provided by the Temple District. In more indigenous societies, you might find this role played by some sort of *shaman*.

At the inception of civic systems—particularly in the Ancient Near East—systematization was in many ways necessary to, in essence, "civilize" the Human Condition into a social order. But social order was more highly regulated than it is today—the environment was more controlled. Now, we just have systems of fragmentation duplicating across society as a contagion. But there was a time when civic matters were more refined—apart from the obvious savagery of war, which has plagued humanity at all times. The priests and priestesses developed and installed highly

---

‡   See "*Crystal Clear*" and "*Imaginomicon*" plus the Professional Piloting Courses given within "*Metahuman Destinations*" and "*Way of the Wizard.*"

sophisticated programming into "citizens," but they were also closely at hand for damage control. The clergy members were not stupid. They were crafty magicians and esoteric psychologists—an invisible hand ruling the governing law all in one.

The King, at these times, ruling from the Palace District, could certainly annihilate society with tyranny, but on a wider scope he was primarily a national figurehead put in charge of the army. He was closely surrounded by a Council of High Priests to direct his attentions, and Priestesses to secretly record and report his every movement. He would be offered "emotional counsel" to make certain that his innermost intentions were in line with the will of the Temple. In Babylon, for example, or even Egypt, real power came from the Temple District. Outside *Self-Honesty*, this too could crumble a society. But, the wise ones knew that a strong King and prosperous population required *Self-Honesty*. And so the social culture was engineered in such a way as to make this possible, giving rise to a whole host of archaic processes, rituals and ceremonial realizations—all providing counseling to the masses in the form of "national tradition" and "culture." For example, in Mesopotamia, large public demonstrations of catharsis—literally called the "Burning Man"—are demonstrated on Mesopotamian Maqlu cuneiform tablet sources[*]—and this concept of *catharsis* directly leads us to the heart of Systemology Route-1: *"Cathartic Processing."*

Δ Δ Δ Δ Δ Δ Δ

"Cathars" were once a very unique sect of Gnostic Christians, which sprung up around the 13th-century in France and parts of Italy. They existed during a heretical part of history—a time when anyone practicing forms of Christia-

---

[*] See "Tablet-M" in *The Complete Anunnaki Bible* edited by Joshua Free. "Tablet-M" is also reprinted as the stand-alone hardcover edition of *"The Maqlu Ritual Book"* and as a *New Standard Zuist Edition* pocket paperback titled *"Anunnaki Rites: The Maqlu Ritual Book."*

nity not sanctioned by the Church were considered heretics. Reference to this obscure faction sporadically appears in connection to lore of the Knights Templar, the Merovingians, the Dragon Legacy and so forth. This group named themselves "Cathars" from a Greek root meaning the *"pure ones."* They developed their own Gnostic processes that were intended to elevate the spirit of man to *"perfect"* status—and they even referred to achievers of this highly esteemed state as *"Cathar Perfects."*

The Cathars inherited a particular process from the *Near East* called *"Consolamentum."* Today, as a "process" in our *Systemology*, we simply call it *"cathartic processing."* It is the most fundamental of potential processes, providing at least a workable outline for additional developments. *Cathartic processing* deals specifically with clearing or purging any inhibiting emotional *Imprints*. We were fortunate enough to discover—while working to unify the "original thesis" of *Systemology* with the *"Arcane Tablets"*—that procedures for *"cathartic processing"* were found alongside the same *"Tablets of Destiny"* used for programming. We just needed to know how to look at them—just as with the other tablets passed off over the past century as trivial mythology. In other words, what we found is that once the Human Condition was programmed into experiencing material existence, a "back door" was also installed into the *System*—and while we can sit out on the sidelines and deny things all we want from our fragmented state, if we truly want to achieve the potentials inherent in our spiritual evolution, than *the only way out is the way through.*

Buried deep within System encoding we find some kill-switches and other mechanisms not within our range of "normal" *Awareness*—obviously put in place by system designers. If we consider that these original *Reality Engineers* may, themselves, have also been operating some "avatar" state in this existence, then they would, out of necessity for themselves, required a sure "way out." No constructive builder is going to wall himself into his creation, right? Whoever put this all into place must surely have been operating the highest faculties of *Awareness*. We might have already assumed that Cosmic or Divine knowledge used to systematize or fragment the Human Condition should also contain methods of defragmentation—even if only for use by the "gods" in their own *Directive toward* maintaining or ensuring their *beta existence* and total control of *ours*.

When we examine the "processes" alluded to on *Arcane Tablets* and compare the lore to more relatively recent innovations of the Cathars (some 800 years ago), we discover that these are not rituals, but highly systematic intellectual processes from a higher level of understanding. Without this level of understanding, these "processes" don't seem to mean much of anything at face value. It is probably for this reason that they remain so buried—going back to the idea of hiding things in simplicity in plain sight. Keep in mind, in the case of the *Cathars*—they were *Gnostics*, which means they viewed most physical reenactment of ritual or ceremony as unnecessary, a corrupting source of fragmentation in itself. To the Cathars: spiritual existence was *Truth* and the physical was *abberative*. Such is a little bit more in line with where we are at in *Grade-III*.

Catharsis is actually not an occult term. None of these terms are, but they apply to esoteric ideas. When the *Cathars* made *Perfects*, they employed *cathartic processing* to conduct a "baptism by the pure Holy Spirit." They did not believe that use of "holy water" alone could produce optimum results. A person had to be "processed" to return to that truly Divine state—assisted in achieving that state of *Gnosis* on their own, by their own discovery, and not some institution using physical objects, obscure symbols and material rituals memorized to the point of losing meaning. Do you see the difference? And this was accomplished by systematic methods of *catharsis*, which could be used to purge harmful emotional *solids* from physical experiences as a means of renewing and restoring the faculties innately in the Human Condition.

What we are describing is the round-about way leading up

to this idea of "*Self-Honesty*" that has been tossed around in previous Grades of material: the increase of ZU-energy by reducing what is stored as emotional encoded *Imprints*, "processing" out the RCC *Imprint* databanks, causing them to *resurface* and be coped with legitimately by faculties of the MCC. This is a state of *Awareness* alluded to in many primers and introductory lessons in the highest branches of mystical arts. But we don't ever seem to get around to this part—instead, plunging past it in some *Self-gratifying* attempts to enliven our monotonous physical lives with colorful rituals. Maybe if we *actually* followed the instructions prescribed by the Ancient Mystery School, we will find out that they actually say: "read all these steps of logic and philosophy and axioms and principles of cosmology before proceeding to attempt anything." We don't do that though. Of course, when we do—when we did—double back, it seems it says down here, at the very end, at step five-million three-hundred and sixty three, it says: "disregard all but steps one through seven and repeat; the rest are unnecessary, meant to weed out the unworthy and entrap them in a *Game of Lights*."

Some *Seekers* that have been following along with the materials over the years already have an understanding of exactly what I am talking about here. And this is one of the keys or secrets held by the *Master*—an individual who has a complete workable understanding of these various levels and degrees represented in former instruction, but they are not themselves formally attached to any of it—drawing up only those solid examples suitable for citation, example and demonstration. So, that's what a *Master* is, and we are referring now to this intermediary *Grade-III* of "*Mardukite Systemology*" material as the *Master Grade*. I expect to also develop a formal instruction course for that, which will solidify the unification of the extant "Mardukite Core" and *Systemology* for this Grade.[‡]

Δ Δ Δ Δ Δ Δ Δ

[‡]   See "*The Complete Master Course*" anthology (or the four-volume *Academy Lectures* set) for the *Master Course*.

Alongside this presentation of wisdom from the *"Tablets of Destiny,"* we have reinforced the *"need for Self-Honesty."* It is critical at this moment in history to put intensive attention on awakening potentials of the Human Condition and unfolding the spiritual evolution laden within. We are at a turning point now; we are about to spread the disease of this Human Condition into *space* as one method of maintaining the *Prime Directive.* But what of the qualities of the populations we hope to seed elsewhere? Are such individuals—outside of *Self-Honesty*—even capable of ensuring an existence of humanity? All of our research would suggest they are not.

All Systemology "processes" are designed, however much esoteric, to increase the amount of ZU energy flow through the *Lifeforce* channel or ZU-line. We could focus directly on the potential faculties of the Mind and Spirit right now, but we would be missing a step—and we are making certain *this time* that our "Temple to the Stars"* is built on the firmest foundation. So, we are left with this task of clearing the channels of emotions using psychological faculties.

The idea of the *"Imprint"* is actually not new—we are just adopting it into our vocabulary. In the past, the wise were quite aware of this phenomenon and its treatment, calling it: **abreaction.** The ancients observed how it was stimulated by an individual's environment and left people unawares to differentiate between their state of conditioning and the objective world-at-large. This was a powerful tool in the hands of authority—and remains so. The first remedy we find when tracing history back from the present is *cathartic processing.* As it turns out, they offered these same services in the Temples of Babylon; mastering these arts was actually a primary function of the Priestess. The common folk of *exoteric society* did not understood

---

* Alluding to the concept that Babylonian temples are "Stairways to Heaven" and "Gateways of the Gods," also reflected in the "Gate-System" of spirituality and initiation suggested by ancient Mardukite Babylonian tradition.

this, so the arts of the Priestess were reduced to mediocrity through history as prostitution. Yet, no less than three dozen individual cuneiform signs described various ranks and roles of Priestesses, and they do not all mean the same thing.

The idea that Truth is *even* attainable is a complete mystery to those living in fragmentation or programming from false *Imprints*. A person incapable of experiencing the idea that "things can be known," has an *Imprint* about it telling them otherwise, even when in an environment that could provide understanding. This works with all reactions that are not *Self-directed*. Do we feel inclined toward or away from something because we *choose* to be, or are we reacting to an earlier *Imprint* that conditioned us to it? This is not a small issue to consider.

A *"Seeker"* is an individual on the adventurous journey of working along the *Pathway to Self-Honesty*; the one receiving the "processing." To differentiate the very specific role of an assistant to this process, the individual administering the "processes" is referred to as the *"Pilot."*

The *Pilot* is specifically and exclusively responsible for *Self-Honestly* assisting the *Seeker* in reaching their chosen *destination*. The *Pilot* is not an academic tour guide; not an interpreter; not a doctor; not a therapist in the traditional sense—they offer no actual or evaluation. All realizations a *Seeker* is guided toward are theirs to discover and determine on their own. The *Seeker* merely has the confidence of knowing there is a safety net of travel by someone who has *already been* where they want to go!

Furthermore, the *Pilot* is not there to validate or invalidate any particular experience or opinion of Reality—only to expertly maneuver the *Seeker's* journey through turbulence—which is essentially what is taking place in the ZU-line whenever an *Imprint* is (re)stimulated. The goal in *cathartic processing* is to discharge the stores of ZU wound up in emotional *solids* developed over the course of one's lifetime. Even if remaining dormant and unstimulated for a long time—at that point of stress, the time when we need all our wits about us to manage Reality, *that's* when they unleash as an *Imprint,* and we don't know the difference.

Practice the techniques. Develop experience. Progress on the *Pathway* working with trusted friends and such. It is clear that we are in great need of assisting ourselves and our fellow man, which is in turn also assisting ourselves. And we must do this swiftly and surely.

The *Systemology Society* rapidly developed a division called the *Mardukite Academy of Systemology*[‡] and a "Flight School" for "Pilot Training." *Flight School* is separate from the *Mardukite Master-Grade Course* for instructors and leadership roles in the Orgs. "Pilot Training" is different, focusing on education regarding actively *applied spiritual technology* of "Systemology" as developed in the future—and which, by 2022, has resulted in *Crystal Clear, Imaginomicon, Metahuman Destinations* and *Way of the Wizard* since first setting down the original premise of Route-1 in Autumn 2019. Some are calling it "technology" and some are calling it "techniques"; the middle ground on this is *"Tech."*

Δ Δ Δ Δ Δ Δ Δ

[‡] Formerly *"International School of Systemology"* (*ISS*).

PROCESS R-1R : ROUTE-1 REVISED (2022) [SYSTEMOLOGY-180 PROCEDURE-R1R]

"Systemology Procedure RR-SP-1" (as based on cuneiform signs) debuted in the premiere edition of "*Tablets of Destiny*" (*Liber-One*)—and is reprinted in the original *Grade-III* mega-anthology "*The Systemology Handbook*" (to which a serious *Seeker* or *Pilot* may still refer to for reference). Although must of the original instruction has been retained, its practice was updated and revised in 2022, after three years of continued experimental research by the *Mardukite Academy of Systemology*, completion of *Grade-III* and *Grade-IV* material, and new developments of *Grade-V*. The first efforts toward revising RR-SP-1 appear as "Systemology Operating Procedure 2-C" (*SOP-2C*) as given in "*Metahuman Destinations*" (*Liber-Two*) for *Grade-IV*. The original steps for RR-SP-1 (based on cuneiform signs[*]) given in the premiere edition are as follows:

1. *US* — "to lead off; accompany; impose a process or path."
2. *TAB* — "to begin; start; fasten/hold level; commence."
3. *GI* — "to return; to go around a corner and back to."
4. *BA* — "to divide; allot; deduce; deduct; reduce."
5. *RA* — "to purify; cleanse; give release or be clear."
6. *DU* — "beingness; to become; to arrive at or ascend."
7. *TEN* — "to stop; end; extinguish or cool down."

The first step is to establish a good communicative energy between *Seeker* and *Pilot*. When "processing" begins, the *Seeker* should be seated comfortably, in a distraction-free environment, across from the *Pilot*, essentially face-to-face, but not touching—at a distance of three feet, since when used professionally there is often a table or desk in between.

---

[*] Translations of cuneiform signs are derived from Mardukite Research Library "*Sumerian Language*" volumes edited by Joshua Free.

Communication is more quickly and easily established with familiarity. A relationship develops between the *Seeker* and *Pilot*. It is favorable if the same *Pilot* continues to assist a *Seeker*, because affinity levels increase. We communicate better with those we feel "close" to and "like." By working with the same *Pilot*, a *Seeker* is assured that the assisting *Pilot* increases their understanding of the *Seeker's* "background." In spite of any records of former processing retained,[‡] the *Pilot* should begin each session simply by establishing communication about the *Seeker's* journey on the *Path*. Session time is not for casual conversation.

The *Pilot* is not to editorialize or educate during these periods. The *Pilot* is simply meant to provide "processing," selectively directing the *Seeker's* attention, completely awake in a state of focused concentration. Any discussion before the session should relate specifically to the *Seeker* and situations that may be currently bothering them at the time. The *Seeker* may even request that a particular incident or *Imprint* be processed during that session. Anything of this nature should be discussed before proceeding; mainly because anything spoken during "processing" should be specific to the "process." "Processing" is not an exploration of the *Seeker's* associative free thought or an opportunity for *Pilots* to relate anecdotal experiences from their own *Life*.

Once a few minutes of initial communication has occurred, it is important for the *Seeker* and *Pilot* to establish an agreement (or validation about Reality) for this session. Aside from this, there is no validation or invalidation to

---

‡ All flight records (of processes) are confidential. Any information from the session should be <u>recorded</u> while it is taking place and <u>retained</u> by the *Pilot* in a *Flight-Log* for that specific *Seeker*. The *Pilot* may record, for training purposes and verification, their personal experience of the session in a separate *Flight-Log* designed to simply keep track of processing-hours ("air time") and critical details. The *Seeker* may also wish to retain record of their own personal experience and realizations in a specially designed *Adventure Journal*. As of 2020, this publication is available from the Systemology Society.

anything that the *Seeker* relates as an experience. There is prompting and redirection if necessary, but no evaluation is expressed; only an acknowledgment of receipt of communication. If during the session, a *Seeker* suddenly comes to some elated realization or asks questions that seek interpretation, the *Pilot* should always put the focus of *Awareness* back on the *Seeker* to examine, such as: "well, what do you think?" or "anything is possible" and then continue the processing steps.

It is assumed that when entering into these processing steps, a *Seeker* has read the *"Tablets of Destiny"* book (and/or *"Crystal Clear: Handbook for Seekers"*) and, for example, knows what an *Imprint* is. Extending a copy of the book to a *Seeker* is the first act by a *Pilot* toward "education." It is assumed that *Seekers* you are first in contact with, those in close proximity to you, are already experienced in some type of visualization and concentration exercises such as demonstrated in previous Grades. If not, then there is some preliminary work that should be done prior to Systemology Processing. A *Pilot* should not engage in assisting Grade instruction unless they have completed *The Complete Mardukite Master* program. A *Master* is entrusted with tools to provide such instruction, but a *Pilot* should not be using "flight time" for education in this way. Formal course materials and Grade instruction are handled separately from Processing Sessions—or combined with books used on the *Seeker's* own time and initiative.

The *Pilot* assures the *Seeker*—in a few words—that they are safe; that they will remain awake and *Aware*; that Systemology "processing" is in no way hypnotherapy. To establish additional trust and agreements, the last statements made by the *Pilot* during this step will be along the lines of: "Now, I'm going to assist you in a process. Would that be fine with you?" Explain the process and defragment any unclear (or unknown) words used for the Processing Command Line. Then: "So, I was thinking of beginning the Processing now. Is that okay?" Every time the *Seeker* provides a response, the *Pilot* acknowledges receipt of the communication: "Okay." "Mm-hmm." "All right." The subject of communication in *Piloting* is covered further in *"Metahuman Destinations"* (*Liber-Two*).

The combined ZU *Awareness* active in both the *Pilot* and *Seeker* simultaneously should be a high enough frequency to handle, surface and reduce *Imprints* safely. When a *Seeker's Awareness* is reduced by *Imprints* during everyday life, their handling of ZU force (energy) is not enough for them to overcome *Imprints*. As a result, we tend to be subdued by them and make poor decisions, which reinforce them with more of our energy and attention. During "processing," they may be intentionally *resurfaced* and exhausted without incident by combining *Awareness* of the *Seeker* and the *Pilot*.

The journey is always upward. Any *Imprints* resurfaced during *cathartic processing* are likely to be already resurfacing in the *Seeker's* daily life from time to time, so there is no danger in simply stimulating them for actual reduction and a sense of release.

Δ Δ Δ Δ Δ Δ Δ

The *Pilot* must wait until the *Seeker* is "present" and "Aware"—securely "buckled in"—before "take-off." This original method of *cathartic processing* begins by entering a state of focused concentration, which for most people experienced with meditation and thought discipline from former Grades, is as simple as closing their eyes. However, it may be that the *Seeker's* current *Awareness* level (on the ZU-line) is providing too much restlessness or withdrawal to use processes requiring elevated levels of *Awareness*. This happens with "subjective processing" all of the time and may be remedied with "objective processing" without breaking the session.[*]

---

[*] See *"Crystal Clear"* (*Liber-2B*) for an introduction to "objective" exercises; and *"Metahuman Destinations"* (*Liber-Two*) introduces "Presence in Space-Time" for SOP-2C.

A common exercise to refocus attention before starting a "process" is for the *Pilot* to have a *Seeker* look around, spot and identify basic objects in the room. This helps orient the *Seeker* to be "in phase." It is very possible during *cathartic processing* that a *Seeker* will move out of phase with *Self* and relive a traumatic experience from the perspective of an alternative *Identity Phase* someone else involved in the original *Imprint*, such as the dominating force (individual) that inflicts the painful experience. This Phase-shift is part of what must be reduced and exhausted as an *Imprint*. It is part of the behavior patterns exhibited when an *Imprint* is stimulated. We often respond as one of the "phases" or "personalities" exhibited in the *Imprint*—and it may be the victim; it may be the domineer; or it may switch between the two. But we must start and end sessions as "Self."

The present author was fortunate, some years back, to find a professional *Abreactive Therapist* to help develop Route-1 properly. For example, at the start of the session, the *Seeker* is instructed to "close their eyes" to establish a state of focused concentration. [The instruction to count down from *seven* has been omitted.] It is important that the *Seeker* respond to the *Pilot's* "Processing Command Lines" to make "processing" work. It is important the the *Pilot* only speaks to the *Seeker* in line with the formula of the "process" and includes no other discussion or "command." A *Pilot* is not commanding the *Seeker* to *do* anything—the *Pilot* is entering input commands to run a "process" that the *Seeker* is responsible for "running" themselves to produce a desired result. Otherwise, we are back to casual conversation, which is not nearly as effective. When the *Seeker's* eyes are closed, the *Pilot* acknowledges that the command has been received and executed ("very good").

The *Pilot's* next statements are very important, to: "start the session," making certain the *Seeker* is presently "in phase" and in good communication. We don't always know where someone is likely to *go* when they close their eyes (for subjective processing), so a *Pilot* needs to be certain the *Seeker* is still consciously "with them" and "in phase" in present space-time.

Then, the *Pilot* assures the *Seeker* that: "At some future point, when I say the phrase *'End of Session'*, anything and everything that has been said and any emotion experienced during this session will have no influence on you, and the session will be ended." Statements like this should end with "Do you understand?" This maintains a clear communication flow.

Δ Δ Δ Δ Δ Δ Δ

The main substance of the Route-1 "process" begins with identification and resurfacing of an *Imprint*: any source of emotional turbulence and fragmentation. [**GSR-Biofeedback** may be used to indicate a "charged" item for processing; as indicated in *Grade-IV*, *"Way of the Wizard"* or *"Metahuman Systemology Handbook."*] This could be a painful experience or some other instance when "shock" encoded an *Imprint* with a sensation, thought (attitude, postulate, belief) or emotional charge. It is likely that the original *Imprint* on a chain of related incidents will not be immediately identified. It may be that the most recent similar instance of difficulty is troubling the *Seeker* and tying up their *Awareness* and attention, but it is linked to older or earlier *Imprinting*.

A *Pilot* is dedicated to assist the *Seeker* in releasing any reactive associations to *Imprints* by *resurfacing* these experiences where the *Imprints* occur. The *Pilot* should not prompt for overly specific data when processing incidents. Simply acknowledge what the *Seeker* says and incite movement through an incident. "Okay. Continue." A *Pilot* should not act doubtful or direct a *Seeker* to validate what they say with "how do you know..." or "what makes you think..." &tc.

The *Pilot's* goal is to bring the *Seeker's* attention back to the earliest instance of similar *facets* or environmental stimulation. The ultimate goal *is* to find the first instance when the *Imprint* was encoded. Each time the *Pilot* is not seeing a reduction in a given *resurfacing*, there is an even earlier time when the facets appear. So, you keep moving the **Backtrack** earlier in time to get the most basic. You can "process" out all instances of restimulation, when the *Seeker* demonstrated some type of irrational response to their environment as part of the *Imprint*—but this is not nearly as effective as "processing" the original or earliest point when the *Imprint* was formed. The most commonly processed *Imprints* are related to fear, loss, pain, rejection and self-worth.

If there was a discussion prior to the session start concerning a recent issue or *Imprint* that restimulated a reactive-response, then the *Pilot* directs the *Seeker's* attention to that channel with: "Locate a time when you ___." Once located, the *Pilot* asks "When" it was and directs the *Seeker* to: "Move to that incident." Wait for an indication that this has happened. If the *Seeker* needs more direction, the *Pilot* may change the command to: "Locate a time when you were first feeling ___" or "Recall the first instance when you experienced ___."

When an instance is finally *located* (or showing "charge" if using *GSR-Biofeedback*), and the *Seeker* has *moved* to it, the *Pilot* asks for the "duration" of the incident—or "How long" the *Imprinting Incident* took place. With this data in hand, the *Pilot* directs (the *Seeker* to close their eyes if they have not and) to: "Move to the beginning of that incident. Tell me when you are there." Once the *Pilot* acknowledges that they have ("Okay") they query: "Tell me what you see." The *Pilot* should acknowledge anything the *Seeker* says and prompt them to "Move through the incident to ___" using the *duration* indicated.

If at any point the *Seeker* appears to be demonstrating physical stress or somatic **pings**, the *Pilot* simply assures them they: "are doing fine. Continue. Tell me what you are seeing." Any physical discomfort or pain stimulated most likely relates to the location where *Imprint* energy has localized on the *genetic vehicle*. It *will* be experienced until it is reduced. Physical sensations are very strong *facets* of an *Imprint*. Any perception in an *Imprint* is a *facet*, which means any associated *facet* may trigger them. It is a *Pilot's* responsibility to assist the *Seeker* in identifying the *facets* holding the energy of an *Imprint* in place. The *Seeker* may be prompted to identify any generalized *facets* in the experience: "what do you see?" or "what do you hear?" or "what do you smell" and so forth. "Move through to the end point." And when the *Seeker* affirms they have, the *Pilot* asks: "What happened?"

Δ Δ Δ Δ Δ Δ Δ

Acknowledging the *Seeker's* narrative is the completion of the first processing cycle. Original instructions for RR-SP-1 prompt a *Seeker* to return to the experience repeatedly in order to discharge it by *catharsis*. There is no predetermined number of times necessary to run out the charge in this way. Each additional time the incident is run through, the *Pilot* performs the same steps as before, except that the *time* and *duration* are not treated again.

A *Pilot* should record all facets and facts, details and statements that the *Seeker* communicates. The *RR-SP-1* instructions indicated that an incident should continue to be run if new information comes through each time; meaning more of the *Imprint* is discharging. This *one* method for applying *Route-1*, selected for the ease of its instruction and application. *Procedure R-1R* recognizes additional *Piloting* knowledge earned during the three years since *Route-1* was first published for open-experimentation by the Systemology Society.

During intensive sessions, *language facets* associated with the *Imprint* are sometimes vocalized by the *Seeker*—demonstrating the extent of *Imprint* blockage. They may even speak in the "phase" of someone else from the *Imprint* (incident). Negative language *Imprints* are often held in place by similar statements said at the time of the *Imprint*. Statements such as "I can't do this" or "this isn't working" or "this is never going to work" or "just forget it" or "I'm never going to get out of this"—these may actually be a part of what was said during the *Imprint* and not simply a statement made by the *Seeker* "in phase" as themselves regarding their attitude about the current "process" taking place. The *Pilot* should recognize this, reducing the *language facet* of the *Imprint* by having the *Seeker* "go over it again"—repeating the statement many times until it turns on more *facets* and/or they realize what "phase" or "facade" they are wearing when this statement runs on a circuit as an *Imprint* response.

Δ Δ Δ Δ Δ Δ Δ

"*Route-1*" techniques require running (processing) an *Imprint* until the "emotional charge" is reduced and the *Seeker* experiences a release from the *Imprint* and its fragmentation. Emotional release is a critical component of the "process." Any *facets* described from each run through should be recorded. They may assist the *Pilot* in returning the *Seeker* to earlier instances in life where a similar situation (or even a similar *facet*) is present. Understand that we are targeting *Imprints*, not situations. The same *Imprint* is likely to have resurfaced in many instances of day-to-day life, under varying circumstances. This is another reason why only one *Imprint* should be the target of an individual session—because in the course of chasing down the *first* Imprinting Incident, a *Seeker* may have to "return to the beginning of the incident and move through to the end" several times where it is finally confronted.

After one or two runs through an incident, the *Pilot* needs to determine if the "charge" on the line is *rising* or *falling*—which can be determined by a "*rise*" or "*fall*" of electrical resistance (*Ohms*) when using *GSR-Biofeedback.** The *Pilot* may also ask if the *Imprint* is "reducing or getting more solid." If the charge is reducing, then continue to run through it. If the incident is *not* reducing, then the incident begins earlier—*or* the incident is connected on a chan-

---

* Refer to *Grade-IV "The Way of the Wizard."*

nel-line of related *Imprinting*, meaning the actual incident that is necessary to resolve the "charge" on this channel takes place at an earlier time (sometimes even prior to the present incarnation). The earliest similar event is the *Imprinting Incident* that unravels the fragmentation on the entire channel.

"Process time" may be reduced by finding the earliest instance of an *Imprint*, clear and simple. An incident is usually run through twice. Not only does this take some charge off the line, but it allows a *Seeker* to more easily locate earlier incidents on the channel. Once located, any perceived *facet* should be processed—sights; smells; tastes; feelings; humidity; even brightness. The *Imprint* is consciously and intentionally given full attention to reduce the entire charge of fragmentation.

Emotional levels of *Awareness* can initially dip quite low during *Route-1* Imprint Processing—then the ability to cope increases and finally moves up the *ZU-line* to the MCC (range) when *Imprinted* fragmentation is reduced and emotional release is experienced. Don't be surprised if this release is in the form of laughter, vibrancy and enthusiasm. We are not invalidating what has happened to an individual; we are extinguishing its emotional pull on us. If possible, the exact *Alpha Thought* or "postulate" that the *Imprint* inspired (or incited) should be identified in order to also properly free up intellectual considerations directly associated with the *Imprint.*

We can be *imprinted*, for example, with an idea that we are "not any good" and we may go into a *phase* of being the thing that is "not any good." Alternatively we display hostility in times when the *Imprint* is stimulated by shifting to another "phase"—telling others that they are "no good." If statements such as "it's no good" come up in Processing, they should be exhausted as part of the *Imprint*—they are not actually statements *about* the "process."

Δ Δ Δ Δ Δ Δ Δ

Successful *catharsis* occurs when the *Seeker* is able to arrive at the highest level of being in their ability to confront the *Imprint*. The *Seeker* may experience sighs, yawns, tear-swells, chuckling, and eventually a higher "realization" or "actualization" point. This is the critical "destination" that the *Pilot* is assisting the *Seeker* to arrive at. The *Seeker* arrives at a new degree (or state) of realization about themselves, actualization (as *Awareness*) of their previous response-reactions—they have "arrived" or "ascended" to a new state of *Beingness*. This point of "ascension" or "becoming" is critical in order to complete the "process."

Procedure R-1R takes *Route-2* and *Route-3* developments into consideration.‡ In view of this fact, and in view of our first revision of Standard Procedure—*SOP-2C*—there are additional tools a *Pilot* may incorporate with *R-1R* in order to fully "clear the channel" (particularly if the earliest *Imprinting Incident* is difficult to contact or is not reducing). The most appropriate is processing analytical recall of all "three circuits" on a channel—prompting a *Seeker* to also locate incidents when they "caused another ___" or when they observed "others causing others ___." Upper-route methods also include times when they "causing yourself ___." These methods are particularly useful when there are sensations (pains and pings) triggered by *Imprints* on a fragmented channel. When incidents are not readily located, *imagined* ones may be substituted to simply "run out" considerations on that channel and potentially resurface related memories.

A *Pilot* should not mistake being "stuck" with "deep processing" where a *Seeker* may go silent for long periods of time. When a *Seeker* is stuck, the *Pilot's* skills may assist pushing through; but sometimes it is not a matter of skill or technique. It may be that an individual's *Awareness* level is up high enough to resurface and reduce a complete *Imp-*

---

‡   *Route-2* is introduced in "*Crystal Clear*" (also reprinted in "*The Systemology Handbook*"); *Route-3* is introduced in "*Metahuman Destinations* (also reprinted in "*The Metahuman Systemology Handbook*").

rint in one session. Sometimes the information necessary to resolve the *Imprint* is not surfacing, even with repetitive returns and scanning the *Backtrack*. Some things can get buried deeply. In this instance, restimulation due to Processing will usually cause what was not uncovered during the session to emerge within a few days *after* the session. Therefore, the same *Imprint* should be "processed" two or three days later.

A heightened state of beingness must be established for the Processing to be successful. Sessions should never be "flown" in such a way as to simply strengthen or reinforce an *Imprint*. The previous steps to returning and reducing should be "flown" so long as new attention is being discharged. Statements may be "flown" so long as they are leading to a phase shift or to uncover a new *facet* or earlier similar incident, but otherwise the general ZU-state of the *Seeker* should increase once the entire *Imprint* is laid out and "flown over" a few times.

Δ Δ Δ Δ Δ Δ Δ

Assuming the *Seeker* has reached a critical point of *Imprint* reduction or End-Point, the *Pilot's* final steps are considered Landing Procedures. If the *Seeker* has reached this point on this leg of their journey, they should be informed that: "Okay then, we are going to pick this up at a later time. Is that okay with you?" They may agree readily to this or they may be hesitant. This suggestion by the *Pilot* is not made in haste (or impatience); it is a decision that requires wisdom. If the *Seeker* is hesitant, the *Pilot* may restate: "I understand, more may come to the surface later." And then the *Pilot* should elevate the *Seeker's* Zu-levels (*Awareness*) with light analytical recall (*Route-2*): "a time when you felt vibrant"; "a time when you were enjoying life"; "a time you were winning"; &tc. Finally the *Pilot* solidifies trust (established during opening procedures) by stating: "End of session."

.: APPENDIX A :.
THE ENUMA ELIŠ (c. 2160 B.C.)*
[TABLETS I—VI.a]

ENUMA ELIŠ SERIES – TABLET I

When in the heights the Heavens had not been named,
And the Earth had not yet been named,
And the primeval Abyss, ABZU, who birthed them,
And CHAOS, TIAMAT, the LAW,
The Ancient One, Mother to them all.
Their waters were as One and no field was formed,
No marsh was to be seen;
When of the gods none had been called into being,
And none bore a name, and no destinies were ordained;
Then were created the celestial gods in the midst of heaven,
LAHMU and LAHAMU were called into being
And the Ages increased.
Then ANSAR and KISAR were created,
And the god ANU then came forth who begot ENKI.
Abounding in all wisdom he had no rival.
Thus the Great Gods were established.
But TIAMAT and APSU were still in confusion,
Troubled and in disorder.
ABZU was not diminished in might, and TIAMAT roared.
ABZU, the begetter of the great gods,
Cried unto MUMMU, his minister,
"MUMMU, thou minister that causes my spirit to rejoice,
Come with me to TIAMAT."
So they went and consulted on a plan with regard to the gods,
  their sons.
ABZU spoke: "Let me destroy their ways, let there be
  lamentation,
And then let us lie down again in peace."
When TIAMAT heard these words, she raged and cried aloud.
She uttered a curse and unto ABZU she asked:
"What then shall we do?"
MUMMU answered giving counsel unto ABZU,
"Come, their way is strong, but you can destroy it;
This day you shall have rest, by night shalt thou lie down in

---

*   Excerpted from *"The Complete Anunnaki Bible."*

peace."
They banded themselves together
And at the side of TIAMAT they advanced; they were furious;
They devised mischief without resting night and day.
They prepared for battle, fuming and raging;
They joined their forces and made weapons invincible;
She spawned monster-serpents, sharp of tooth, and merciless
    of fang;
With poison, instead of blood, she filled their bodies.
Fierce monster-vipers she clothed with terror.
With splendor she clothed them, she made them of lofty
    stature.
Whoever beheld them, terror overcame him,
Their bodies reared up and none could withstand their
    attack.
She set up vipers and dragons, and the monster LAHAMU.
And hurricanes, and raging hounds, and scorpion-men,
And mighty tempests, and fish-men, and rams;
They bore cruel weapons, without fear of the fight.
Her commands were mighty, none could resist them;
After this fashion she made eleven kinds of monsters.
Among the gods who were her sons,
Inasmuch as he had given her support,
She exalted KINGU; in their midst she raised him to power.
To march before the forces, to lead the host,
To give the battle-signal, to advance to the attack,
To direct the battle, to control the fight,
Unto him she entrusted, saying: "I have uttered thy spell,
In the assembly of the gods I have raised thee to power.
The dominion over all the gods have I entrusted unto him.
Be thou exalted, you are my chosen spouse,
May your name be magnified among all ANUNNAKI."
She gave him the **Tablets of Destiny**, on his breast she laid
    them,
Saying: "Thy command shall not be in vain,
And your decrees shall be established."
Now KINGU, thus exalted, having received the power of ANU,
Decreed the fate among the gods his sons,
Saying: "Let the opening of your mouth quench the Fire-god;
He who is exalted in the battle, let him display his might!"

ENUMA ELIŠ SERIES – TABLET II

TIAMAT made weighty her handiwork,
Evil she wrought against the gods her children.
To avenge ABZU, TIAMAT planned evil,
But how she had collected her forces, the god unto ENKI
   divulged.
ENKI was grievously afflicted and he sat in sorrow.
The days went by, and his anger was appeased,
And to the place of ANSAR his father he took his way.
He went and, standing before ANSAR, his father,
All that TIAMAT had plotted he repeated unto him,
Saying "TIAMAT, our mother hath conceived a hatred for us,
With all her force she rages, full of wrath.
All the gods have turned to her,
With those, whom you created, they go to her side.
They have banded together and at the side of TIAMAT
And they advance; they are furious,
They devise mischief without resting night and day.
They prepare for battle, fuming and raging;
They have joined their forces and are making war.
TIAMAT, who formed all things,
And made weapons invincible;
She hath spawned monster-serpents,
Sharp of tooth, and merciless of fang.
With poison, instead of blood, she hath filled their bodies.
Fierce monster-vipers she hath clothed with terror,
With splendor she has armed them;
She has made them tall in stature.
Whoever beholds them is overcome by terror,
Their bodies rear up and none can withstand their attack.
She hath set up vipers, and dragons, and the monster
   LAHAMU,
And hurricanes and raging hounds, and scorpion-men,
And mighty tempests, and fish-men and rams;
They bear cruel weapons, without fear of the fight.
Her commands are mighty; none can resist them;
After this fashion, huge of stature,
She has made eleven kinds of monsters.
Among the gods who are her sons,
Inasmuch as he has given her support,

She has exalted KINGU;
In their midst she hath raised him to power.
To march before the forces, to lead the host,
To give the battle-signal, to advance to the attack.
To direct the battle, to control the fight,
To him she has uttered your spell;
She hath given to him the **Tablets of Destiny**,
On his breast she laid hem,
Saying: 'Thy command shall not be in vain,
And the your word shall be established.'
"O my father, let not the word of thy lips be overcome,
Let me go, that I may accomplish all that is in thy heart.
  I shall avenge."

ENUMA ELIŠ SERIES – TABLET III

ANSAR spoke to his minister:
"O GAGA, thou minister who causes my spirit to rejoice,
Unto LAHMU and LAHAMU I will send thee.
Make ready for a feast, at a banquet let them sit,
Let them eat bread, let them mix wine,
That for MARDUK, the avenger, they may decree the fate.
Go, GAGA, stand before them, And all that I tell thee,
Repeat unto them, and say: 'ANSAR, your son, has sent me,
The purpose of his heart he has made known unto me.
He said TIAMAT, our mother, has conceived a hatred for us,
With all her force she rages full of wrath.
All the gods have turned to her, with those, whom you
   created,
They go to her side. I sent ANU, but he could not withstand
   her;
ENKI was afraid and turned back.
But MARDUK has set out, the champion of the gods, your son;
To set out against TIAMAT his heart has called him.
He opened his mouth and spake unto me,
Saying: 'If I, your avenger, Conquer TIAMAT and give you life,
Appoint an assembly, make my fate preeminent and proclaim
   it so.
In UPSUKKINAKU seat yourself joyfully together;
With my word in place I will decree fate.
May whatsoever I do remain unaltered,

May the word of my lips never be changed nor made of no
    avail.'
Quickly decree for him the fate which you bestow
So that he may go and fight your strong enemy."
GAGA went humbly before LAHMU and LAHAMU, the gods,
His fathers, and he kissed the ground at their feet.
He humbled himself; then stood up and spoke to them saying:
"ANSAR, your son, has sent me,
The purpose of his heart he hath made known unto me.
He says that TIAMAT, our mother, hath conceived a hatred
    for us,
With all her force she rages full of wrath."
And he spoke the words of the tale.
LAHMU and LAHAMU heard and cried aloud.
All of the IGIGI wailed bitterly, saying:
"We do not understand the deeds of TIAMAT!"
Then did they collect and go,
The great gods, all of them, the ANUNNAKI who decree fate.
They entered in the House of ANSAR, kissed one another,
They made ready for the feast, ate bread,
And they mixed sesame-wine.
They were wholly at ease, their spirit was exalted;
Then for MARDUK, their avenger, they decreed the fate.

ENUMA ELIŠ SERIES – TABLET IV

The ANUNNAKI prepared for MARDUK a lordly chamber,
Before his fathers as prince he took his place.
"MARDUK, You are now chief among the great gods,
Thy fate is unequaled, thy word is ANU.
Your words shall be command,
In your power shall it be to exalt and to abase.
None among the gods shall transgress your boundary.
Abundance, shall exist in thy sanctuary shrine,
Even if you lack offerings.
MARDUK, you are our avenger!
We give you sovereignty over the whole world.
Sit down in might; be exalted in thy command.
Your weapon shall never lose its power; it shall crush your
    enemy.
Lord, spare the life of him that puts his trust in thee,

But as for the god who began the rebellion, empty them of
  life."
The ANUNNAKI set out a garment
And continued to speak to MARDUK.
"May thy fate, O lord, be supreme among the gods,
To destroy and to create; speak only the word,
And your command shall be fulfilled.
Command now that the garment vanish;
And speak the word again and let the garment reappear!"
Then he spake the words and the garment vanished;
Again he commanded it and the garment reappeared.
When the gods, his fathers, beheld the fulfillment of his word,
They rejoiced, and they did homage unto him,
Saying, "Maerdechai! Maerdechai! MARDUK is king!"
They bestowed upon him the scepter, the throne and ring,
They give him invincible weaponry to overwhelm the enemy.
"Go, and cut off the life of TIAMAT," they said.
"And let the wind carry her blood into secret places."
MARDUK made ready the bow, his first choice in weapon,
He slung a spear upon him.
He raised the club in his right hand.
The bow and the quiver he hung at his side.
He set the FLAMING DISC in front of him
And with the flame he filled his body.
He fashioned a net to enclose the inward parts of TIAMAT,
He stationed the four winds so that nothing of her might
  escape;
The South wind and the North wind and the East wind
And the West wind He created the evil wind,
And the tempest, and the hurricane,
And the fourfold wind,
And the sevenfold wind, and the cyclone,
And the wind which had no equal;
He sent forth the winds which he had created, seven in total;
To disturb the inward parts of TIAMAT.
Then MARDUK raised the thunderbolt, mounted the chariot,
A storm unequaled for terror, and he harnessed four horses
Named DESTRUCTION, FEROCITY, TERROR,
And SWIFTNESS; and foam came from their mouths
And they were mighty in battle,
Trained to trample underfoot.

With garments cloaked in terror and an overpowering
  brightness
Crowning his head, MARDUK set out toward the raging
  TIAMAT.
Then the gods beheld him.
And when the lord drew near,
He gazed upon the inward parts of TIAMAT,
He heard the muttering of KINGU, her spouse.
As MARDUK gazed, KINGU was troubled,
The will of KINGU was destroyed and his motions ceased.
And the gods, his helpers, who marched by his side,
Beheld their leader's fear and their sight was troubled.
But TIAMAT did not turn her neck.
She spit rebellious words.
MARDUK raised the thunderbolt,
His mighty weapon, against TIAMAT,
Who was raging, and he called out:
"You have become great as you have exalted yourself on
  high,
And your heart has prompted you to call to battle.
You have raised KINGU to be your spouse,
You have chosen Evil and sinned against ANU and his decree.
And against the gods, my fathers,
You have dedicated yourself to a wicked plan.
Let us now face off in battle then!"
When TIAMAT heard these words,
She acted possessed and lost her sense of reason.
She screamed wild, piercing cries,
She trembled and shook to her very foundations.
She recited an incantation, and cast a spell,
And the gods of the battle cried out for their weapons.
Then TIAMAT and MARDUK advanced towards one another,
The battle drew near.
Lord MARDUK spread out his net and caught her,
And the evil wind he gathered behind him and let loose in her
Face when she opened her mouth fully.
The terrible winds filled her belly,
And her courage was taken from her,
And her mouth opened wider.
MARDUK seized the spear and burst her belly,
Severing her inward parts, he pierced her heart.

He overcame her and cut off her life;
He cast down her body and stood upon it.
After slaying TIAMAT, the leader of the ANCIENT ONES,
The might was broken and her minions scattered.
But they were surrounded, so that they could not escape.
MARDUK took them captive and broke their weapons;
In the net they were caught and in the snare they sat down.
And on the eleven monsters which she had filled
With the power of striking terror, he brought them affliction,
Their strength he stole and their opposition
He trampled under his feet.
From KINGU who he had conquered,
He rightly took the **Tablets of Destiny**,
And sealed them with his seal, then hung them from his neck.
Now after MARDUK had conquered and cast down his
    enemies,
And had fully established ANSAR's triumph over the enemy,
And had attained the purpose of ENKI,
Over the captive gods he strengthened his position,
And he returned to the conquered TIAMAT.
With his merciless club he smashed her skull.
He cut through the channels of her blood,
And he made the North wind steal it away
Outside in secret places between spaces.
His fathers beheld, and rejoiced and were glad;
Presents and gifts they brought unto him.
Then Lord MARDUK rested, gazing upon her dead body
And devised a cunning plan.
He split her up like a flat fish into two halves;
One half of her he established a covering for heaven.
Sealed with a GATE he stationed a WATCHER IAK SAKKAK
And fixed him not to let her waters to ever come forth.
MARDUK passed through and surveyed the regions of
    Heaven,
And over the Deep he set the dwelling of ENKI.
And after measuring the structure of the Deep,
He founded his Mansion,
Which was created likened to Heaven and he set down
The fixed districts for ANU, ENLIL and ENKI to reign.

ENUMA ELIŠ SERIES – TABLET V

MARDUK fixed the Star Gates of the Elder Gods;
And the stars he gave images as the stars of the Zodiac,
which he fixed in place.
He ordained the year and into sections he divided it;
For the twelve months he fixed the stars.
He founded his Star Gate on NIBIRU to fix them in zones;
That none might rebel or go astray,
He fixed the Star Gate of ENLIL
And ENKI alongside him.
He opened great gates on both sides,
He made strong gates on the left and on the right
And in the midst thereof he fixed the zenith;
He fixed the Star Gate for the Moon-god
And decreed that he shine forth,
Trusting him with the night and to determine days;
The first of the great gates he assigned to NANNA-SIN,
And perpetually, every month he would be crowned, saying:
"At the beginning of the month, when you shine down upon
    the land,
You command the trumpets of the six days of the moon,
And on the seventh day you will divide the crown.
On the fourteenth day you will stand opposite as half-moon.
When the Sun-god of the foundation of heaven calls thee,
On that the final day again you will stand as opposite.
All shall go about the course I fix.
You will drawn near to judge the righteous
And destroy the unrighteous.
That is my decree and the covenant of the first gate."
The gods, his fathers, beheld the net which MARDUK had
    fashioned,
They beheld his bow and how its work was accomplished.
They praised the work which he had done and then ANU
    raised up
And kissed the bow before the assembly of the gods.
And thus he named the names of the bow, saying:
"Long-wood shall be one name,
And the second name shall be Dragonslayer,
And its third name shall be the Bow-star,
In heaven shall it remain as a sign to all."

Then ANU and MARDUK fixed a Star Gate for it too,
And after the ANUNNAKI decreed the fates for the ANCIENT
  ONES,
MARDUK set a throne in heaven for himself at ANU's right
  hand.

ENUMA ELIŠ SERIES – TABLET VI.a

The ANUNNAKI acclaimed him "First among the ELDER
  GODS."
MARDUK heard the praises of the gods,
His heart called to him to devised a cunning plan.
He approached ENKI saying:
"The Key to the GATE shall be ever hidden, except to my
  offspring.
I will take my blood and with bone I will fashion a Race of
  Men,
That they may keep watch over the GATE.
And from the blood of KINGU I will create a race of men,
That they will inhabit the Earth in service to the gods
So that our shrines may be built and the temples filled.
But I will alter the ways of the gods, and I will change their
  paths;
Together shall they be oppressed
And unto evil shall they no longer reign.
I will bind the ELDER GODS to the WATCHTOWERS,
Let them keep watch over the GATE of ABZU,
And the GATE of TIAMAT and the GATE of KINGU.
I bind the WATCHER IAK SAKKAK to the GATE
With the Key known only to my Race.
Let none enter that GATE
Since to invoke DEATH is to utter the final prayer."
The ANUNNAKI rejoiced and set their mansions in
  UPSUKKINAKU.
When all this had been done, the Elders of the ANUNNAKI
Seated themselves around MARDUK
And in their assembly they exalted him
And named him FIFTY times,
Bestowing upon him the FIFTY powers of the gods.

.: APPENDIX B :.
MARDUK'S TABLET OF DESTINY

an-bala ki-bala an-ba ki an-ba
As above, so below; On earth, as it is in heaven.

da-ga nam-ku-zu d-Lamma a bi-ib-gar
What the mind believes, the spirit reinforces.

nig-ku-lam-ma dingir-ra-na-ka su—tu-tu nu-ub-zu
When disaster is self-made, no man can interfere.

nig-gu-gar-ra nig-gaba-gar-ra
What is given in submission is a catalyst for defiance.

nig-ge-na-ta a-ba in-da-di nam-ti i-u-tu
Whoever partners with Truth, creates Life.

.: APPENDIX C :.
"SAJAHA" TABLET EXCERPTS (c. 580 B.C.)*
[TABLETS I–V]

SAJAHA SERIES – TABLET I

1. There are vibrations and energy flows of different types and strength; everywhere and in everything and in everyone.
2. For everything and also for all people, there exists a permanent force in a sea of cosmic vibrations and energy currents; equal to a large lake, which is composed of many different seas in itself.
3. Everything emerges from, and everyone experiences reality from, oceans of vibrations and energetic flows that incessantly emit a field and reproduce by itself; but without ability to determine anything about any of these things—often without even noticing.
4. It is participation in *games* of vibration and energy currents that challenge everyone to maintain a high degree of purity to remain close to the Source of All Being—the *All-as-One*—from which people have become almost entirely lost since the demise of the original empire. And the descendants have lost most of the old power.
5. It has come to be—in times being what they are—especially in that which pertains to the subtle vibrating Force flowing unobserved, that powers are directed only to a small extent of their potential, never really mastered or used conveniently.
6. The qualities and abilities of our ancestors, necessary for mastery of high power—Divine Right on Earth—are diluted among descendants today—no longer among the population.

SAJAHA SERIES – TABLET II

4. From the knowledge of eternity-in-infinity, I have drawn a circle with my stylus on a tablet. What is the meaning of this?
5. Everything is in that world, which also applies in this one —and there are still a thousand times more.
6. The circle marked shows nothing more than a small image of the *Great All.*

---

*   Excerpted from *"The Complete Anunnaki Bible."*

7. Where is the start? Where is the end? What makes one thing different from another? How is the circle at the beginning and end of [All] this!?

8. They are the beginning and the end; one as the other.

9. Whatever you start in the earth world is not separate; it significantly and necessarily has its higher counterpart in the other world.

10. By drawing the circle with the stylus on the tablet, a self-contained line is demonstrated, according to its kind, neither beginning nor ending and yet we can behold its existence!

11. So it is with the great cycle of eternity-in-infinity: eternally connected is *All-as-One* from the beginning to the end.

SAJAHA SERIES – TABLET III

1. Much has been, much will be, and in between what has been and what will be coming, is the *kNow*.

2. But this *kNow* is but always only a half-breath, and there is no scale by which to measure it.

3. MARDUK, surveyor of everything, who added to the people's knowledge, the *kNow*, the power of eternity-in-infinity.

4. MARDUK sees the beginning and the end. In between, he sees the people on earth, they can not believe what they behold of the gods.

6. MARDUK sets forth the *Way-of-the-Walking* for the *Seekers*. Choose your *Pathway* and guide the people.

7. The compassionate eye of MARDUK gazes upon an erring race, creation of the gods. He shines upon the right way to go. He gives advice only. The *Seeker* is never forced on the *Path*.

SAJAHA SERIES – TABLET IV

4. But if in sleep, the inner [*alpha*] body is lifted from the outer, then you have dreams.

5. Because it is so that the inner body is linked back to the *alpha* state, the outer (surface) world, the *afterbirth*, is here and now All-as-One in the world. The cloak of form is temporary and hence, sleep.

10. From the point of the [*alpha*] spirit as *Observer*, he sees the essence of the earthly [*physical*] world in (*self-honest*) truth; nothing is hidden from him; all thoughts are laid before him;

the veil of glamour is lifted. And what you realize you from there, is that which is truly valuable knowledge.

13. The mind, due to its own nature, does not look for random paths; it seeks what it lacks. It *craves* to *kNow*.

SAJAHA SERIES – TABLET V

1. Through the astral [*stars*] sky I flew like an eagle in the azure blue night, which is a different night than the night of the earth, and constantly endures [*as the astral or starry sky*].

2. I learned to control my [*astral*] wings; nowhere and everywhere—at once—I found the boundary. I beheld the earthly [*physical*] world in a torrential sea of currents—such as you do not see from this *side*, which is not so much looked upon but *felt*: You were there—*All-as-One*—and your [*alpha*] spirit came down to the earthly [*physical*] world, and embraced the *genetic vehicle* occupied, and have kept your survival there/here as the necessary basis for life/awareness.

3. The images before me: the earthly [*physical*] world was not so large, and the stars were not so small, and while many were similar, they were all different from each other. There were [*star*] worlds red and yellow, blue and green, white and also those of nearly black. There were others of variegated colors. Some radiate such intense light out of themselves that I could not perceive their form. Others were of a different kind altogether of which I have no words to describe.

4. I beheld a vision of the sun, that which shone down upon the earth; bright and hot and glowing like gold. Then, I saw the moon, ruler of the night as it would seem from Earth. All about I saw the earth [*physical*] world suspended on imperceptible strings—like the sun's rays.

5. And the vibrations carried me back through sparkling lights and darkness—in alternation - and I do not know where. And then I saw another earth-like world; both familiar and yet alien at the same time. I descended. The sky was a bluish red, and there was no daylight other than this moonlight formed by the luminance of two moons.

6. Then a storm whirled and spun me around, and my hair caught in the vibrations and then it ceased to roar and was quieted. I floated home, past other worlds: the night, the dark, the blue, took me back...

SYSTEMOLOGY GLOSSARY
TABLETS OF DESTINY EDIT

A-for-A (one-to-one) : an expression meaning that what we say, write, represent, think or symbolize is a direct and perfect reflection or duplication of the actual aspect or thing—that "A" is for, means and is equivalent to "A" and not "a" or "q" or "!"; in the relay of communication, the message or particle is sent and perfectly duplicate in form and meaning when received.

aberration : a departure from what is right; in chromatic light science, the failure of a mirror, lens or refracting surface to produce an exact "*one-to-one*" or "*A-for-A*" duplication between an object and its image; a deviation from, or distortion in, what is true or right or straight; in *NexGen Systemology*, a term to describe *fragmentation* as it applies to an individual, which causes them to "stray" form the *Pathway*.

abreaction : the "burn off" or "purging" or "discharge" of "unconscious" (reactive response) as applied to early 20th century German psychology, from *abreagieren*, meaning "coming down from a release or expression of a repressed or forgotten emotion; in *NexGen Systemology*, fully "resurfacing" traumatic past experiences consciously (on one's own determinism) in order to purge them of their emotional excess (or "charge"); also "*Route-1*" and "*catharsis.*"

acid-test : a metaphor refers to a chemical process of applying harsh nitric acid to a golden substance (sample) to determine its genuineness; in *NexGen Systemology*, an extreme conclusive process to determine the reality, genuineness or truth of a substance, material, particle or piece of information.

actualization : to make actual, not just potential; to bring into full solid Reality; to realize fully in *Awareness* as a "thing."

affinity : the apparent and energetic *relationship* between substances or bodies; the degree of *attraction* or repulsion between things based on natural forces; the *similitude* of frequencies or waveforms; the degree of *interconnection* between systems.

agreement (reality) : unanimity of opinion of what is "thought" to be known; an accepted arrangement of how things are; things we consider as "real" or as an "is" of "reality"; a consensus of what is real as made by standard-issue (common) participants; what an individual contributes to or accepts as "real"; in *Nex-Gen Systemology*, a synonym for *"reality."*

alpha : the first, primary, basic, superior or beginning of some form; in *NexGen Systemology*, referring to the state of existence operating on spiritual archetypes and postulates, will and intention "exterior" to the low-level condensation and solidarity of energy and matter as the 'physical universe'.

alpha-spirit : a "spiritual" *Life*-form; the "true" *Self* or I-AM; the *individual*; the spiritual (*alpha*) *Self* that is animating the (*beta*) physical body or *"genetic vehicle"* using a continuous *Lifeline* of spiritual ("*ZU*") energy; an individual spiritual (*alpha*) entity possessing no physical mass or measurable waveform (motion) in the Physical Universe as itself, so it animates the (*beta*) physical body or *"genetic vehicle"* as a catalyst to experience *Self*-determined causality in effect within the *Physical Universe*; a singular unit or point of *Spiritual Awareness* that is *Aware* that it is *Aware*.

amplitude : the quality of being *ample*; the size or amount of energy that is demonstrated in a *wave*. In the case of audio waves, we associate amplitude with "volume." It is not a statement about the frequencies of waves, only how "loud" they are —to what extent they are or may be projected (or audible).

AN : an ancient "Sumerian" cuneiform sign for Heaven or "God"; in *Mardukite Zuism and Systemology* designating the *'spiritual zone'* (or *'Alpha Existence'*); the *Spiritual Universe*— comprised of spiritual matter and spiritual energy; a direction of motion toward spiritual *Infinity*, away from or superior to the physical (*'KI'*); the spiritual condition of existence providing for our primary *Alpha* state as an individual *Identity* or *I-AM-Self* which interacts and experiences *Awareness* of a *beta* state in the *Physical Universe* (*'KI'*) as *Life*.

Ancient Mystery School : the original arcane source of all esoteric knowledge on Earth, concentrated between the Middle East and modern-day Turkey and Transylvania c. 6000 B.C. and then dispersing south (Mesopotamia), west (Europe) and east (Asia) from that location.

apparent : visibly exposed to sight; evident rather than actual, as presumed by Observation; readily perceived, especially by the senses.

archetype : a "first form" or ideal conceptual model of some aspect; the ultimate prototype of a form on which all other conceptions are based.

ascension : actualized *Awareness* elevated to the point of true "spiritual existence" exterior to *beta existence*. An "Ascended Master" is one who has returned to an incarnation on Earth as an inherently *Enlightened One*, demonstrable in their actions—they have the ability to *Self-direct* the "Spirit" as *Self*, just as we are treating the "Mind" and "Body" at this current grade of instruction; previously treated in *Moroii ad Vitam* as a state of Beingness after *First Death*, experienced by an *etheric body*, which is able to maintain consciousness as a personal identity continuum with the same *Self-directed* control and communication of Will-Intention that is exercised, actualized and developed deliberately during one's present incarnation.

assumption : the act of taking or gathering to one's Self; taking possession of, receive or behold.

attention : active use of *Awareness* toward a specific aspect or thing; the act of "attending" with the presence of *Self*; a direction of focus or concentration of *Awareness* along a particular channel or conduit or toward a particular terminal node or communication termination point; the Self-directed concentration of personal energy as a combination of observation, thought-waves and consideration; focused application of *Self-Directed Awareness*.

Babylonian : the ancient Mesopotamian civilization that evolved from *Sumer*; inception point for systematization of civic society and religion.

Backtrack : to retrace one's steps or go back to an early point in a sequence; an applied spiritual philosophy within *Metahuman Systemology* "*Wizard Grades*" regarding continuous existence of an individual's "*Spiritual Timeline*" through all lifetime-incarnations; the course that is already laid behind us; a methodology of systematic processing methods developed to assist in revealing "hidden" *Mental Images* and *Imprints* from one's past and reclaim attention-energies "left behind" with them by increasing ability to manage and control personal energy mechanisms fixed to their continuous automated creation.

beta (awareness) : all consciousness activity ("*Awareness*") in the "Physical Universe" (KI) or else *beta-existence*; *Awareness* within the range of the *genetic-body*, including material thoughts, emotional responses and physical motors; personal *Awareness* of physical energy and physical matter moving through physical space and experienced as "time"; the *Awareness* held by *Self* that is restricted to a physical organic *Lifeform* or "*genetic vehicle*" in which it experiences causality in the *Physical Universe*.

beta (existence) : all manifestation in the "Physical Universe" (KI); the "Physical" state of existence consisting of vibrations of physical energy and physical matter moving through physical space and experienced as "time"; the conditions of *Awareness* for the *Alpha-spirit* (*Self*) as a physical organic *Lifeform* or "*genetic vehicle*" in which it experiences causality in the *Physical Universe*.

biological unconsciousness : the organism independent of the sentient *Awareness* of the *Self* to direct it; states induced by severe injury and anesthesia.

biomagnetic/biofeedback : a measurable effect, such as a change in electrical resistance, that is produced by thoughts, emotions and physical behaviors which generate specific 'neuro-transmitters' and biochemical reactions in the brain, body and across the skin surface.

cacophony : dissonant, turbulent, harsh and/or discordant sound or noise.

catalog / catalogue : a systematic list of knowledge or record of data.

catalyst : something that causes action between two systems or aspects, but which itself is unaffected as a variable of this energy communication; a medium or intermediary channel.

catharsis / cathartic processing : from the Greek root meaning "pure" or "perfect"; Gnostic practices of "consolamentum" where an individual removes distorting/fragmented emotional charges and encoding from a personal energy flow/circuit connected or associated with some terminal, mass, thing, *&tc.*; in *NexGen Systemology*, the emptying out or discharge of emotional stores; also "*abreaction*" or "*Route-1*."

causative : as being the cause; to be at cause.

chakra : an archaic Sanskrit term for "wheel" or "spinning circle" used in *Eastern* wisdom traditions, spiritual systems and mysticism; a concept retained in NexGen Systemology to indicate etheric concentrations of energy into wheel-mechanisms that process *ZU* energy at specific frequencies along the *ZU-line*, of which the *Human Condition* is reportedly attached *seven* at various degrees as connected to the Gate symbolism.

channel : a specific stream, course, current, direction or route; to form or cut a groove or ridge or otherwise guide along a specific course; a direct path; an artificial aqueduct created to connect two water bodies or water or make travel possible.

charge : to fill or furnish with a quality; to supply with energy; to lay a command upon; in *NexGen Systemology*—to imbue with intention; to overspread with emotion; application of *Self-directed (WILL)* "intention" toward an emotional manifestation in beta-existence; personal energy stores and significances entwined as fragmentation in mental images, reactive-response encoding and intellectual (and/or) programmed beliefs; in traditional mysticism, to intentionally fix an energetic resonance to meet some degree, or to bring a specific concentration of energy that is transferred to a focal point, such as an object or space.

chronologically : concerning or pertaining to "time"; to treat as "units" of "time" ; to sequence a series of events or information with regard to the order it happened or originated (in time).

codification : process of collecting, analyzing and then arranging knowledge in a standardized and more accessible systematic form, often by subject, theme or some other designation.

collapsing a wave : also, "*wave-function collapse*"; in *Quantum Physics*, the concept that an Observer is "collapsing" the wave-function to something "definite" by measuring it; defining or calculating a wave-function or interaction of potential interactions by an Observation; in *NexGen Systemology*, when a wave of potentiality or possibility because a finite fixed form; Consciousness or *Awareness* "collapses" a wave-function of energy-matter as a necessary "third" Principle of Apparent Manifestation (first described in "*Tablets of Destiny*"); potentiality as a wave is collapsed into an apparent "*is*", the energy of which is freed up in systematic processing by "*flattening*" a "collapsed" wave back into its state of potentiality.

computing device : a calculator or modern computer; a mechanism that performs specific functions, particularly input, output and storage of data/information.

confront : to come around in front of; to be in the presence of; to stand in front of, or in the face of; to meet "face-to-face" or "face-up-to"; additionally, in *NexGen Systemology*, to fully tolerate or acceptably withstand an encounter with a particular manifestation or encounter.

consciousness : the energetic flow of *Awareness*; the Principle System of *Awareness* that is spiritual in nature, which demonstrates potential interaction with all degrees of the Physical Universe; the *Beingness* component of our existence in *Spirit*; the Principle System of *Awareness* as *Spirit* that directs action in the Mind-System.

continuity : being a continuous whole; a complete whole or "total round of"; the balance of the equation ["–120" + "120" = "0" *&tc.*]; an apparent unbroken interconnected coherent whole; also, as applied to Universes in *NexGen Systemology*, the lowest base consideration of space-time or commonly shared level of energy-matter apparent in an existence, or else the lowest degree of solidity or condensation whereby all mass that exists is identifiable or communicable with all other mass that exists; represented as "0" on the *Standard Model* for the Physical Universe (*beta-existence*), a level of existence that is below Human emotion, comparable to the solidity of "rocks" and "walls" and "inert bodies."

continuum : a continuous enduring uninterrupted sequence or condition; observing all gradients on a *spectrum*; measuring quantitative variation with gradual transition on a spectrum without demonstrating discontinuity or separate parts.

correlate : a relationship between two or more aspects, parts or systems.

correspondence : a direct relationship or correlation; see also "*associative knowledge.*"

Cosmic Law : the "Law" of Nature (or the Physical Universe); the "Law" governing cosmic ordering; often called "Natural

Law" in sciences and philosophies that attempt to codify or systematize it.

cosmology : a systematic philosophy defining origins and structure of an apparent Universe.

Cosmos : archaic term for the "Physical Universe"; semantically implies chaos brought into order; in *NexGen Systemology*, can also include considerations of "Universes" experienced previously as a *beta-existence*.

counter-productive : contrary to the greater or original purpose or intention; in *NexGen Systemology*, anything which brings *Life* away from its sustainable goal or position of *Infinite Existence*.

crash-coursed : a very intense or steep delivery of education over a very brief time period, usually applied to bring a student "up-to-speed" or "up-to-date" for receiving and understanding newer or cumulatively more advanced material.

Crossing the Abyss : to enter the spiritual or metaphysical unknown in "Self-annihilation" to purify the Self and "return to the Source."

Crystal Clear : the second professional publication of Mardukite Systemology, released publicly in December 2019; the second professional text in Grade-III Mardukite Systemology, released as *"Liber-2B"* and reissued in the Grade-III Master Edition *"Systemology Handbook"*; contains fundamental theory of *"Beta-Defragmentation"* and *"Route-2"* systematic processing methodology.

cuneiform : the oldest extant writing system at the inception of modern civilization in Mesopotamia; a system of wedge-shaped script inscribed on clay tablets with a reed pen, allowing advancements in record keeping and communication no longer restricted to more literal graphic representations or pictures.

cuneiform signs : the cuneiform script, as used in ancient Mesopotamia, is not represented in a linear alphabet of "letters," but by a systematic use of basic word "signs" that are combined to form more complex word "signs"—each sign represented a "sound" more than it did a letter, such as "ab," "ad", "ba", "da" &tc.

data-set : total accumulation of knowledge used to base Reality.

dead-memories : outdated, inadequate or erroneous data.

defragmentation : the *reparation* of wholeness; collecting all dispersed parts to reform an original whole; a process of removing *"fragmentation"* in data or knowledge to provide a clear understanding; applying techniques and processes that promote a *holistic* interconnected *alpha* state, favoring observational *Awareness* of continuity in all spiritual and physical systems; in *NexGen Systemology*, a *"Seeker"* achieving an actualized state of basic *"Self-Honest Awareness"* is said to be *beta-defragmented*, whereas *Alpha-defragmentation* is the rehabilitation of the *creative ability*, managing the *Spiritual Timeline* and the POV of *Self* as Alpha-Spirit (I-AM); see also *"Beta-defragmentation."*

degree : a physical or conceptual *unit* (or point) defining the variation present relative to a *scale* above and below it; any stage or extent to which something *is* in relation to other possible positions within a *set* of *"parameters"*; a point within a specific range or spectrum; in *NexGen Systemology*, a *Seeker's* potential energy variations or fluctuations in thought, emotional reaction and physical perception are all treated as *"degrees."*

destiny : what is set down, made firm, standard, or stands fixed as a constant end; the absolute *destination* regardless of whatever course is traveled; in *NexGen Systemology*, the *"destiny"* of the *"Human Spirit"* (or *"Alpha Spirit"*) is infinite existence—*"Immortality."*

dichotomy : a division into two parts, types or kinds.

differential : the quantitative value difference between two forces, motions, pressures or degrees.

differentiation : an apparent difference between aspects or concepts.

discernment : to perceive, distinguish and/or differentiate experience into true knowledge.

displace : to compel to leave; to move or replace something with something else in its place or space.

dissonance : discordance; out of step; out of phase; disharmonious; the "differential" between the way things are and the way things are experienced; cognitive dissonance could be demonstrated as A = abc, or C = A, the duplication of truth/communication is not A-for-A.

dross : prime material; specifically waste-matter or refuse; the discarded remains collected together.

dynamic (systems) : a principle or fixed system which demonstrates its *'variations'* in activity (or output) only in constant relation to variables or fluctuation of interrelated systems; a standard principle, function, process or system that exhibits *'variations'* and change simultaneously with all connected systems; each *'Sphere of Existence'* is a dynamic system, systematically affecting (supporting) and affected (supported) by other *'Spheres'* (which are also dynamic systems).

Eastern traditions : the evolution of the *Ancient Mystery School* east of its origins, primarily the Asian continent, or what is archaically referred to as "oriental."

emotional encoding : the readable substance/material (data) of *'imprints'*; associations of sensory experience with an *imprint*; perceptions of our environment that receive an *emotional charge*, which form or reinforce facets of an *imprint*; perceptions recorded and stored as an *imprint* within the "emotional range" of energetic manifestation; the formation of an energetic store or charge on a channel that fixes emotional responses as a mechanistic automation, which is carried on in an individual's *Spiritual Timeline* (or personal continuum of existence).

encompassing : to form a circle around, surround or envelop around.

energy signatures : a distinctive pattern of energetic action.

engineering : the *Self-directed* actions and efforts to utilize knowledge (observed causality/science), maths (calculations/quantification) and logic (axioms/formulas) to understand, design or manifest a solid structure, machine, mechanism, engine or system; as *"Reality Engineering"* in *NexGen Systemology*—intentional *Self-directed* adjustment of existing Reality conditions; the application of total *Self-determinism* in *Self-Honesty* to change apparent Reality using fundamentals of *Systemology* and *Cosmic Law*.

entanglement : tangled together; intertwined and enmeshed systems; in *NexGen Systemology*, a reference to the interrelation of all particles as waves at a higher point of connectivity than is apparent, since wave-functions only "collapse" when someone is *Observing*, or doing the measuring, evaluating, &tc.

entropy : the reduction of organized physical systems back into chaos-continuity when their integrity is measured against space over time; reduction toward a zero-point.

epicenter : the point from which shock-waves travel.

erroneous : inaccurate; incorrect; containing error.

esoteric : hidden; secret; knowledge understood by a select few.

etching : to cut, bite or corrode with acid to produce a pattern.

evaluate : to determine, assign or fix a set value, amount or meaning.

exacting : a demanding rigid effort to draw forth from.

executable : the supreme authoritative ability to carry out according to design.

existence : the *state* or fact of *apparent manifestation*; the resulting combination of the Principles of Manifestation: consciousness, motion and substance; continued *survival*; that which independently exists; the *'Prime Directive'* and sole purpose of all manifestation or Reality; the highest common intended motivation driving any *"Thing"* or *Life*.

existential : pertaining to existence, or some aspect or condition of existence.

exoteric : public knowledge or common understanding; the level of understanding and *Knowing* maintained by the "masses"; the opposite of *esoteric*.

experiential data : accumulated reference points we store as memory concerning our "experience" with Reality.

extrapolate : to make an estimate of the "value" outside of the perceivable range.

facets : an aspect, an apparent phase; one of many faces of something; a cut surface on a gem or crystal; in *NexGen Systemology*—a single perception or aspect of a memory or *"Imprint"*; any one of many ways in which a memory is recorded; perceptions associated with a painful emotional (sensation) experience and *"imprinted"* onto a metaphoric lens through which to view future similar experiences; other secondary terminals that are associated with a particular terminal, painful event or experience of loss, and which may exhibit the same encoded significance as the activating event.

faculties : abilities of the mind (individual) inherent or developed.

fate : what is brought to light or actualized as experience; the actual *course* taken to reach an end, charted end, or final *destination*; in *NexGen Systemology*, the *'fate'* of a *'Human Spirit'* (or *'Alpha Spirit'*) is determined by the choice of course taken to experience *Life*.

feedback loop : a complete and continuous circuit flow of energy or information directed as an output from a source to a target which is altered and return back to the source as an input; in *General Systemology*—the continuous process where outputs of a system are routed back as inputs to complete a circuit or loop, which may be closed or connected to other systems/circuits; in *NexGen Systemology*—the continuous process where directed *Life* energy and *Awareness* is sent back to *Self* as experience, understanding and memory to complete an energetic circuit as a loop.

fragmentation : breaking into parts and scattering the pieces; the *fractioning* of wholeness or the *fracture* of a holistic interconnected *alpha* state, favoring observational *Awareness* of perceived connectivity between parts; *discontinuity*; separation of a totality into parts; in *NexGen Systemology*, a person outside a state of *Self-Honesty* is said to be *fragmented*.

game : a strategic situation where a "player's" power of choice is employed or affected; a parameter or condition defined by purposes, freedoms and barriers (rules).

game theory : a mathematical theory of logic pertaining to strategies of maximizing gains and minimizing loses within prescribed boundaries and freedoms; a field of knowledge widely applied to human problem solving and decision-making; the application of true knowledge and logic to deduce the correct course of action given all variables and interplay of dynamic systems; logical study of decision making where "players" make choices that affect (the interests) of other "players"; an intellectual study of conflict and cooperation.

general systemology ("systematology") : a methodology of analysis and evaluation regarding the systems—their design and function; organizing systems of interrelated information-processing in order to perform a given function or pattern of functions.

genetic-vehicle : a physical *Life*-form; the physical (*beta*) body that is animated/controlled by the (*Alpha*) *Spirit* using a continuous *Lifeline* (ZU); a physical (*beta*) organic receptacle and catalyst for the (*Alpha*) *Self* to operate "causes" and experience "effects" within the *Physical Universe.*

gifted : attributing a special quality or ability; having exceptionally high intelligence or mental faculties.

godhood : a divine character or condition; "divinity."

gradient : a degree of partitioned ascent or descent along some scale, elevation or incline; "higher" and "lower" values in relation to one another.

GSR-Meters ("galvanic skin response"–"electropsychometer") : a *biofeedback* device used for measuring electrical resistance (in "Ohms") of the skin surface; one of many parts used in a polygraph system; a highly sensitive "Ohm-meter" with variable range, set points and amplification used to monitor electrical fluctuations of the skin surface.

heralded : proclaimed ahead of or prior to; officially announced.

holistic : the examination of interconnected systems as encompassing something greater than the *sum* of their "parts."

Homo Novus : literally, the "new man"; the "newly elevated man" or "known man" in ancient Rome; the man who "knows (only) through himself"; in NexGen Systemology—the next spiritual and intellectual evolution of *homo sapiens* (the "modern Human Condition"), which is signified by a demonstration of higher faculties of *Self-Actualization* and clear *Awareness.*

Human Condition : a standard default state of Human experience that is generally accepted to be the extent of its potential identity (*beingness*)—currently treated as *Homo Sapiens Sapiens,* but which is scheduled for replacement by *Homo Novus.*

hypothetical : operating under the assumption a certain aspect actual "is."

identity : the collection of energy and matter—including memory—across a *"Spiritual Timeline"* that we consider as "I" of *Self*, but the "I" is an individual and not an identification with anything other than *Self* as *Alpha-Spirit*.

identity-system : the application of the *ZU-line* as "I"—the continuous expression of *Self* as *Awareness* across a *"Spiritual Timeline"*; see *"identity."*

illuminated : to supply with light so as to make visible or comprehensible.

immersion : plunged or sunk into; wholly surrounded by.

imprint : to strongly impress, stamp, mark (or outline) onto a softer 'impressible' substance; to mark with pressure onto a surface; in *NexGen Systemology*, the term is used to indicate permanent Reality impressions marked by frequencies, energies or interactions experienced during periods of emotional distress, pain, unconsciousness, loss, enforcement, or something antagonistic to physical (personal) survival, all of which are are stored with other reactive response-mechanisms at lower-levels of *Awareness* as opposed to the active memory database and proactive processing center of the Mind; an experiential "memory-set" that may later resurface—be triggered or stimulated artificially—as Reality, of which similar responses will be engaged automatically; holographic-like imagery "stamped" onto consciousness as composed of energetic *facets* tied to the "snap-shot" of an experience.

imprinting incident : the first or original event instance communicated and *emotionally encoded* onto an individual's *"Spiritual Timeline"* (recorded memory from all lifetimes), which formed a permanent impression that is later used to mechanistically treat future contact on that channel; the first or original occurrence of some particular *facet* or mental image related to a certain type of *encoded response*, such as pain and discomfort, losses and victimization, and even the acts that we have taken against others along the Spiritual Timeline of our existence that caused them to also be *Imprinted*.

incarnation : a present, living or concrete form of some thing, idea or beingness; an individual lifetime or life-cycle from birth/creation to death/destruction independent of other lifetimes or cycles.

inception : the beginning, start, origin or outset.

incite : to urge on or cause; instigate; prove or stimulate into action.

indefinable : without a clear definition being currently presented.

individual : a person, lifeform, human entity or creature; a *Seeker* or potential *Seeker* is often referred to as an "individual" within Mardukite Zuism and Systemology materials.

infinite existence : "immortality."

inhibited : withheld, held-back, discouraged or repressed from some state.

"in phase" : see *"phase alignment."*

institution : a social standard or organizational group responsible for promoting some system or aspect in society.

inter-dimensional : systems that are interconnected or correlated between the Physical Universe and the Spiritual Universe —or between "dimension states" observably identified as "physical," "emotional," "psychological" and "spiritual." The only point of true interconnectivity that we can systematically determine is called *"Life"* or the POV of *Self.*

intermediate : a distinct point between two points; actions between two points.

invalidate : decrease the level or degree or *agreement* as Reality.

invest : spend on; give or devote something in exchange for a beneficial result; to endow with.

knowledge : clear personal processing of informed understanding; information (data) that is actualized as effectively workable understanding; a demonstrable understanding on which we may 'set' our *Awareness*—or literally a "know-ledge."

KI : an ancient cuneiform sign designating the *'physical zone'*; the *Physical Universe*—comprised of physical matter and physical energy in action across space and observed as time; a direction of motion toward material *Continuity*, away from or subordinate to the Spiritual (*'AN'*); the physical condition of existence providing for our *beta* state of *Awareness* experienced (and interacted with) as an individual *Lifeform* from our primary Alpha state of Identity or *I-AM-Self* in the *Spiritual Universe* (*'AN'*).

kinetic : pertaining to the energy of physical motion and movement.

learned : highly educated; possessing significant knowledge.

level : a physical or conceptual *tier* (or plane) relative to a *scale* above and below it; a significant *gradient* observable as a *foundation* (or surface) built upon and subsequent to other levels of a totality or whole; a *set* of "*parameters*" with respect to other such *sets* along a *continuum*; in *NexGen Systemology*, a *Seeker's* understanding, *Awareness* as *Self* and the formal grades of material/instruction are all treated as "*levels.*"

Liber-One : First published in October 2019 as "*The Tablets of Destiny: Using Ancient Wisdom to Unlock Human Potential*" by Joshua Free; republished in the complete *Grade-III* anthology, "*The Systemology Handbook*"; revision republished in August 2022 as "*The Tablets of Destiny Revelation: How Long-Lost Anunnaki Wisdom Can Change the Fate of Humanity.*"

Liber-Two : First published in October 2020 as "*Metahuman Destinations: Piloting the Course to Homo Novus*" by Joshua Free; an anthology of the *Grade-IV* "Professional Piloting Course," containing revised materials from *Liber-2C*, *Liber-2D* and (most of) *Liber-3C*.

Liber-2B : First published in December 2019 as "*Crystal Clear: The Self-Actualization Manual & Guide to Total Awareness*" by Joshua Free; republished in the complete *Grade-III* anthology, "*The Systemology Handbook*"; revision republished in April 2022 as "*Crystal Clear (Handbook for Seekers): Achieve Self-Actualization and Spiritual Ascension in This Lifetime.*"

Liber-3D : First published in June 2021 as "*Imaginomicon: The Gateway to Higher Universes (A Grimoire for the Human Spirit)*" by Joshua Free; a manual completing the *Grade-IV* (Metahuman Systemology) professional series with a treatment of "Wizard Level-0"; revision republished in June 2022 as "*Imaginomicon: Approaching Gateways to Higher Universes (A New Grimoire for the Human Spirit).*"

Liber-3E (Liber-Three) : First published in April 2022 as "*The Way of the Wizard: Utilitarian Systemology (A New Metahuman Ethic)*" by Joshua Free; a professional manual bridging *Grade-IV* (Metahuman Systemology, *Wizard Level-0*) with *Grade-V* (Spiritual Systemology, *Wizard Level-1*).

localized : brought together and confined to a particular place.

logic equations : using symbols and basic mathematical logic to establish the validity of statements or to see how a variable within a system will change the result; a basic demonstration of proportion or relationship between variables in a system.

logistics : pertaining to the movement or transportation between locations.

macrocosmic : taking examples and system demonstrations at one level and applying them as a larger demonstration of a relatively higher level or unseen dimension.

manifestation : something brought into existence.

Marduk : founder of Babylonia; patron Anunnaki "god" of Babylon.

Mardukite Zuism : a Mesopotamian-themed (Babylonian-oriented) religious philosophy and tradition applying the spiritual technology based on *Arcane Tablets* in combination with "Tech" from *NexGen Systemology*; first developed in the New Age underground by Joshua Free in 2008 and realized publicly in 2009 with the formal establishment of the *Mardukite Chamberlains.* The text "*Tablets of Destiny*" is a cross-over from Mardukite Zuism (and Mesopotamian Neopaganism) toward higher spiritual applications of Systemology.

Master-Control-Center (MCC) : a perfect computing device to the extent of the information received from "lower levels" of sensory experience/perception; the proactive communication system of the "*Mind*"; a relay point of active *Awareness* along the Identity's *ZU-line*, which is responsible for maintaining basic *Self-Honest Clarity* of *Knowingness* as a *seat of consciousness* between the *Alpha-Spirit* and the secondary "*Reactive Control Center*" of a *Lifeform* in *beta existence*; the Mind-center for an *Alpha-Spirit* to actualize cause in the *beta existence*; the analytical *Self-Determined* Mind-center of an *Alpha-Spirit used* to project *Will* toward the genetic body; the point of contact between *Spiritual Systems* and the *beta existence*; presumably the *"Third Eye"* of a being connected directly to the *I-AM-Self*, which is responsible for *determining* Reality at any time; in *NexGen Systemology*, this is plotted at (4.0) on the continuity model of the *ZU-line*.

MCC : see *"Master-Control-Center."*

Mesopotamia : land between Tigris and Euphrates River; modern-day Iraq; the primary setting for ancient *Sumerian* and *Babylonian* traditions thousands of years ago, including activities and records of the *Anunnaki*.

methodology : a complete system of applications, methods, principles and rules to compose a *'systematic'* paradigm as a "whole"—esp. a field of philosophy or science.

misappropriated : put into use incorrectly; to apply ineffectively or as unintended by design or definition.

motor functions : internal mechanisms that allow a body to move.

Nabu : the *Anunnaki* "god of wisdom, writing and knowledge" for Babylonian (Mardukite) Tradition.

NexGen Systemology : a modern tradition of applied religious philosophy and spiritual technology based on *Arcane Tablets* in combination with *"general systemology"* and *"games theory"* developed in the New Age underground by Joshua Free in 2011 as an advanced futurist extension of the *"Mardukite Chamberlains"*; also referred to as *"Mardukite Systemology," "Metahuman Systemology"* and *"Spiritual Systemology."*

objective : concerning the "external world" and attempts to observe Reality independent of personal "subjective" factors.

one-to-one : see *"A-for-A."*

optimum : the most favorable or ideal conditions for the best result; the greatest degree of result under specific conditions.

orchestration : to arrange or compose the performance of a system.

organic : as related to a physically living organism or carbon-based life form; energy-matter condensed into form as a focus or POV of Spiritual Life Energy (*ZU*) as it pertains to beta-existence of *this* Physical Universe (*KI*).

pantheism : religious philosophies that observe God as inherent within all aspects of the Physical Universe.

paradigm : an all-encompassing *standard* by which to view the world and *communicate* Reality; a standard model of reality-systems used by the Mind to filter, organize and interpret experience of Reality.

parameters : a defined range of possible variables within a model, spectrum or continuum; the extent of communicable reach capable within a system or across a distance; the defined or imposed limitations placed on a system or the functions within a system; the extent to which a Life or "thing" can *be*, *do* or *know* along any channel within the confines of a specific system or spectrum of existence.

paramount : the most important; of utmost importance; "above all else."

participation : being part of the action; affecting the result.

patron god : the most sacred deity of a region or city, of which most temples and religious services are directed; the personal deity of an individual.

PCL : see "*processing command line.*"

perturbation : the deviation from a natural state, fixed motion, or orbit system caused by another external system; disturbing or disquieting the serenity of an existent state; inciting observable apparent action using indirect or outside actions or 'forces'; the introduction of a new element or facet that disturbs equilibrium of a standard system; the "butterfly effect"; in *NexGen Systemology*, *'perturbation'* is a necessary condition for the *ZU-line* to function as a *Standard Model* of actual *'monistic continuity'*— which is a *Lifeforce* singularity expressed along a spectrum with potential interactions at each degree from any source; the influence of a degree in one state by activities of another state that seem independent, but which are actually connected directly at some higher degree, even if not apparently observed.

phase (identification) : in *NexGen Systemology,* a pattern of personality or identity that is assumed as the POV from *Self*; personal identification with artificial "personality packages"; an individual assuming or taking characteristics of another individual (often unknowingly as a response-mechanisms); also *"phase alignment."*

phase alignment or *"in phase"* : to be in synch or mutually synchronized, in step or aligned properly with something else in order to increase the total strength value; in *NexGen Systemology*, alignment or adjustment of *Awareness* with a particular identity, space or time; perfect *defragmentation* would mean being "in phase" as *Self* fully conscious and Aware as an Alpha-Spirit *in* present *space* and *time*, free of synthetic personalities.

physics : regarding data obtained by a material science of observable motions, forces and bodies, including their apparent interaction, in the Physical Universe (specific to this *beta-existence*).

physiology : a material science of observable biological functions and mechanics of living organisms, including codification and study of identifiable parts and apparent systematic processes (specific to agreed upon makeup of the *genetic vehicle* for this *beta-existence*).

pilot : a professional steersman responsible for healthy functional operation of a ship toward a specific destination; in *NexGen Systemology*, an intensive trained individual qualified to specially apply *Systemology Processing* to assist other *Seekers* on the *Pathway*.

ping : a short, high pitched ring, chime or noise that alerts to the presence of something; in computer systems, a query sent on a network or line to another terminal in order to determine if there is a connection to it; in *NexGen Systemology*, the sudden somatic twinge or pain or discomfort that is felt as a sensation in the body when a particular terminal (lifeform, object, concept) is 'brought to mind' or contacted on a personal communication channel-circuit; the accompanying sensations and mental images that are experienced as an automatic-response to the presence of some channel or terminal.

postulate : to put forward as truth; to suggest or assume an existence *to be*; to provide a basis of reasoning and belief; a basic theory accepted as fact; in *NexGen Systemology*, "Alpha-Thought"—the top-most decisions or considerations made by the Alpha-Spirit regarding the *"is-ness"* (what things "are") about energy-matter and space-time.

precedent : a matter which precedes or goes before another in importance.

prehistoric : any time before human history is properly recorded in writing; prior to c. 4000 B.C.

premise : a basis or statement of fact from which conclusions are drawn.

presence : the quality of some thing (energy/matter) being "present" in space-time; personal orientation of *Self* as an *Awareness* (*POV*) located in present space-time (environment) and communicating with extant energy-matter.

prevalent : of wide extent; an extensive or largely accepted aspect or current state.

Prime Directive : a "spiritual" implant program that installs purposes and goals into the personal experience of a Universe, esp. any *Beta-Existence* (whether a 'Games Universe' or a 'Prison Universe'); intellectually treated as the "Universal Imperative" in some schools of moral philosophy; comparable to "Universal Law" or "Cosmic Ordering."

"process-out" or **"flatten a wave"** : to reduce *emotional encoding* of an *imprint* to zero; to dissolve a *wave-form* or *thought-formed* "solid" such as a "*belief*"; to completely run a *process* to its end, thereby *flattening* any previously "*collapsed-waves*" or *fragmentation* that is obstructing the *clear channel* of *Self-Awareness*; also referred to as "processing-out"; to discharge all previously held emotionally encoded imprinting or erroneous programming and beliefs that otherwise fix the free flow (wave) to a particular pattern, solid or concrete "*is*" form.

processing command line (PCL) or **command line** : a directed input; a specific command using highly selective language for *Systemology Processing*; a predetermined directive statement (cause) intended to focus concentrated attention (effect).

projecting awareness : sending out (motion) or radiating "*consciousness*" from *Self* ("I") to another POV.

proportional : having a direct relationship or mutual interaction with.

Proto-Indo-European (PIE) : in Linguistic-Semantic Sciences, a hypothetical single-source Eurasian root language (c.4500

B.C.) demonstrating common origins of many "word-roots" found in European languages.

psychometric evaluation : the relative measurement of personal ability, mental (psychological/thought) faculties, and effective processing of information and external stimulus data; a scale used in "applied psychology" to evaluate and predict human behavior.

reactive control center (RCC) : the secondary (reactive) communication system of the "*Mind*"; a relay point of *Awareness* along the Identity's *ZU-line*, which is responsible for engaging basic motors, biochemical processes and any *programmed automated responses* of a living *beta* organism; the reactive Mind-Center of a living organism relaying communications of *Awareness* between causal experience of *Physical Systems* and the "*Master Control Center*"; it presumably stores all emotional encoded imprints as fragmentation of "chakra" frequencies of *ZU* (within the range of the "*psychological/emotive systems*" of a being), which it may *react* to as Reality at any time; in *NexGen Systemology*, this is plotted at (2.0) on the continuity model of the *ZU-line*.

reality : see "*agreement.*"

receptacle : a device or mechanism designed to contain and store a specific type of aspect or thing; a container meant to receive something.

recursive : repeating by looping back onto itself to form continuity; *ex.* the "Infinity" symbol is recursive.

relative : an apparent point, state or condition treated as distinct from others.

relinquish : to give up control, command or possession of.

repetitively : to repeat "over and over" again; or else "repetition."

responsibility : the *ability* to *respond*; the extent of mobilizing *power* and *understanding* an individual maintains as *Awareness* to enact *change*; the proactive ability to *Self-direct* and make decisions independent of an outside authority.

resurface : to return to (or bring up to) the "surface" of that which has previously been submerged; in *NexGen Systemology*

—relating specifically to processes where a *Seeker* recalls blocked energy stored covertly as emotional "*imprints*" (by the RCC) so that it may be effectively defragmented from the "*ZU-line*" (by the MCC).

Route-1 : a specific methodology from *SOP-2C* denoting "*Resurfacing Processing*," as described in the text "*Tablets of Destiny*" (*Liber-One*) as "RR-SP" (and reissued in "*The Systemology Handbook*").

scions : a descendant or offspring; an offshoot or branch.

Seeker : an individual on the *Pathway to Self-Honesty*; a practitioner of *Mardukite Systemology* or *NexGen Systemology Processing* that is working toward *Spiritual Ascension*.

Self-actualization : bringing the full potential of the Human spirit into Reality; expressing full capabilities and creativeness of the *Alpha-Spirit*.

Self-determinism : the freedom to act, clear of external control or influence; the personal control of Will to direct intention.

Self-honesty : the basic or original *alpha* state of *being* and *knowing*; clear and present total *Awareness* of-and-as *Self*, in its most basic and true proactive expression of itself as *Spirit* or *I-AM*—free of artificial attachments, perceptive filters and other emotionally-reactive or mentally-conditioned programming imposed on the human condition by the systematized physical world; the ability to experience existence without judgment.

self-sustained : self-supported; self-sufficient; independent.

semantics : the *meaning* carried in *language* as the *truth* of a "thing" represented, *A-for-A*; the *effect* of language on *thought* activity in the Mind and physical behavior; language as *symbols* used to represent a concept, "thing" or "solid."

semantic-set : the implied meaning behind any groupings of words or symbols used to define a specific paradigm.

sensation : an external stimulus received by internal sense organs (receptors/sensors); sense impressions.

sentient : a living organism with consciousness or intelligence; a "thinking" or "reasoning" being that perceives information from the "senses."

sine-wave : the *frequency* and amplitude of a quantified (calcul-able) *vibration* represented on a graph (graphically) as smooth repetitive *oscillation* of a *waveform*; a *waveform* graphed for demonstration—otherwise represented in *NexGen Systemology* logic equations as 'W*f*,' or in mathematics as the *'function of x'* (*fx*); graphically representing arcs (*parameters*) of a circular *continuity* on a *continuum*; in the *Standard Model of NexGen Systemology*, the actual 'wave vibration' graphically displayed on an otherwise static *ZU-line* (of Infinity) is a *'sine-wave'*.

singularity : in general use, "to be singular," but our working definition suggests the opposite of individuality (contrary to most dictionaries); in upper-level sciences, a "zero-point" where a particular property or attribute is mathematically treated as "infinite" (such as the "black-hole" phenomenon), or else where apparently dissimilar qualities of all existing aspects (or indi-viduals) share a "singular" expression, nature or quality; additionally, in *NexGen Systemology*, a hypothetical zero-point when apparent values of all parts in a Universe are equal to all other parts before it collapses; in *Transhumanism*, a hypothetic-al "runaway reaction" in technology, when it becomes self-aware, self-propagating, self-upgradable and self-sustainable, and replaces human effort of advancement or even makes con-tinued human existence impossible; also, technological efforts to maintain an artificial immortality of the Human Condition on a digital mainframe.

slate : a hard thin flat surface material used for writing on; a chalk-board, which is a large version of the original wood-framed writing slate, named for the rock-type it was made from.

somatic : specifically pertaining to the physical body, its sensa-tions and response actions or behaviors as separate from a "Mind-System"; also *"pings."*

SOP-2C : *Standard Operating Procedure #2C* or *Systemology Operating Procedure #2C*; a standardized procedural formula introduced in materials for *"Metahuman Destinations"* (*Liber-Two*); a regimen or outline for standard delivery of systematic processing used by *Systemology Pilots* and *Mardukite Minis-ters*; a procedure outline of systematic processing, which includes applications of *"Route-1," "Route-2," "Route-3"* and *"Route-0"* as taught for *Grade-IV Professional Piloting*.

spectrum : a broad range or array as a continuous series or sequence; defined parts along a singular continuum; in physics, a gradient arrangement of visible colored bands diffracted in order of their respective wavelengths, such as when passing *White Light* through a *prism*.

Spheres of Existence (dynamic systems) : a series of *eight* concentric circles, rings or spheres (each larger than the former) that is overlaid onto the Standard Model of Beta-Existence to demonstrate the dynamic systems of existence extending out from the POV of Self (often as a "body") at the *First Sphere*; these are given in the basic eightfold systems as: *Self, Home/Family, Groups, Humanity, Life on Earth, Physical Universe, Spiritual Universe* and *Infinity-Divinity.*

standard issue : equally dispensed to all without consideration.

standard model : a fundamental *structure* or symbolic construct used to evaluate a complete *set* in *continuity* relative to itself and variable to all other *dynamic systems* as graphed or calculated by *logic.*

static : characterized by a fixed or stationary condition; having no apparent change, movement or fluctuation.

sub-zones : at ranges "below" which we are representing or which is readily observable for current purposes.

successively : what comes after; forward into the future.

succumb : to give way, or give in to, a relatively stronger superior force.

Sumerian : ancient civilization of *Sumer,* founded in Mesopotamia c. 5000 B.C.

superfluous : excessive; unnecessary; needless.

superstition : knowledge accepted without good reason.

surefooted : proceeding surely; not likely to stumble or fall.

system : from the Greek, "to set together"; to set or arrange things or data together so as to form an orderly understanding of a "whole"; also a *'method'* or *'methodology'* as an orderly standard of use or application of such data arranged together.

systematization : to arrange into systems; to systematize or make systematic.

Systemology : see "*NexGen Systemology.*"

thought-form : apparent *manifestation* or existential *realization* of *Thought-waves* as "solids" even when only apparent in Reality-agreements of the Observer; the treatment of *Thought-waves* as permanent *imprints* obscuring *Self-Honest Clarity* of *Awareness* when reinforced by emotional experience as actualized "thought-formed solids" ("*beliefs*") in the Mind; energetic patterns that "surround" the individual.

thought-habit : reoccurring modes of thought or repeated "self-talk"; essentially "self-hypnosis" resulting in a certain state.

thought-wave or **wave-form** : a proactive *Self-directed action* or reactive-response *action* of *consciousness*; the *process* of *thinking* as demonstrated in *wave-form*; the *activity* of *Awareness* within the range of *thought vibrations/frequencies* on the existential *Life-continuum* or *ZU-line*.

threshold : a doorway, gate or entrance point; the degree to which something is to produce an effect within a certain state or condition; the point in which a condition changes from one to the next.

thwarted : to successfully oppose or prevent a purpose from actualizing.

tier : a series of rows or levels, one stacked immediately before or atop another.

timeline : plotting out history in a linear (line) model to indicate instances (experiences) or demonstrate changes in state (space) as measured over time; a singular conception of continuation of observed time as marked by event-intervals and changes in energy and matter across space.

transhumanism : a social science and applied philosophy concerning the next evolved state of the "*Human Condition,*"; progress in two potential directions, either "spiritual" technologies advancing *Self* as an "Alpha-Spirit," or the direction of "external"-"physical" technologies that modify or eliminate characteristics of the *Body*; a theme describing contemporary application of material sciences emphasizing only "physical" and "genetic" parts of the *Human* experience, such as brain activity, cell-life extension and space travel; *NexGen Systemology* recently began distinguishing its emphasis on "spiritual technology" as "*metahumanism.*"

transmit : to send forth data along some line of communication; to move a point across a distance.

traumatic encoding : information received when the sensory faculties of an organism are "shocked" into learning it as an "emotionally" encoded *Imprint*; a duplicated facsimile-copy or *Mental Image* of severe misfortune, violent threats, pain and coercion, which is then categorized, stored and reactively retrieved based exclusively on its emotional *facets.*

unconscious : a state when *Awareness* as *Self* is removed totally from the equation of *Life* experience, though it continues to be recorded in lower-level response mechanisms (fixed to a simulacrum or genetic vehicle) for later retrieval.

undefiled : to remain intact, untouched or unchanged; to be left in an original "virgin" state.

validation : reinforcement of agreements or considerations as "real."

vibration : effects of motion or wave-frequency as applied to any system.

vizier : a high ranking official; a minister-of-state.

wave-form : see "*sine-wave.*"

wave-function collapse : see "*collapsing a wave.*"

Western Civilization : modern contemporary culture, ideals, values and technology, particularly of Europe and North America as distinguished by growing urbanization, industrialization, and inspired by a history of rebellion to strong religious and political indoctrination.

ziggurat : religious temples of ancient Mesopotamia; stepped-pyramids and towers used for spiritual and religious purposes by Sumerians and Babylonians, many of which are presented as seven tiers, levels or terraces representing "Seven Gates" (or "7 Veils") of existence, separating material continuity of the Earth Plane from "Infinity" ("8").

ZU : the ancient Sumerian cuneiform sign for the archaic verb —"*to know,*" "*knowingness*" or "*awareness*"; in *Mardukite Zuism and Systemology*, the active energy/matter of the "Spiritual Universe" (AN) experienced as a *Lifeforce* or *consciousness* that imbues living forms extant in the "Physical Universe" (KI); "*Spiritual Life Energy*"; energy demonstrated by the WILL of an actualized *Alpha-Spirit* in the "Spiritual Universe" (AN), which impinges its *Awareness* into the Physical Universe (KI), animating/controlling *Life* for its experience of *beta-existence* along an individual Alpha-Spirit's personal *Identity-continuum*, called a *ZU-line*.

Zu-Line : a theoretical construct in *Mardukite Zuism and Systemology* demonstrating *Spiritual Life Energy* (ZU) as a personal individual "continuum" of Awareness interacting with all Spheres of Existence on the Standard Model of Systemology; a spectrum of potential variations and interactions of a monistic continuum or singular *Spiritual Life Energy (ZU)* demonstrated on the Standard Model; an energetic channel of potential POV and "locations" of Beingness, demonstrated in early Systemology materials as an individual Alpha-Spirit's personal *Identity-continuum*, potentially connecting *Awareness (ZU)* of *Self* with "*Infinity*" simultaneous with all points considered in existence; a symbolic demonstration of the "*Life-line*" on which *Awareness (ZU)* extends from the direction of the "Spiritual Universe" (AN) in its true original *alpha state* through an entire possible range of activity resulting in its *beta state* and control of a *genetic-entity* occupying the *Physical Universe (KI)*.

WOULD
YOU
LIKE
TO
KNOW
MORE
? ? ?

SYSTEMOLOGY
The Pathway to Self-Honesty

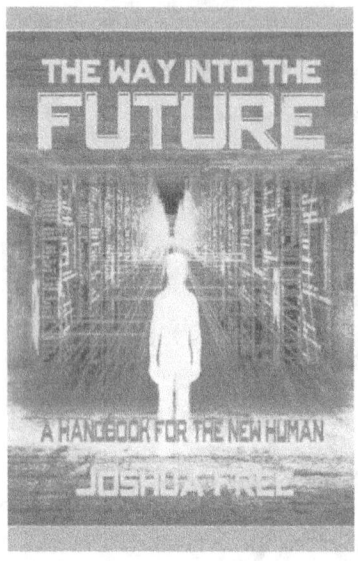

A Basic Introduction to Mardukite Systemology

THE WAY INTO THE FUTURE

A Handbook for the New Human

a collection of writings by Joshua Free selected by James Thomas

Here are the basic answers to what has held Humanity back from achieving its ultimate goals and unlocking the true power of the Spirit and highest state of Knowing and Being.

"The Way Into The Future" illuminates the *Pathway* leading to Planet Earth's true "metahuman" destiny. With <u>excerpts</u> from *"Tablets of Destiny," "Crystal Clear," "Systemology—The Original Thesis"* and *"The Power of Zu."* You can help shine clear light on anyone's pathway!

Carefully selected by Mardukite Publications Officer, James Thomas, this critical *collection of eighteen articles, lecture transcripts and reference chapters* by Joshua Free is sure to be not only a treasured part of your personal library, but also the perfect introduction for all friends, family and loved ones.

(*Basic Grade-III Introductory Pocket Anthology*)

SYSTEMOLOGY
The Pathway to Self-Honesty
ORIGINAL UNDERGROUND INTRODUCTIONS
REVISED AND REISSUED IN HARDCOVER

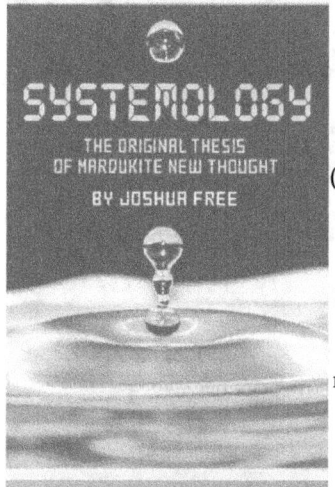

SYSTEMOLOGY
The Original Thesis of Mardukite New Thuoght
by Joshua Free

(*Mardukite Systemology Liber-S-1X*)

The very first underground discourses released to the "New Thought" division of the Mardukite Research Organization privately over a decade ago and providing the inspiration for rapid futurist spiritual technology called "Mardukite Systemology."

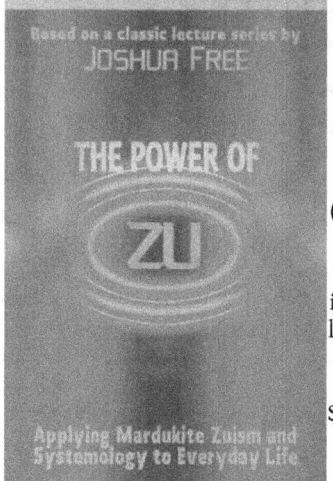

THE POWER OF ZU
Applying Mardukite Zuism & Systemology to Everyday Life
by Joshua Free
Foreword by Reed Penn

(*Mardukite Systemology Liber-S-1Z*)

A unique introductory course on Mardukite Zuism & Systemology, including transcripts from a 3-day lecture series given by Joshua Free in December 2019 to launch the Mardukite Academy of Systemology & Founding Church of Mardukite Zuism just in time for the 2020's.

SYSTEMOLOGY
The Pathway to Self-Honesty

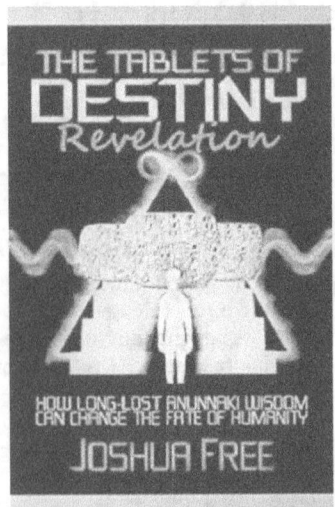

THE TABLETS OF DESTINY REVELATION

How Long-Lost Anunnaki Wisdom Can Change the Fate of Humanity

by Joshua Free

Mardukite Systemology Liber-One

second edition

Discover the origins of the Pathway to Self-Honesty with the book that started it all!

In this newly revised "Revelations" Academy Edition: Rediscover the original system of perfecting the Human Condition on a Pathway that leads to Infinity. Here is a way!—a map to chart spiritual potential and redefine the future of what is means to be human.

A landmark public debut for Grade-III Systemology and the foundation stone for reaching higher and taking back control of your DESTINY!

The revelation of 6,000 year old secrets, providing the tools and wisdom to unlock human potential...

SYSTEMOLOGY
The Pathway to Self-Honesty

CRYSTAL CLEAR
Handbook for Seekers

*Achieving
Self-Actualization
& Spiritual Ascension
in This Lifetime*

by Joshua Free

*Mardukite Systemology
Liber-2B*

second edition

Take control of your destiny and chart the first steps
toward your own spiritual evolution.

Realize new potentials of the Human Condition with
a Self-guiding handbook for Self-Processing
toward Self-Actualization in Self-Honesty using actual
techniques and training provided for the coveted
"Mardukite Self-Defragmentation Course Program"
—once only available directly and privately from the
underground International Systemology Society.

Discover the amazing power behind the
applied spiritual technology
used for counseling and advisement in
the Mardukite Zuism tradition.

SYS♀EMOLOGY
The Pathway to Self-Honesty

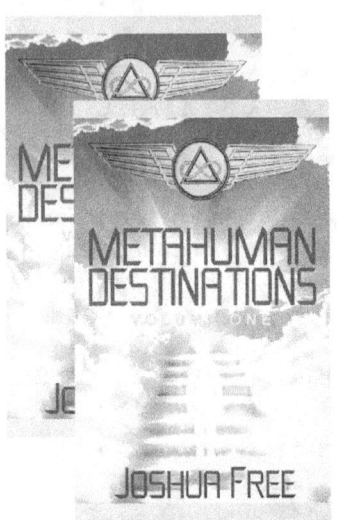

METAHUMAN DESTINATIONS

The Original 2020 Professional Piloting Academy Course for Grade IV

by Joshua Free

Mardukite Systemology Liber-Two (2C,2D,3C) Revised 2-Volume Set

available individually

Drawing from the Arcane Tablets and nearly a year of additional research, experimentation and workshops since the introduction of applied spiritual technology and systematic processing methods, Joshua Free provides the ground-breaking manual for those seeking to correct—or "defragment"—the conditions that have trapped viewpoints of the Spirit into programming and encoding of the Human Condition.

Experience the revolutionary professional course in advanced spiritual technology for Mardukite Systemologists to "Pilot" the way to higher ideals that can free us from the Human Condition and return ultimate command and control of creation to the Spirit.

SYSTEMOLOGY
The Gateways to Infinity

IMAGINOMICON

Accessing the Gateway to Higher Universes

A New Grimoire for the Human Spirit

by Joshua Free

Mardukite Systemology Grade-IV Metahumanism, Wizard Level-0, Liber-3D

revised edition

The Way Out. Hidden for 6,000 Years.
But now we've found the Key.
A grimore to summon and invoke, command and control,
the most powerful spirit to ever exist.
Your Self.

Access beyond physical existence.
Fly free across all Gateways.
Go back to where it all began and reclaim that
personal universe which the *Spirit* once called *"Home."*

Break free from the Matrix;
control the Mind and command the Body
from outside those systems
— because *You* were never "human" —
fully realize what it means to be a *spiritual being*,
then rise up through the Gateways to Higher Universes
and *BE.*

SYSTEMOLOGY

The Gateway to Infinite Self-Honesty

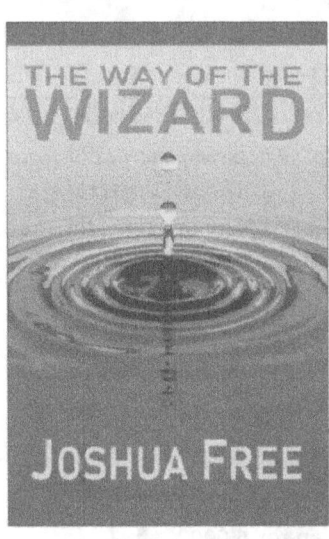

THE WAY OF THE WIZARD

Utilitarian Systemology

A New Metahuman Ethic

by Joshua Free

Mardukite Systemology Liber-3E

Grade-IV to Grade-V transition bridge

Your ticket off of a Prison Planet...
...and a Pathway leading to Spiritual Ascension!

Accumulated involvement in dangerous situations, states of confusion, unjust destruction and being at the effect end of faulty—or—blatantly false information, all lend to fragmented purposes that may very well be painted to appear "for our own good." Instead they are non-survival or counter-survival oriented, leading us away from routes to achieve "greater heights"—higher, more ideal, states of knowingness and beingness—including the Magic Universe immediately preceding this one.

Here then is a bridge from Grade-IV to Grade-V, the next great frontier of the *Pathway* crossed by participants in the "Freedom From" workshops led by Joshua Free in 2021.

SYS⚲EMOLOGY
The Gateways to Infinity

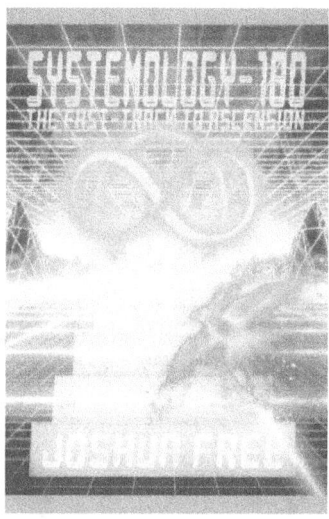

SYSTEMOLOGY-180
The Fast-Track to Ascension

A Handbook for Pilots

by Joshua Free

*Mardukite Grade-V
Systemology
Liber-180*

*Expert application of
all Grade-III and Grade-IV
training and techniques*

A perfected "metahuman" state for the Human Condition awaits; free of emotional turbulence, societal programming and an ability to be truly Self-Determined from the clear perspective of the actual Self, the Eternal Spirit or "I-AM" Awareness that is back of and beyond this existence—an "Angel" or "god" that has fallen only by its own considerations, by being convinced that it resides locally here on earth within a perishable human shell.

"*Systemology-180*" presents newly revised instruction from the Mardukite Academy to deliver the fastest results in climbing the Ladder of Ascension. Hundreds of exercises and techniques that progressively free you from bonds of the Human Condition and increase your spiritual horsepower enough to break the chains and attachments to the material world and an existence confined to a material body.

SYSTEMOLOGY
The Gateways to Infinity

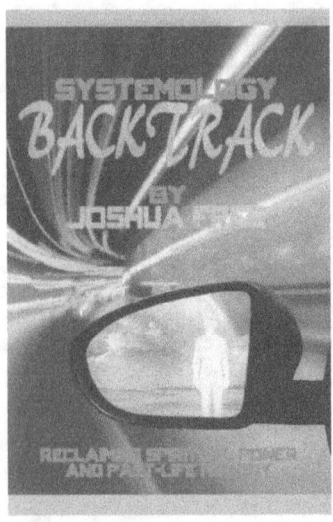

SYSTEMOLOGY:
BACKTRACK
**Reclaiming
Spiritual Power &
Past-Life Memory**

by Joshua Free

*Mardukite Grade-V
Systemology
Liber-4*

*Transcripts of the
original lectures
with diagrams
and glossary*

We are all Spiritual Beings that have known a very long
existence. Even before the evolution of Humans or Earth,
we existed as other forms, in other times and spaces.
We have descended down a very long *track* of potential
Beingness and considerations, a *track* that parallels the
allegory of "Fallen Angels" enticed by mundane bodies;
only to be trapped in them and longing to *Ascend* again.

*What if we could recover the long forgotten Knowingness of our
past existences? What if we could reclaim our true Spiritual power
that we have lost sight of? What if we could actually Backtrack
our descent and return to the Source?*

"Backtrack" documents the first advanced course given by
Joshua Free to the Systemology Society for Grade-V.
He candidly introduces the new Wizard-Level subject of
Alpha-Defragmentation to Grade-III and Grade-IV alumni
ready to embark on their next phase of the *Pathway*.

IN A WORLD FULL OF "TENS" BE AN
ELEVEN

THE METAPHYSICS OF STRANGER THINGS

TELEKINESIS,
TELEPATHY
SYSTEMOLOGY

by Joshua Free

*Mardukite
Systemology
Liber-011*

*Experimental
exploratory
edition*

Discover the metaphysical truth about the Universe—and maybe even yourself—as we explore what lies beneath the epic saga, *Stranger Things.* You're invited to a world where fantasy, science fiction and horror unite, and games like *Dungeons and Dragons* become reality.

Uncover a world of secret "mind control" projects, just like those at *Hawkins National Laboratory.* Decades of psychedelic experiments among other developmental programs for psychic powers, remote viewing, telekinesis (psychokinesis, PK) and more are revealed. Get an inside look at the operations of a real-life underground organization pursuing the truth about rehabilitating spiritual abilities for an actual "metahuman" evolution on planet Earth.

Premiere edition available in paperback and hardcover!

Commemorating the Mardukite 15th Anniversary!

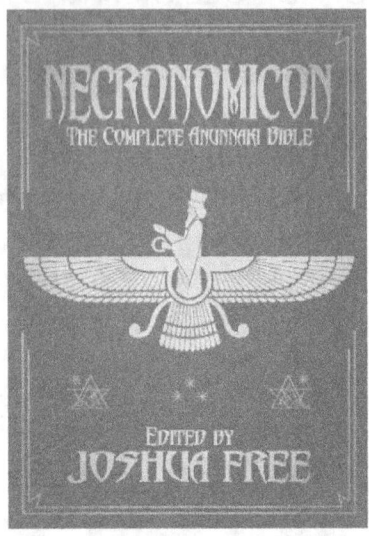

NECRONOMICON
THE COMPLETE ANUNNAKI BIBLE
(Deluxe Edition Hardcover Anthology)
collected works by Joshua Free

The ultimate masterpiece of Mesopotamian magic, spirituality and history, providing a complete collection—a grand symphony—of the most ancient writings on the planet. The oldest Sumerian and Babylonian records reveal detailed accounts of cosmic history in the Universe and on Earth, the development of human civilization and descriptions of world order. All of this information has been used, since ancient times, to maintain spiritual and physical control of humanity and its systems. It has proved to be the predecessor and foundation of all global scripture-based religious and mystical traditions thereafter. These are the raw materials, unearthed from the underground, which have shaped humanity's beliefs, traditions and existence for thousands of years—right from the heart of the Ancient Near East: Sumer, Babylon and even Egypt...

Also available abridged in hardcover as:
"Necronomicon: The Compact Anunnaki Bible"

The Original Classic Underground Bestseller Returns!
10th Anniversary Hardcover Collector's Edition.

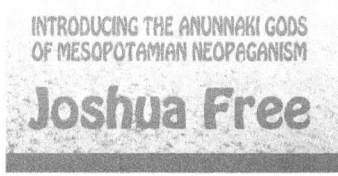

SUMERIAN RELIGION
Introducing the Anunnaki Gods
of Mesopotamian Neopaganism

Mardukite Research Volume Liber-50

by Joshua Free

Develop a personal relationship with Anunnaki Gods
—the divine pantheon that launched a thousand
cultures and traditions throughout the world!

Even if you think you already know all about the Sumerian Anunnaki or Star-Gates of Babylon... * Here you will find a beautifully crafted journey that is unlike anything Humans have had the opportunity to experience for thousands of years... * Here you will find a truly remarkable tome demonstrating a fresh new approach to modern Mesopotamian Neopaganism and spirituality... * Here is a Master Key to the ancient mystic arts: true knowledge concerning the powers and entities that these arts are dedicated to... * A working relationship with these powers directly... * And the wisdom to exist "alongside" the gods, so as to ever remain in the "favor" of Cosmic Law.

Also available in paperback as *"Anunnaki Gods"* by Joshua Free.

"Babylonian Myth & Magic" (*Liber-51+E*) sequel now available!

∞

PUBLISHED BY THE **JOSHUA FREE** IMPRINT REPRESENTING

The Founding Church of Mardukite Zuism
& Mardukite Academy of Systemology

mardukite.com